YEAR

AN ANNUAL RECORD OF CURRENT PICTORIAL
HISTORY COVERING EVERY IMPORTANT WORLD EVENT

SHARED RESPONSIBILITY FOR PEACE OF WORLD IS REFLECTED BY GRAVE, THOUGHTFUL FACES OF PRESIDENT EISENHOWER, KHRUSHCHEV

YEAR

THE PICTURE NEWS ANNUAL

1,000 PICTURES • 3,000 SUBJECTS • 75,000 WORDS • FULLY INDEXED

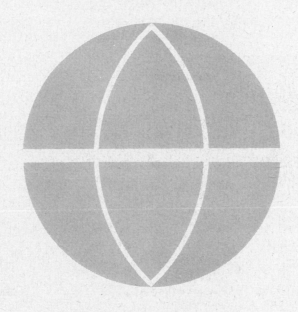

Foreword by Richard M. Nixon, Vice President of the United States

PICTURE NEWS ANNUALS, PICTURE HISTORY BOOKS AND PICTURE NEWS MAGAZINES

BY THE EDITORS OF YEAR AND NEWS FRONT

News Front

EDITOR AND PUBLISHER Baldwin H. Ward

EXECUTIVE EDITOR Thomas Simonton

• • •

MANAGING EDITOR Jane Kronholtz

ART DIRECTOR Donald Ritter

CONTRIBUTING EDITORS

Louis Alexander	Stevens Hammer	J. Malcolm Morris
Jewell Bown	Merian Kirchner	Alvin Schuster
John Callahan	Leonard Lefkow	Robert Sobel
Edwin Diamond	Marilyn Lukashok	Irwin Stambler
Isabel Dicker	John Martin	Carroll Swan
Bernard Goldman	Charles Miller	Ben Weberman
	Richard Waldstein	

EDITORIAL ASSISTANTS Maxine Hochman   Thomas Kahn

ART DEPARTMENT
Art and Production   Jacqueline Cleveland, *Manager*   Fred Poffenberger
Gwen Major   Barbara Totka

Camera   Jerry Bertet, *Manager*   William Carlisle   Moses Pelham

PUBLISHING DEPARTMENT   N. Donald Edwards, *Assistant to the Publisher*

Frances F. Dunning	Dorothy McGratty
Lucille Felix	Polly Pond
Doris Goodwin	Miriam Saunders
Ebba Gustafson	Joanne Ward
Aleen W. Kiel	Mary Wiekel

FOREIGN NEWS REPRESENTATIVES

M. O. Rodriguez	ARGENTINA
C. P. Smith	AUSTRALIA
Albert E. Norman	
Paul Lendvai	AUSTRIA
Joao Ribeiro Dantas	BRAZIL
George J. Sanderson	CANADA
P. A. Ongray	CHILE
Carlos A. Tellez	CUBA
Lois Grjebine	FRANCE
Marjorie Gilles	GREAT BRITAIN
Henry R. Moore	
Gretel Spitzer	GERMANY
Phillip Drew	
Stanley Rich	HONGKONG
Laurence P. Atkinson	INDIA
Guido Botta	ITALY
Melton S. Davis	
Kazuo Takita	JAPAN
Alastair Matheson	KENYA
Marilu Pease	MEXICO
Li Wan-Chu	NAT. CHINA
G. Leeflang	NETHERLANDS
J. G. Erne Adams	NEW ZEALAND
Paul R. Block	SOUTH AFRICA
W. E. Arnold	S. RHODESIA
Marcel Schulte	WEST GERMANY

Published by YEAR, Incorporated, 21 West 45th Street, New York 36, N.Y. Library of Congress Catalog Card No. 48-11192. Printed and bound in the U.S.A. Printed by Safran Printing Co., Detroit, Mich. Bound by Publishers Bookbinding. Inc., New York, N.Y. Typography by Sullivan Typesetting, Los Angeles 25, Calif. Printed on Publication Coated Text by Oxford Paper Co., New York 17, N.Y.

Richard M. Nixon,
Vice President
of the
United States

FOREWORD

During the year 1959 it has become more and more clear that man's quest for peace in an era of cold war competition will not be marked by the spectacular breakthroughs which have recently taken place in the field of science and which have brought us into the "space age."

Responsible world leaders have recognized that there is no magic formula which will settle the differences between the free world and the Communist bloc; no conferences at the summit which will, in itself, dramatically end world tensions. The road to peace is long and hard and, if we are to stay on it, both our people and our leaders must display patience and understanding to a maximum degree.

As this book records in picture and word, the year was highlighted by a new series of personal discussions between world leaders. President Eisenhower's strong leadership was hailed by millions.

We have welcomed the idea of peaceful competition between nations and systems of government—competition which if directed into peaceful channels can only result in improving the lot of all mankind. But we believe that if competition is to be practiced it must be fair competition. If certain rules of the game are not followed by all parties concerned, healthy competition cannot develop.

So long as Americans remain true to the principles of freedom which are our heritage, we can face, with faith and confidence, any competition that may lie ahead.

Our hope will be that under these conditions, the vast energies which nations now devote to weapons of war will instead be used to clothe, house and feed the people of the world. This is the only goal worthy of our aspirations. Competing in this way, all mankind will gain.

Richard Nixon

"I found that I was fitted for nothing so well as for a study of truth; as having a mind nimble and versatile enough to catch the resemblances of things (which is the chief point), and at the same time steady enough to fix and distinguish their subtler differences; as being gifted by nature with desire to seek, patience to doubt, fondness to meditate, slowness to assert, readiness to consider, carefulness to dispose and set in order; and as being a man that neither affects what is new nor admits what is old, and that hates every kind of imposture. So I thought my nature had a kind of familiarity and relation with truth."

—FRANCIS BACON (1561-1626)

PUBLISHER'S NOTE

YEAR 1959, the twelfth Edition in our annual series, brings you, in pictorial format with captions and text, the significant news events of the year.

As in preceding issues, YEAR'S purpose is to present the memorable world-wide happenings and personalities of the past 12 months, edited in long-range perspective through the combined media of pictures and text.

The time span covered in this 1959 Edition represents the editorial year from September to September. The 12-month period is adhered to in each successive volume because news cycles in most fields of human endeavor follow a seasonal rather than a calendar year.

The major news and photo services, and YEAR'S correspondents from nearly every part of the world, have contributed to make YEAR 1959 an impartial treatment of the history of our time.

The Editors of YEAR delved through more than 75,000 new photographs to select the better than 1,000 appearing in this volume. The approximate 75,000 words of captions and text were checked and double-checked for accuracy, reference value and a balanced presentation.

To increase the interest and reference use of YEAR 1959 the number of Special Features at the back of each issue of YEAR has been greatly increased. For further

lasting value, YEAR 1959 has been printed on improved quality paper.

YEAR, *Inc.* also publishes NEWS FRONT, The National Picture News Magazine for Management. NEWS FRONT is not available to the public either on the newsstand or by paid subscription but goes only to management executives (officers and key department heads) in U.S. business, industry, finance, government and the military.

NEWS FRONT'S editorial content each issue embodies 12-15 picture news articles on the subjects of Business, World and National Affairs.

Its articles are not concerned with spot news or day to day developments but instead are interpretive background articles dealing with long-term aspects of the news.

YEAR'S companion series of pictorial history books (see below) include: *The Pictorial History of the World, Bible and Christianity, The Turbulent 20th Century, Pictorial History of America, Science and Engineering,* and *Flight.* All of these special titles follow the YEAR picture-caption-text format.

Our expressed thanks go to Richard M. Nixon, Vice President of the U.S., who graciously wrote the foreword to YEAR 1959.

BALDWIN H. WARD, *Publisher*

Special Titles in the Pictorial History Series published by the Editors of YEAR

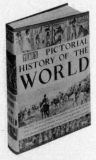     

| PICTURE HISTORY OF THE WORLD | SCIENCE & ENGINEERING | BIBLE & CHRISTIANITY | PICTURE HISTORY OF AMERICA. | FLIGHT | TURBULENT 20TH CENTURY |

TABLE OF CONTENTS

NATIONAL AFFAIRS

WORLD AFFAIRS

AMERICAN SCENE

SPECIAL FEATURES:

NATIONAL AFFAIRS -- 1959

Eisenhower prestige survives despite lame-duck term, Democratic Congress

POLITICALLY 1959, contrary to the pundits' prognostications, turned out to be an Eisenhower year.

Congress liked him (despite overwhelming Democratic majorities, it upheld all of his major vetoes) the people of the U.S. liked him (in the polls, his popularity stood higher than ever) and the people of Western Europe pinned their hopes for peace on him (witness the millions who paid him spontaneous homage in Bonn, London and Paris).

The 86th Congress had been expected to go its Democratic course, brushing aside the Administration program and, with its eye on the 1960 Presidential election, enacting its own vote-catching "platform."

In practice, however, it did not work out that way.

As the session neared its end, the real leader seemed to be, not the Democratic high command of Senate Majority Leader Lyndon Johnson and House Speaker Sam Rayburn, but Dwight D. Eisenhower. He had beaten them on such major issues as farm subsidies and housing and won overwhelming House approval for a "get-tough" labor bill. (Much of this Congressional success was due to the unadmitted but very real revival of the Republican-Southern Democratic coalition, a revival which made prospects of a civil rights bill with "teeth" dim indeed.)

The President emerged as the champion of cutting expenses, balancing the budget and, in an era of unprecedented domestic prosperity, leaving things alone as much as possible.

This was the national mood, and his influence and power seemed to be increased rather than diminished by his constitutional inability to succeed himself in 1960.

He stood above the battle, one which throughout the year waxed ever hotter, and underlaid most political maneuvering in and out of Congress.

On the Republican side, Vice President Richard M. Nixon, who had made more of that office than any predecessor, piled up what seemed a commanding lead. Most Republican professionals preferred him, and he had demonstrated both competence and courage not only domestically but before South American mobs and in toe-to-toe exchanges with Nikita Khrushchev.

Only cloud on Nixon's nomination horizon was New York's Gov. Nelson Rockefeller, a sensational, aggressive campaigner whose appeal to the voters was not lessened by well-publicized international qualifications of his own.

The Democratic race throughout the year remained wide open. There was no Democratic Nixon.

The front runner, Sen. John Kennedy of Massachusetts, hurt by the failure of Congress to adopt his labor bill, lost ground with the politicians if not in the polls.

Twice-defeated Adlai Stevenson, protesting he would not "seek" the nomination, nevertheless remained the choice of many. Sen. Hubert Humphrey, of Minnesota, on paper the ideal "liberal" candidate, and Sen. Stuart Symington of Missouri, who on paper seemed to appeal to practically everyone, made little noticeable progress.

Biggest uncertain factor was California's Gov. "Pat" Brown, who would control the second largest bloc of delegates, and he was not talking.

The death of John Foster Dulles, the President's "strong right arm" in foreign affairs since he first took the oath of office in 1953, was a great personal loss.

But it also turned out to be the occasion of the President's grasping the helm of Free World leadership more firmly than ever before, and, ably seconded by his new Secretary of State, Christian Herter, seizing the Cold War initiative.

Only in defense did the Eisenhower leadership come under serious fire. But disclosures of mounting Soviet strength and U.S. weakness failed to arouse the nation. People still trusted the "General in the White House." Besides, they were convinced that all-out nuclear war would be so horrible that it would never actually occur. (A Congressional committee warning that a full-scale attack would cause 50 million deaths, 20 million injuries caused little stir.)

HONOLULU HULAS
AS HAWAII BECOMES NO. 50

Drastic cuts were made in the Nike defenses planned against manned aircraft, emphasis shifting to anti-missile missiles. On the retaliatory side, there was a shift away from fixed missile bases which an enemy could easily locate—and destroy—to submarines and other fast-moving, hard-to-find missile platforms.

Unification, which most experts agreed was inevitable, inched toward realization.

In civil aviation, 1959 saw the jets take over. 400-600 mph flights became commonplace.

Peace, to prosperous 1959, seemed so necessary that it was inevitable, and politicians and people predicated everything on its continuance.

POLITICAL PHENOMENON OF YEAR WAS PRESIDENT EISENHOWER'S DOMINANCE OVER CONGRESS DESPITE INELIGIBILITY FOR REELECTION

9

CHRISTIAN A. HERTER was sworn in to succeed Secretary of State Dulles and was engaged much of the year in negotiations with the Russians. President Eisenhower watches the ceremony as Frank K. Sanderson, White House Administrative officer, administers oath. The Senate voiced its approval of the former Massachusetts governor by a vote of 93 to 0. C. Douglas Dillon *(r.)* was made Under Secretary.

IKE TAKES HELM
ABROAD AND AT HOME

Hopes Khrushchev visit exchange will "melt a little of the ice;"

veto threat proves strong weapon

in pushing his domestic program

LOSS OF HIS Secretary of State, a projected exchange of visits with Nikita Khrushchev, battles with Congress over legislation and appointments, differences with the USSR over Berlin and worries over national economic trends were more than enough to keep President Eisenhower well occupied during the past year.

It was a great blow to the President when John Foster Dulles died on May 24 after a long fight with cancer. The President had leaned heavily on Dulles for more than six years to shape U.S. foreign policy.

Ironically, Dulles' death came precisely on the deadline set—but not acted on—by Moscow, six months before, for turning control of Western access to Berlin over to the Communist East Germans.

While Dulles' successor, Secretary of State Christian A. Herter, and his British and French counterparts strove lengthily but unsuccessfully to reach agreement on Berlin with Soviet Foreign Minister Andrei Gromyko, the President himself remained under great pressure for a summit meeting.

The upshot was the invitation to the Soviet Premier to come to the U.S., which, while it did not technically constitute a "summit," was nevertheless a great concession to Khrushchev.

But, as the President described the Khrushchev visit and his own projected trip to Moscow, he hoped to "melt a little of the ice that seems to freeze our relationships."

As a preliminary, he scheduled flights to West Europe to confer with the chiefs of the U.S. allies.

He thus seemed to be instigating a new era of personal diplomacy.

On the domestic front, the President found himself at the beginning of the session facing the third Democratic Congress elected during his tenure. He did not expect and he did not get ready acquiescence to all his proposals. However, more than once he was able to get his way through the use of his veto power and the Democrats, once again, failed to override any of his major vetoes.

This was the next to last full year of the President's White House tenure, but the polls showed nevertheless that his popularity was at one of its peaks. This popular support, of course, did much to strengthen his chances in congressional battles.

The President began a series of stag dinners for members of the regular White House press corps and discussed much of his current thinking.

The year began for Eisenhower with his proclaiming Alaska a state at 12:02 p.m., Jan. 3 with the help of six pens. He later sent a series of messages to Congress ranging from his annual state of the union, budget and economic messages to special ones on civil rights and labor reform.

The budget his Administration prepared for the fiscal year 1960 was a precariously balanced one, estimating Federal spending and income at around $77 billion.

Administration officials conceded that any number of things could upset it, but the President worked hard all through the year in stressing the need for fiscal integrity and warning of the dangers of "creeping" infla-

tion. Although a year earlier, he had been gravely concerned about a recession, he reported to the country on Jan. 9 that the "recession was fading into history without gigantic, hastily improvised public works projects or untimely tax reductions."

On Jan. 31 he created a permanent Cabinet Committee on Price Stability for Economic Growth to make a continuing anti-inflation study. At its helm he put Vice President Nixon, who thereby got his first formal administrative job in the Executive Branch.

The President, before embarking on his journey to Moscow, had his share of international visitors at home. The year began with Mikoyan, Soviet Deputy Premier, coming to Washington to confer with Eisenhower. Prime Minister Macmillan of Great Britain arrived in March and met with the President for three days at the Presidential retreat, Camp David, near Thurmont, Md. King Hussein of Jordan also visited with Ike in the U.S. and a long-time friend and colleague—Winston Churchill—was a visitor.

ANTAGONISTS in one of the bitterest nomination fights of session were Mrs. Clare Booth Luce, named by President to be Ambassador to Brazil, and Senator Wayne Morse, Oregon Democrat, who charged her with "emotional instability" and lack of necessary qualifications. Senate confirmed her, but she resigned upon advice of her husband, *Time-Life* editor Henry Luce. President accepted with regret; named career diplomat John Cabot to post

11

OGDEN REID'S nomination as Ambassador to Israel led Senate Foreign Relations Chairman Fulbright to express great concern over standard of ambassadorial appointments. He renewed the protest against handing out appointments as political rewards. The former president of New York *Herald Tribune* was confirmed, however, after a hearing at which he was flanked by N.Y.'s Republican Senators Kenneth B. Keating and Jacob K. Javits *(r.)*. Reid denied any political ambitions, expressed self-confidence in new job as ambassador.

JOHN A. McCONE, *(r.)* successor to Strauss as AEC Chairman, kept busy during year with problems of atomic power program, fallout, and nuclear test ban talks. He clashed with Joint Atomic Energy Comm. over atom plans; he announced an advisory group report on fallout that gave reassuring picture and commended Commission's handling of radiation problem; and later attended Geneva atomic test ban talks.

FIRST CABINET NOMINEE in thirty-four years to be refused Senatorial approval was Lewis Strauss, rejected by close 49-46 vote. President said country was loser by Senate's action; nominated Frederick H. Mueller to the post. He was confirmed with no difficulty. Factors in Strauss' defeat were reported to include his personality, lobbying by high Administration officials which was resented, mistakes in presenting case.

FOUR DEMOCRATIC SENATORS who helped defeat Strauss were *(l.* to *r.)*, Joseph C. O'Mahoney (Wyo.), Clinton Anderson (N. Mex.), Wayne Morse (Ore.), and Gale McGee (Wyo.). Every Senator but Senator Fulbright, Foreign Relations Chairman, went on record in Strauss voting. Opponents argued that Strauss' past record and "conduct and demeanor" showed he lacked "degree of integrity and competence essential" for the job. They accused him of "misleading statements" and "unnecessary truths" and of withholding information from Congress when he was Atomic Energy Commission Chairman. Supporters argued there was no doubt about his "honesty and integrity, competence and his long record of willing cooperation with Congress." Strauss said he was confident history would vindicate his record. Senators Margaret Smith and William Langer were only GOPs who voted against him.

STATE DEPARTMENT shifts included the departure of Walter S. Robertson (*l.*) as Assistant Secretary of State for Far Eastern Affairs. Robertson, one of the staunchest supporters of Nationalist China and one of most vigorous opponents of UN membership or U.S. recognition of Red China, was replaced by J. Graham Parsons, a career foreign service officer. Other department changes: Robert Murphy moved up to Under Secretary for Political Affairs; Livingston Merchant to Deputy Under Secretary for Political Affairs.

NATIVE OF RUSSIA became the new Presidential Science Advisor to Eisenhower succeeding Dr. James R. Killian. Dr. George B. Kistiakowsky, 58, Harvard Chemistry Professor (shown with wife and dog, "Penny"), a member of President's Science Advisory Comm. had won the President's Medal for preparing the explosive charge used to detonate 'first A-bomb. Dr. Killian returned to MIT where he had been named Chairman. Advisory group headed by Killian proposed May 23 that the nation's annual investment in education for its youth at least be doubled.

13

DULLES TRAVELED 560,000 MILES AS SECRETARY; SAW NEHRU, TITO; SIGNED MUTUAL DEFENSE PACT WITH NATIONALIST CHINA IN TAIPEI

FREE WORLD MOURNS DULLES' DEATH

John Foster Dulles, Secretary of State since Eisenhower's Administration began in 1953, died May 24, of cancer. He was the President's chief advisor, representative to Congress and agent abroad in the realm of foreign affairs. Despite controversy, it could not be denied that he was the strongest personality of the Cabinet; that he had great ability as persuader, and that he had extraordinary vitality in carrying out his missions. He had prepared for his diplomatic career in international law, and had practiced for thirty-eight years before retiring to devote his remaining years entirely to government service with his country.

DULLES' BROTHER, Allen Dulles, *(r.)* was CIA Dir. His sister had position in State Department's German Affairs office.

VISITORS at Walter Reed Hospital in the declining days of Dulles' life included Pres. Eisenhower, Winston Churchill.

HE MET WITH RUSSIAN LEADERS BULGANIN AND KHRUSHCHEV AT GENEVA; KOREA'S PRESIDENT RHEE AT SEOUL; CHIANG AT FORMOSA

CHRISTIAN HERTER helps Dulles keep dry on his return from talks with DeGaulle.

DULLES-IKE met regularly. Ike said: "We, who were privileged to work with him, have lost a dear and close friend, as all Americans have lost a champion of freedom."

SECRETARY rested in Fla. He resigned Apr. 15; was made Special Consultant.

FUNERAL of Dulles brought international dignitaries, including Soviet's Andrei Gromyko, French and British Foreign Ministers who came with Herter from Geneva.

PRESIDENT got bipartisan backing from congress leaders on Berlin situation at White House briefing. Congress went on record as being in full accord with President in crisis.

TWENTY YEAR reign of Rep. Joseph Martin as leader of House Republicans ended when Rep. Charles Halleck (l.) won vote by GOP members. Martin blamed defeat on election losses.

CONGRESSMEN YIELD TO ECONOMY

President defeated on Strauss; wins over "spenders"

THE 86TH Congress was the first to represent 50 states of the Union, seating the first Senators and Representatives from Alaska and Hawaii. This, however, was only one of the distinctions of this Congress.

had been untouched since 1949, was pushed through.

The old rule required vote of two-thirds of the entire Senate membership to shut off debate. The change permits two-thirds of the Senators on the floor at the time to shut off debate. Northern Liberals had hoped for a more drastic change.

In a surprise climax to an unex-

pected revolt, House Republicans voted to replace Rep. Joseph W. Martin, Jr., their leader in every Congress since 1939, with Rep. Charles A. Halleck as minority floor leader.

With internal matters disposed of, Congress turned to the business of legislation and the battle between the Republican President and the Democratic Congress was on.

SHARP ATTACK on congressional leadership of Senator Lyndon Johnson came from fellow Democrat William Prox-

mire *(l.)*. He argued that Johnson was running Senate without consulting rank and file. Johnson replied it was "myth".

REPORTS congressmen packed payrolls with relatives created furor. Rep. Randall Harmon's wife worked from home.

Armed with big majorities in both Houses, the Democrats embarked on what seemed to be a "do-the-President-one-better" campaign.

It was a campaign, however, that was soon to slow down in the face of presidential vetoes and in so doing was to split the Democrats themselves over Congressional strategy.

Three vetoes that came early in the session, none of which was overridden, helped force the Democrats to give ground to President Eisenhower's economy offensive.

First was the politically significant veto of a minor bill dealing with the Rural Electrification Administration. Then the President refused to sign Democratic farm bills to control prices and production of wheat and tobacco. The third was his veto of the $1.4 billion Democratic housing bill on the grounds it was "excessive" and "extravagant."

A result was that the Democrats in Congress began curbing their more ambitious plans on such issues

as airport construction, public works and aid to depressed areas.

A major controversy was debt management. The Administration proposed removing the 4½% interest ceiling on long-term government bonds. Congress approved another Administration request in this area— the raising of the permanent ceiling on the national debt from $283 billion to $288 billion. In addition, it approved a "temporary" increase in the ceiling to $295 billion until June 30, 1960.

Congress also voted statehood for Hawaii, a $126 million two-year program of airport construction, a one-year extension of the corporate and excise taxes adopted during the Korean war, a vote of confidence in the Administration's handling of the Berlin crisis, and a foreign aid bill of $3.1 billion.

Other dominant issues included a civil rights bill extending the life of the Civil Rights Commission, a labor reform bill aimed at labor racketeering, and a proposal to finance the highway program by raising Federal gasoline taxes.

The Democratic majority pushed

through a bill giving the Tennessee Valley Authority a go-ahead to finance itself by selling $70 million in bonds. The President signed it after assurances that Congress would remove a provision he regarded as infringement on presidential powers.

AUTHOR of Democratic housing bill vetoed by Eisenhower was Sen. Sparkman (D.-Ala.). Ike called bill "extravagant".

FILIBUSTER FIGHT was first of new session as *(l. to r.)* Sens. Clifford Case (R.-N.J.); Paul H. Douglas (D.-Ill.), and Jacob Javits (R.-N.Y.) joined efforts to make it easier to end filibuster. They wanted rule change to permit Senate majority to end prolonged debate. Johnson "compromise" won out. It permits shut-off of debate by two-thirds of Senators present and voting. It was first change in so-called Cloture rule in 10 years and represented a big victory for Johnson over northern liberals.

SEN. EVERETT M. DIRKSEN (R.-Ill.) *(above)* was elected Senate GOP minority leader. The "conservative" defeated "liberal" nominee J. Sherman Cooper (Ky.).

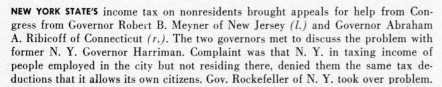

NEW YORK STATE'S income tax on nonresidents brought appeals for help from Congress from Governor Robert B. Meyner of New Jersey *(l.)* and Governor Abraham A. Ribicoff of Connecticut *(r.)*. The two governors met to discuss the problem with former N. Y. Governor Harriman. Complaint was that N. Y. in taxing income of people employed in the city but not residing there, denied them the same tax deductions that it allows its own citizens. Gov. Rockefeller of N. Y. took over problem.

GOP SENATORS took interest as fight developed over N.Y.s billion dollar Title I slum clearance program. Key figure was Robert Moses, Chairman of N.Y. Mayor's Comm. on slum clearance, who said attacks were unfounded. A congressional investigation of whole program was slated. In program, blighted land is sold to private developers at markdown after being condemned.

SUPREME COURT ended session after disposing of 1781 cases. Among rulings was one upholding power of House Un-American Activities Committee to question witnesses about communism. It also ruled that neither Congress nor President had authorized denial of security clearance to defense plant workers without giving them chance to confront accusers. Seated (*l. to r.*) are Justices Douglas, Black, Warren, Frankfurter, Clark; standing: Whittaker, Harlan, Brennan, Stewart.

PRESIDENT named Potter Stewart to succeed Burton. At 43, he is court's youngest member. His father, Judge James G. Stewart of Ohio Supreme Court (*l.*), congratulated him as son's wife looks on. Stewart had been on Court of Appeals.

HAROLD BURTON (*r.*) retired Oct. 13 as Associate Justice after serving since 1945 when he was appointed by President Truman. A 70-year-old Republican, Burton is former Senator from Ohio. He retired in accordance with "medical advice".

POLITICIANS PREPARE FOR 1960

GOP HOPES in retaining White House in 1960 will rest with one of these two men, Nixon *(l.)*, or Rockefeller. They met over breakfast in Oct. '58 to end reports they were at odds.

Democratic hopefuls jockey for position; Nixon finds rival as Rockefeller's victory gives GOP another candidate

LOUISIANA was shaken by the collapse of Gov. Earl Long who was committed to mental hospital. Long fought confinement and won a quick release after firing the hospital head.

DEMOCRATS AND REPUBLICANS spent 1959 preparing for the 1960 battle for triumph in the White House.

It was a jubilant group of Democrats who read the election returns of the 1958 congressional fight. They increased their control of the Senate from a 49-47 margin to 63-34. In the House, their lead jumped from 235-200 to 283-153. They were confident of holding control.

But despite their tremendous victory, the Democrats were having their difficulties. The old North-South split over civil rights was still in evidence, as well as differences between the liberal factions and the congressional moderates led by Sen. Johnson and Speaker Rayburn.

The Democratic National Chairman, Paul Butler, joined in criticism of the congressional leadership. Mr. Johnson's supporters fired back, some demanding Butler's resignation, but all was ostensibly ironed out at a Butler-Johnson-Rayburn "truce" meeting on Capitol Hill.

While the liberals and moderates within the Democratic party were thus at variance, the party's potential presidential nominees were jockeying for the spotlight. Sen. John Kennedy (Mass.) led the hopefuls. Sen. Hubert Humphrey (Minn.) hoped to strengthen his standing as a statesman by going to Moscow where he had a much publicized eight-hour talk with Khrushchev. On July 14 a Humphrey-for-President organization was announced, the first such group for any of the potential candidates.

HUBERT HUMPHREY   **STUART SYMINGTON**   **JOHN KENNEDY**   **LYNDON JOHNSON**

DEMOCRATIC ELIGIBLES spent year trying to create best possible public image. Humphrey was first in action by giving blessing to Humphrey-for-President organization. Kennedy kept after

labor racketeering; Johnson after good congressional record; and Symington after Administration on defense policy. Speculation included Stevenson, who insisted he would not run.

GOV. EDMUND BROWN (California) said he would be a "favorite son" candidate in 1960 election giving him control of important bloc of convention delegates. He might get No. 2 spot.

REPUBLICANS got new national chairman in Sen. Thruston B. Morton (Ky.), *(l.)*. Mrs. Morton watches retiring Chairman Meade Alcorn lift Morton's hand in uncontested victory.

Sen. Stuart Symington (Mo.) kept after the Administration on defense policies. And Sen. Johnson, too, was frequently mentioned.

The Republicans, while worrying considerably about ways to win back control of Congress, worried less about presidential nominees. Vice President Nixon seemed to have things under control. His trip to Russia, complete with public arguments with Khrushchev, all helped to enhance his political prestige. But there was still an undercurrent of anti-Nixon feeling among some Republicans who were overjoyed when Nelson Rockefeller triumphed over Gov. Averell Harriman in N. Y.'s gubernatorial contest. Rockefeller stated he would rely on what the public opinion polls indicated in determining whether he would strive to catch the front-running Nixon.

Meanwhile, the President remained silent during the year, refusing to disclose any preference for either man. He did let it be known, however, that he had a list of several Republicans he felt were qualified for the office, including Richard Nixon and Nelson Rockefeller.

MISSILE LAG WORRIES NATION

Short–cuts sought as USSR strides ahead

TO FIGHT ARMY BATTLES among Joint Chiefs of Staff is Gen. Lyman L. Lemnitzer, 58, who succeeded Gen. Taylor.

RESEARCH DIRECTOR Herbert F. York, 37, was first appointee to new post ranking directly after three service secretaries.

During 1959 the new re-organization plan for the Armed Services was pushed out of the limelight by Congressional discussion and public concern over the U.S. missile lag.

Defense Secretary Neil McElroy acknowledged to Congress that the Soviets would maintain a three-to-one lead in intercontinental missiles as far into the future as 1962. Sen. Stuart Symington (D-Mo.), former Air Force Secretary, gloomily declared he thought the ratio would be an absolute six-to-one.

The USSR test fired its first intercontinental missile about 18 months ahead of the U.S. McElroy estimated that in mid-July Moscow had up to 10 ICBM's. Meanwhile, the operational date for the first U.S. Altas

ICBM was repeatedly pushed back.

However, military planners and factory scientists discussed possible short cuts for regaining supremacy.

One was to speed development and production of the Nike-Zeus anti-missile missile.

Another was to put more money and effort into the development of solid-fuel missiles such as Polaris and Minuteman, which can be fired without the delays that liquid-fuel missiles undergo.

Controversy also raged, in Congress and between the Air Force and the Army, over whether defense requires both the Army's Nike-Hercules and the Bomarc. The Nike-Hercules is a "point" and the Bomarc is an "area" missile, but both are defense only against manned bombers, and not against other missiles. The argument led Secretary McElroy to submit to Congress a White-House approved "master plan" for missile age defense. The plan cut $600 million from Nike-Hercules and $900 million from Bomarc. It added $137 million toward the development of Nike-Zeus.

The Senate accepted the master plan but restored part of the cuts to both Nike-Hercules and Bomarc.

Progress toward unification in the Defense Department inched ahead. Seven joint committees were eliminated when the new organization of the Joint Chiefs of Staff got under way. One by one, eight unified commands were moved out from the in-

NEW DEPUTY DEFENSE SECRETARY is Thomas S. Gates, Jr., being congratulated by President Eisenhower. When Donald A. Quarles, 64, who was in line to succeed Defense Secretary McElroy, died in his sleep on May 8 of a heart attack, Navy Secretary Gates, 53, of Philadelphia, reversed his plans for retirement from public service. He helps McElroy run government's biggest, most expensive department.

ARE BOMBER DEFENSES NECESSARY? Many Nike-Hercules batteries (80 mile range, nuclear warhead) were in place to defend major cities and defense installations. Army turned 24 batteries over to National Guard units. Defense master plan cut $600 million from appropriation, subcommittee restored part.

ANOTHER PAWN IN MISSILE-LAG DEBATE was Bomarc (200-400 mile range) interceptor missile. Two sites were under construction, 12 more designated. Defense master plan cut **Air Force** Bomarc program back by $900 million, gave more to Zeus anti-missile, but again subcommittee only went part way.

dividual Air Force, Navy and Army departments to the direct control of the Joint Chiefs, starting (in Sept., 1958) with Air Force General Norstad's unified European Command.

The Navy combined the Bureau of Ordnance and the Bureau of Aeronautics into a single Bureau of Naval Weapons. The Army improved upon its 1957 conversion of "triangular" divisions into "pentomic" infantry divisions by reorganization.

To the undersea laurels won by the *Nautilus* trip under the North Pole, the Navy added more records. The

Seawolf stayed below the surface for two months. In April, 1959, with five members of Congressional Joint Committee on Atomic Energy aboard, the nuclear-powered *Skipjack* set a new depth record—below 400 feet—and a speed record for that depth—of over 20 knots.

A Navy party boarded the Soviet trawler *Novorossisk*, following reports of five breaks in the trans-Atlantic cable off Newfoundland. Both the U.S. and Russia were signatories to an 1884 international convention which classified deliberate damage to

cables as a punishable offense.

The Army disclosed "now available" nerve gasses that kill if a single droplet touches the skin. An Army general speculated about warfare with chemicals that do not kill but just paralyze—physically or by fear—and called them "psychochemicals."

The nation was not the least bit ready for attack, civil defense reports early in 1959 indicated. On the other hand,—following Moscow's reneging on its May 27 West Berlin deadline—the USSR had not conducted any air raid drills recently either.

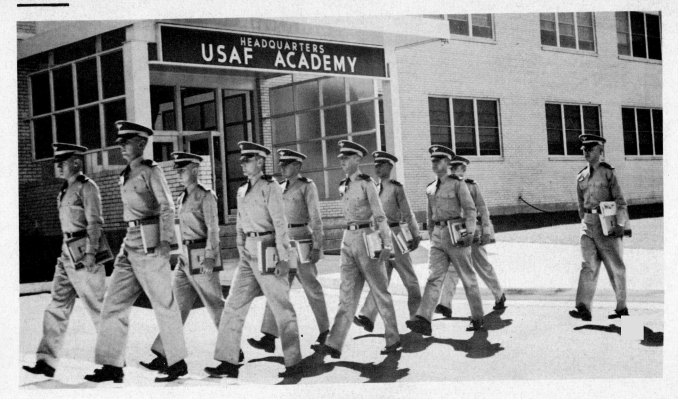

NEW AIR FORCE ACADEMY has almost everything (cost: $136 million) except an airfield where cadets can learn to fly. The Air Force could not justify cost of construction while there were two others (Peterson Field and Lowery Air Force Base) within 60 miles of Colo. campus.

SHRINKAGE OF THE WORLD was demonstrated in late 1958 by Air Force Gen. Curtis LeMay, vice chief of staff, who piloted KC-135 jet tanker the 7100 miles from Tokyo to Washington non-stop in record time of 12 hours, 28 minutes. When he arrived in Washington the Air Force's No. 2 man went on record as favoring unification of armed services.

SOVIET-BUILT JETS ATTACKED this Navy P-4M plane on patrol June 19 over the Sea of Japan, but gunners could not respond; their armament was unusable. The Soviet-built plane's guns (manned possibly by Red Chinese) blew large hole in the tail gun turret, shattered the glass over the gunner's seat and wounded him. Incident caused criticism in U.S. because the plane flew without guns adequate for protection.

"FATHER" AND ATOMIC SUBS of his "family" won honors. Rear Adm. Hyman Rickover, called father of nuclear submarines, was nominated for Vice Admiral, won right to inspect Soviet atompowered icebreaker during Leningrad visit. Crew of *Nautilus* was acclaimed in England after crossing under North Pole. Other atomic subs set submersion (60-days) and depth (400 feet) records.

MASTER PLAN TO OVERCOME MISSILE LAG was discussed by Defense Secretary Neil McElroy *(l.)*, Gen. Nathan Twining, chairman of Joint Chiefs of Staff, and Sen. Richard Russell (D-Ga.) *(r.)* chairman of Armed Services committee. A Senate subcommittee approved McElroy's master plan, which cut back expenditures for defense against manned bombers and increased appropriations for missile defense.

PRICE OF PROGRESS was evidenced by this scrap heap of obsolete jet planes standing in the desert at Davis-Montham Air Force Base in Arizona. Planes would be melted down and metal re-used.

JETS RULE WORLD SKIES

Rocket–powered X–15 leads advance; commercial jet air travel

FIRST MANNED SPACECRAFT, rocket powered X-15, is placed in position under wing of giant B-52 mother ship. Research craft is launched from bomber at altitudes of 30-40,000 ft. for assault on boundaries of earth's atmosphere. At controls for first free flight (power off) test last June was North American pilot Scott Crossfield (bottom r.). In later tests, USAF, NASA or Navy pilots will take X-15 to speeds of 3-4000 mph, and will fly at altitudes of 800,000 ft.

VIGILANTE A3J-1 Navy attack plane is one of newest craft to enter nation's inventory. This carrier-based, supersonic plane (North American) is powered by two J79-2 engines, delivering over 15,000 lbs. of thrust each. Craft has novel feature of delivering missiles through an opening in its tail.

booms as
new control agency
is born

On JUNE 8, 1959, the historic first free flight of the North American Aviation X-15, with test pilot Scott Crossfield at the controls, advanced the dawn of the space age. Continuing tests of this rocket-powered plane by the National Aeronautics & Space Administration (NASA), USAF and the Navy, will lead to flights of 3-4000 mph, right up to the edge of outer space.

By the end of 1959, 4-600 mph jet and turboprop airliners were carrying passengers to a rapidly increasing list of key cities in the U.S. and throughout the world. By midyear, the handful of pure jets in service had already flown an estimated 500,000 passengers with long waiting lists for most flights.

But even as the revolutionary jets took over the commercial airways, the X-15 program pointed to even more fantastic events in the near future. All researchers agreed that Mach 3-5 passenger transports could be placed in operation within the next decade, spanning the U.S. coast-to-coast in just one hour. Preliminary designs for such planes already are being drawn up by all leading aircraft manufacturers.

The past year also saw the birth of a new, central government regulatory board for aviation, the Federal Aviation Agency, charged with streamlining the country's aviation system to meet the needs of today's high performance aircraft. The old Civil Aeronautics. Administration (CAA) was merged into the new agency, whose first administrator was E. R. Quesada.

Military spending continued to shift away from conventional aircraft with a new factor, spacecraft, entering the picture. Expenditures for aircraft in Fiscal Year 1960 were ex-

VTOL DEVELOPMENTS in 1959 included first order for commercial use in U.S. of new British-designed Fairey Rotodyne convertiplane *(below)*. Five of these craft, to carry 65 passengers, up to 200 mph, were ordered by New York Airways for delivery in 1964. Military sponsored experimental projects included Hiller's tilt-wing X-18, Ryan's deflected slipstream VTOL, Doak Aircraft's Model 16 *(shown above)*.

pected to be $6.6 billion as against $7.1 billion in 1959. But missile spending will go up. New planes in production during '59 included North American's Vigilante, carrier-based attack bomber and the Northrop N-156F. The latter, a lightweight fighter designed to be produced by U.S. allies, highlighted the growing importance of foreign markets. Lockheed, for example, signed to deliver 96 F-104s to West Germany.

The business aircraft market kept moving at a healthy pace. As demand mounted throughout the year, it appeared likely that '59 production would exceed the 6414 planes turned out in 1958.

BUSINESS BAROMETERS HIT NEW RECORDS

Recovery from 1958 dip tops expectations

A STRONGLY RISING ECONOMY ran head-on into a lengthy steel strike during 1959, and successfully passed this test of the recovery that had carried the nation's business to new records.

Spurred partly by advance buying of steel and partly by strength in virtually every sector of the economy, the Gross National Product rose to a record $490 billion by mid-year, up $52.5 billion from the recession low of a year earlier.

It was a recovery that came much faster than almost every expert had predicted. The Federal Reserve Board index of industrial production hit 155 per cent of the 1947-1949 average by June, compared with 126 at the low in mid-April 1958.

The problem of unemployment took care of itself as less than one worker out of 20 was out of a job compared with one out of 15 a year earlier. By mid-summer, jobs had reached 68 million, highest in Labor Department records.

Consumer demand received credit, more than any other factor, for lifting the country out of what could have been a serious recession.

Although numerous stories were repeated about the feared effects of a recession, individuals, using both their salaries and bank accounts during 1958, started the economy off on a round of prosperity that might top anything before in U.S. history.

For example, sales of 1959 automobiles got off to a fair start in the final quarter of 1958 as they were introduced. Volume continued to accelerate as buyers did not hesitate to place firm orders. Several times during the year, manufacturers upped production and sales quotas as results topped expectations. Production passed the 3 million mark before mid-

year, many months ahead of 1958.

Retail lines, predominantly hard goods such as furniture and appliances, shared in the business improvement. Sales of apparel stores and general merchandise kept pace.

Consumers did not provide the sole props for the boom. Businessmen, too, were filled with optimism as indicated by the firm recovery in

EVEN THE STEEL STRIKE, which made cold and idle the furnaces which produce

plant and equipment expenditures.

Business spending for modernization and expansion rose to an annual rate of $33.5 billion right after mid-year 1959 from a low of $29.6 billion a year earlier.

With virtually everyone feeling optimistic about the outlook, it was not surprising that heavy demand for common stocks sent prices soaring to

85-90% of the basic material of U.S. heavy industry, and temporarily cost

what turned out to be an all-time high.

The Dow-Jones industrial average passed the 600 mark in 1959 for the first time ever and continued to rise until reaching 678.10.

As money went into equities, and as fixed income securities lost their appeal, interest rates continued their sharp climb.

Top rated corporations found that they had to pay more than 5 per cent interest, in contrast to only 3½ per cent on loans made a year earlier.

Even the U.S. Treasury ran head-on into a law prohibiting its borrowing at more than 4¼ per cent interest. With the going level over that President Eisenhower asked Congress to raise the statutory interest on government borrowings.

Prosperity had reached an unprecedented peak, and business barometers pointed to bright skies for 1960.

600,000 persons their jobs, failed to slow the upsurge of the U.S. economy.

EMPLOYMENT SET NEW RECORDS, rising to 68 million at mid-year. Those out of work dropped to 4 million, only 5.6 per cent of the total labor force.

WARNING AGAINST STOCK MANIPULATORS was given by Securities and Exchange Commissioner Edward N. Gadsby. Head of a 900-man staff, he battled unprincipled promoters. Increased public participation in the market was stimulated by lure of quick profit on rising prices. Unscrupulous "boiler shops" increased at rate of 200 a week.

RAILWAY EXPRESS AGENCY, owned by all the country's railroads, got a new lease on life in mid-year. Threatened revolts by N. Y. Central and the Chicago and Northwestern were quieted by compromise which covered routing, payments to carriers.

EXPORT-IMPORT PROBLEMS plagued U.S. industry as competition for world markets put pressure on sales and profits of manufacturers. Senators Norris Cotton, (R., N.H.) *(second from l.)* and Strom Thurmond, (D., S.C.) *(third from l.)* discuss ways to protect the American textile industry with trade officials.

MATERIALS TESTING REACTOR built by General Electric Co. is installed at Vallecitos Atomic Laboratory, Pleasanton, Calif. The new unit, within a matter of hours, can stimulate months and even years of irradiation under actual operating conditions.

OIL IMPORT QUOTAS went into effect March 10 in an effort to bring excessive supplies of crude oil and products into satisfactory balance with the rising demand. Consumption in 1959 increased 7 per cent to a new peak but could not absorb the flood of output unleashed by the Suez crisis in 1957-58.

ALEXANDER GUTERMA failed as a "financial wizard". When his empire of approximately a dozen big and small companies began to crumble as banks "called" insolvent loans, the SEC took unprecedented action, to assure his whereabouts, of arresting him on criminal charge of not filing required reports.

STEEL STRIKE strained labor-management relations as employers refused to increase wages or otherwise contribute to further inflation of the economy. Union chiefs insisted that they share in the fruits of very profitable record steel output. Steel users, meanwhile, were well stocked for "long siege."

SURPLUSES STILL HEADACHE

Farm program cost soars to $7.3 billion; no solution seen

EXPENDITURES for agriculture in 1959 were surpassed in magnitude only by outlays for national security and interest on the public debt. The rising tide of surpluses, especially wheat, caused government farm spending to soar from 1954's $2.6 billion to $7.3 billion for 1959. The two main farm problems were:

Technological improvements which caused great expansion in surplus farm products, and the hotly debated program of price supports.

The administration wanted to restrict or discontinue price supports; the farm bloc, its political strength faltering, wanted them expanded.

The Senate Agricultural Committee approved a wheat bill reducing supports for farmers planting full acreage allotment, increasing them for those cutting acreage 20%. However, farm prices rose in livestock, fruits and vegetables, none of which had price support guarantees.

High props were leading more growers to sacrifice quality in order to boost yield. While U.S. bakers and millers shunned poor grain, much of it was being shipped overseas. Conferences to decide on a "Food for Peace" plan were suggested by President Eisenhower. An international conference of this type would explore steps to the establishment of world food deposits for famine or disaster relief on all continents.

The critical depression that plagued the nation's poultry industry began to slack off. Egg prices soared from 28 to 40 cents a dozen, partly due to unusually warm weather which caused hens to lay fewer eggs.

An amendment to the Pure Food, Drug and Cosmetic Act provided that the Food and Drug Administration must approve the use of food additives. This, in effect, requires a food to be proved safe before it can be marketed to consumers.

Research on farm production resulted in the development of new work and time-saving devices. One of these is a machine that picks up hay in the field, compresses it into wafers, and delivers them to a wagon. Hay biscuits are said to help cows to digest more easily.

SOLUTION to the wheat problem was proposed by Secretary of Agriculture Ezra Taft Benson as he continued his campaign for lower price supports. His proposal was that the government give up farm programs gradually and let conditions of a free market control production and determine income. Farm bloc Congressmen, on the other hand, wanted government to do more, even to support prices at such a high level that rigid production controls would be required. President Eisenhower advocated giving Benson more latitude in setting price supports, cutting parity and discouraging production.

GOLDEN field of Minnesota wheat that stretches as far as the eye can see is typical of thousands in the grain region. Government is storing wheat surplus of 1.2 billion bushels.

PICKETING Congress, wives of poultry farmers hold protest signs outside hearing room of House Agriculture Subcommittee. Faced with growing surplus of chickens and eggs, subcommittee investigated poultry prices. Heavy impact of agricultural programs on federal budget is mainly result of high production and the farmers' confusion in cutting crops.

AUTOMATIC PILOT for use with hydraulic power steering on farm tractors is demonstrated by designer, Louis Liljedahl, U.S. Department of Agriculture engineer at University of Minnesota. Sensitive feelers straddle row, signal pilot to close switches when tractor moves too close or far from row.

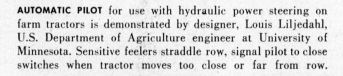

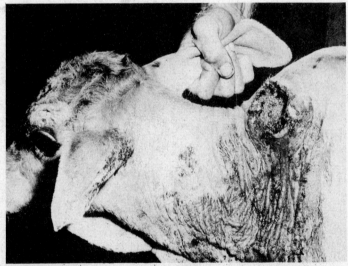

SCREWWORM FLY, whose larvae literally eat animals alive, is now being wiped out by a unique method. Billions of male screwworms are collected, sterilized to prevent reproduction by powerful gamma rays from radioactive cobalt, and "seeded" by air over infected areas. As more and more females mate with these sterilized males, the government hopes species will become extinct and end $20 million a year cost to Georgia and Florida livestock owners.

WHEAT REBEL Stanley Yankus and family post "for sale" sign on Dowagiac, Michigan chicken farm. Penalties amounting to $4300 were levied against Yankus for planting excess wheat acreage to feed chickens. Yankus sold the farm and moved to Australia.

AFL-CIO staged mass Washington rally in April to demand increased spending, other government action to eliminate unemployment. Delegates *(r.)* swarmed from all parts of nation into capital. But April drop in unemployment of whopping 750,000 took wind from labor sails, although 3.6 million remained jobless.

CONGRESS EXPOSES LABOR RACKETS

NON-PROFESSIONALS, mostly low paid Puerto Ricans, Negroes, struck N.Y. City volunteer hospitals, won benefits.

Strikes lose appeal as wages, jobs set record; dues–paying labor union membership falls

RANK-AND-FILE apathy, a "get tough" attitude on the part of top management, political uncertainty and public disillusionment because of racketeering and "featherbedding" all made life difficult for labor's U.S. chieftains in 1959.

Adding to their woes was the rearguard and, from the long-range viewpoint, losing battle they were fighting against automation, which, if it promised to create many new jobs, was certain to abolish many of those now existing.

The political conflict centered about the attempt of Congress, on the second time around, to write new legislation which would prevent in future the racketeering exposed by the continuing Senate committee headed by Sen. John L. McClellan D-Ark.).

This had to be accomplished without, if possible, alienating the AFL-CIO and the powerful independent unions. The task was not made easier by the widening shadow of the 1960 Presidential election, and the fact that some Senators most identified with

LABOR SECRETARY James Mitchell (l.), Senator Kennedy, confer prior to Mitchell's testimony to Kennedy committee. Mitchell asked ban on "blackmail" pickets and was confident of employment rise.

WALTER REUTHER of Auto Workers, and Electrical Workers' James Carey, aid local strikers during AFL-CIO Executive Council meeting in Puerto Rico. President Eisenhower criticized session in balmy tropics, was assailed by AFL-CIO President Meany for excessive hours on golf course.

LABOR'S "BLACK SHEEP," Harry Bridges (l.), Jimmy Hoffa (far l.), retained tight control of their giant unions. Teamsters' chief Hoffa appeared often before McClellan Committee, showed agility in dodging questions, criticism for failing to clean up union. Bridges presided over International Longshoremen's San Francisco convention, received overwhelming vote of confidence.

labor legislation had their eyes on the Democratic nomination.

Any new law, if adopted, seemed certain to be based on the once defeated bill sponsored by Sen. John Kennedy of Massachusetts (front runner among Democratic aspirants and brother of the McClellan Committee's chief counsel) and former Sen. Irving Ives (R-N.Y.).

The threat of a strike by one of the giant mass production unions, once labor's ace in the hole, seemed to have lost much of its terrors. This was made clear by the backing and filling which attended the bitter dispute preceding the steel strike. (Both President Eisenhower and Vice President Nixon intervened to try to avert an open rupture.)

The mass of union members seemed to have lost all heart for a renewal of the titanic conflicts of the '30s. Pay, on the average, was the highest in history, conditions were generally good. Few — wives in particular — wanted to risk the new house or prospects of a 1960 model car for a few highly-taxed dollars more per week.

There was a proportionate decline in dues-paying members facing such disparate unions as the United Auto Workers and the American Newspaper Guild with the problem of "free loaders" who enjoy union benefits without joining up.

Walkouts, however, were widespread, ranging from airlines to coal, food retailing to newspapers.

But the "climate of opinion," even among union members, was against strikes, unless abundantly justified.

COAL MINERS in West Virginia and Kentucky struck in April, but their major target was not operators but sickness of industry whose product had largely been superseded by other fuels. Surveys agreed only solution was cutback in production, new coal uses, relocation of miners whose jobs seemed permanently lost. Veteran union head John L. Lewis *(l.)* agreed privately age of solid fuel had ended, but hoped new uses, automation might rescue industry. Another sickness— juke box racketeering — was exposed by Senate *(below)*.

PROTESTING American Airlines ticket agent is joined by his daughter as he pickets pilot walkout which took place early in the year. Highly-paid pilots demanded elimination of non-pilot flight engineers in jets. Strike idled 18,000 other employees at American Airlines, disrupted all flight schedules.

HANDS ACROSS TABLE symbolize agreements which put end to danger of paralyzing, industry-wide auto walkout. Smiling at each other are John S. Bugas (l.), Ford industrial relations vice president, and UAW's Reuther. Prolonged strike would have frustrated industry's hope of a 5.5 million-car year.

HANDCLASP, however, between Steel Workers' President David J. MacDonald, U.S. Steel's R. Conrad Cooper, was only preliminary to week after week of unsatisfactory discussions in attempt to reach a new agreement. Management, with almost all major companies united in common front, displayed much harder attitude than in previous years, wanted to "freeze" existing pact for another year. Union complained it was attempting to take over its role as champion of worker. Nation continued to show indication of becoming more impatient with endless round of wage, then price increases.

ALOHA is greeting expressed here as Representative John J. Rivers (D-Alaska) greets Delegate John Burns (D-Hawaii). The two rubbed noses, Eskimo style, after House passed Hawaiian statehood bill by vote of 323 to 89 March 12. Rivers and Burns wear leis about their necks to help celebrate event. Campaigning for chance to represent Hawaii went into high gear as soon as it was heard that Congress approved entrance of 50th state of Union.

SERENITY is present in Hawaii even in busy business sections. This is Bishop Street in Honolulu, looking mountain-ward. Chief product of the islands has long been sugar, with pineapple, live stock, coffee and rice industries in second place. Mainly an agricultural country, Hawaii's landscape is dotted with farms and plantations, which have been greatly improved by scientific work and labor-saving devices. Manufacturing is increasing to serve the local market.

HULAS HAIL HAWAII STATEHOOD

HALF-MOON of Waikiki extends from the Royal Hawaiian Hotel (foreground) to the famous landmark of Diamond Head. A mecca for thousands of tourists a year, Waikiki is part of the picturesque Hawaiian Islands that were brought to the attention of the Western World in 1778 when British explorer James Cook "discovered" them. Hawaii shifted from kingdom to republic in 1894; to U.S. possession in 1898; and to U.S. territory in 1900. As a Pacific crossroads it has acquired over the years a population of 578,000 that constitutes a great racial melting-pot. People of Japanese origin predominate (35%), followed by whites (25%) and Asians other than Japanese accounting for 19%. Pure or mixed Hawaiians make up most of the remainder. The question of statehood for Hawaii arose almost as soon as the islands became a territory. First Hawaiian statehood bill before Congress was introduced in 1919, others in 1947-1953.

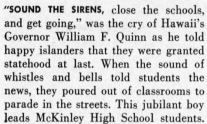

"SOUND THE SIRENS, close the schools, and get going," was the cry of Hawaii's Governor William F. Quinn as he told happy islanders that they were granted statehood at last. When the sound of whistles and bells told students the news, they poured out of classrooms to parade in the streets. This jubilant boy leads McKinley High School students.

SMILING VICTORS in Hawaii's first national election are GOP's Sen. Hiram Fong *(below, with wife)*, Democrats' Sen. Oren Long *(l.)*, Rep. Daniel Inouye *(r.)*. Mainland-born Long, 70, was territorial governor, senator. Millionaire Fong, 54, war hero Inouye, 34, both were born in new state, are first persons of Chinese and Japanese descent elected to the U.S. Congress.

CELEBRATIONS to welcome Hawaii into the union included pageants and hula shows for camera fans and tourists. Here a group of joyful islanders pose with letters spelling out the reason for their happiness. Statehood gives local sovereignty and voice to all Hawaiians in Presidential and Congressional elections, formulation of national policy.

39

WORLD AFFAIRS -- 1959

Soviet Communists try smiling while Chinese Communists keep on snarling

INTERNATIONAL Communism, in 1959, presented several faces to the world, like the ancient god Janus, or, better yet, like Cerberus, the dog that in Greek mythology guarded the gates of Hell.

Which to believe was the Free World's problem.

The "friendly" face was that of Moscow. It was typified by the man-to-man bluff heartiness of Nikita Khrushchev, who sought to spread the image of colossal but essentially reasonable power, prepared to come to a "live and let live" accommodation with the West, and, in particular, the U.S.

But this "friendliness" had its price.

If Khrushchev, after the many futile weeks of the Foreign Ministers' Geneva Conference, tacitly dropped his threat to turn control of land travel to West Berlin over to his East German puppets, he won for these same East Germans a place, if not at the conference table, at least in the conference room, and thus grudging quasi-recognition.

And, of much more importance, he won for himself what he had long and apparently vainly coveted, an invitation to visit the U.S. and a matching Eisenhower trip to Moscow.

The exchange of visits provided a double opportunity for the two-power talks the Kremlin craved.

It was this latter prospect which, if it aroused hope among the peoples, aroused fear among Allied statesmen. It caused President Eisenhower, as an essential preliminary, to make a fence-mending swing around Bonn, Paris and London to shore up NATO and promise solemnly that he planned to shun any semblance of bilateral agreement, or even negotiation, with Khrushchev.

Another, openly snarling face was that of Red Peking.

China, while the USSR was preaching reasonableness, increased in pitch its bitter, incessant press and radio attacks on the U.S., the West and Free Asia.

And, where it could, it suited action to its words.

The pledged autonomy of Tibet, Himalayan cloud-kingdom just north of India, was drowned in native blood and smothered under the weight of forced Chinese mass immigration. Tibet's theocratic ruler, the young Dalai Lama, escaped with only his life and the extremely slender hope of UN intervention.

China also determinedly revived ancient claims to the two Indian frontier protectorates of Bhutan and Sikkim.

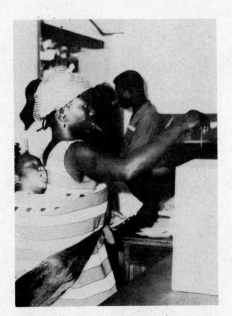

AFRICAN MOTHER CASTS VOTE FOR FUTURE

(However, the rape of Tibet, the threat to the two border states and Peking's contemptuous rudeness in the face of India's persistent proffers of friendship caused a revulsion of Indian feeling, and shook even Nehru's cherished neutralism. The West, thus, might become the ultimate gainer.)

Potentially even graver, since here the U.S. was directly concerned, was the Chinese-backed Red threat to Laos, which had received independence at the 1954 Geneva conference which had ostensibly brought peace to Indo-China.

Communist "liberation" forces, defying existing agreements, resumed operations from their bases in Red North Viet Nam, and quickly developed a potentially dangerous threat to the main communications arteries and the capital, Ventiane, itself.

Fall of Laos would outflank two Western allies, North Viet Nam and Thailand, and imperil all the rest of Southeast Asia.

(A sinister sidelight was the fact that Khrushchev, when he accepted the Eisenhower invitation, already had blessed the new aggression.)

Communism's third face, that turned to freedom-intoxicated Africa and the fermenting Caribbean, was that of benevolent big brother—and fisher in troubled waters.

Everywhere, Moscow was attempting to counter Western aid with help offers of its own. Everywhere, Red intrigue was playing on the strings of new, self-conscious nationalism and resentment of U.S. economic supremacy and former French and British tutelage.

In Africa, several of the republics set up by the De Gaulle regime seemed about to sever their last links with Paris—and Moscow was eager to move in.

In the Caribbean, Cuba's new, touchy and economically fuzzy-minded Castro government had shown a measure of friendship to local Communists—and this, the Kremlin planners hoped, might provide a Red base of operations in Latin America.

But the U.S., undismayed, continued its search for a just, lasting peace for all humanity. President Eisenhower, as he left on his visit of reassurance to West European leaders, answered critics by stating:

"We are talking about the human race and what is going to happen to it."

EISENHOWER DESIRE TO MELT COLD WAR ICE IS SYMBOLIZED BY STATE DINNER GIVEN FOR KHRUSHCHEV AND WIFE AT WHITE HOUSE

U.S., USSR CHIEFS STAGE FACE-TO-FACE TALKS

Eisenhower-Khrushchev discussions follow Geneva deadlock; could lead to full Summit parley, even Berlin agreement

PRESIDENT EISENHOWER ushered in a distinctly new era in the East-West cold war in 1959. He invited Soviet Premier Nikita Khrushchev, avowed rival of the U.S., to see the U.S. for himself in late September. This was to be followed by his own unprecedented tour of the USSR.

This was a new chapter of personal diplomacy at the highest level. It was not an attempt to end the cold war. But it was a step in a long-range plan to do so, and at least an attempt to start an immediate thaw. On the

Soviet side, the Khrushchev-Eisenhower exchange was part of a drive, begun late in 1957, to achieve a Big Four summit conference of government leaders to deal with the critical Berlin and German issues.

For a year-and-a-half the leaders of the major powers had debated the idea of a summit parley as a way of trying to break the ice in Soviet-Western relations. The idea was pushed mainly by Moscow, accepted by London, and opposed variously by Washington, Paris, and Bonn.

WEST GERMAN CHANCELLOR KONRAD ADENAUER (R.) MEETS GENIAL EISENHOWER AT START OF LATTER'S TALKS WITH THE ALLIES.

Vice President Nixon's summer tour of the Soviet Union, his unusual public debate with Khrushchev, and the warmth of his reception gave impetus to a feeling that the U.S. should invite Khrushchev to Washington. Failure of the Big Four foreign ministers' conference in Geneva also was a factor influencing President Eisenhower.

So, on Aug. 3, a wholly new chapter began. The President announced: "In the effort to melt a little bit of the ice that seems to freeze our relationships . . . with the Soviets . . . possibly a visit such as I now have proposed would be helpful."

Premier Khrushchev followed by saying: "The important thing is to find through these exchanges a common language and a common understanding of questions we are to settle."

The arrangement was unprecedented in that it was the first time any Russian head of government set foot in the U.S., and the first time that a U.S. president would publicly visit the Soviet Union. (President Roosevelt's wartime journey to Yalta was a secret mission.)

Khrushchev's itinerary, which began Sept. 15, was a fairly wide one condensed into a brief period. It called for two days of ceremonies in Washington, including a question-and-answer session at the National Press Club

and talks with the President, then entertainment in New York and an address to the UN General Assembly. Before returning to Washington for more talks with the President, the Khrushchev tour called for eight days of visits in Los Angeles, San Francisco, Des Moines and Pittsburgh. A stellar attraction for Khrushchev was a visit to the big Iowa corn belt. One of the Soviet leader's greatest passions has been a drive to increase Soviet farm production.

All this gave those charged with the security of both leaders an enormous task. This was true especially in the case of Khrushchev. As head of a government which was hated bitterly by emigre groups, the Soviet leader was an automatic invitation to protest, even violence.

Despite some heavy criticism, the President's effort to break the East-West deadlock met with general approval at home and abroad. But there was anxiety among the Allies that a Big Two conference might make deals of convenience at their expense. To reassure the major Allies, President Eisenhower flew to Bonn, London and Paris, for talks with the Allied leaders. It was a great personal triumph, yet he did not quite succeed in removing all doubts of Allied leaders on the wisdom of Big Two talks, or even Big Four talks.

West German Chancellor Konrad Adenauer met the President when he arrived at Wahn airport, along with an estimated 315,000 persons who cheered General Eisenhower on the route to Bonn, the West German capital.

"The American people stand by your side in insuring that the loyal, free people of free Berlin will, like yourselves, continue always to enjoy that great privilege (of freedom)."

These words by the President were what the Germans ached to hear. They meant that he did not intend to make any independent agreements with Khrushchev whereby the U.S. would abandon West Berlin to the East German puppet government.

President Eisenhower next visited Great Britain. He saw Queen Elizabeth at Balmoral Castle in Scotland and talked with Prime Minister Harold Macmillan. An estimated one million Londoners turned out to cheer the former Supreme Commander of Allied Forces in Europe.

Another huge crowd gathered to see the President when he flew to Paris for talks with France's President Charles de Gaulle. General Eisenhower was received with affection and hospitality in France, where he renewed the standing invitation to de Gaulle to visit the United States, and where he visited his old NATO headquarters.

Diplomats, remembering that a short time ago de Gaulle had described the Eisenhower decision to meet Premier Khrushchev as the act of a "lone horseman" going to talk to the other side, said the change of atmosphere was remarkable after "Ike's" personal visit.

President Eisenhower was greeted by a big crowd upon his return to Washington Labor Day. This tremendous store of good will he had built up at home and abroad was needed in his projected effort to convince the Soviet masses and their leaders that he was dedicated to peace— but a peace with justice.

The crisis over Berlin, one that the Soviets have kept alive ever since World War II, involved a Soviet challenge to the right of the Big Three western powers to maintain troops in the former German capital and to have free access to it across the 110 miles of Communist

U.S. SECRETARY OF STATE CHRISTIAN HERTER REMAINS FIRM ON BERLIN AT FINAL BIG FOUR FOREIGN MINISTERS' GENEVA PARLEY.

East Germany that separate the city from West Germany.

After seven weeks of negotiations—interrupted by a recess in late June and early July—the atmosphere in Geneva was one of hopeless deadlock. The announced Eisenhower-Khrushchev exchange of visits gave the Big Four foreign ministers a means of gracefully adjourning that futile parley. Statements summarizing their position on Berlin showed these main differences:

Status quo: The West sought a five-year extension of the present situation in divided Berlin, with Western rights to continue until agreement on a new status. The USSR offered an 18-month extension but refused to commit itself to any extension or recognition of Western right after that.

Germany: Moscow insisted agreement on Berlin be linked with establishment of an all-German committee to discuss the future of Germany. The West, seeing this as a device to force Western recognition of East Germany, called for agreement on Berlin alone, with the question of Germany's future left for discussion by the Big Four

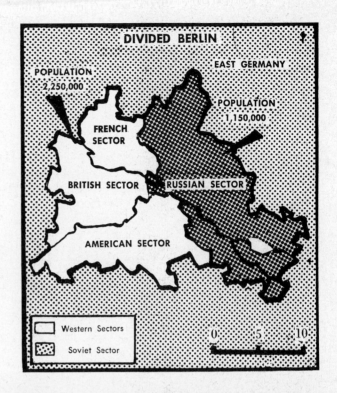

BIG FOUR FOREIGN MINISTERS: SELWYN LLOYD (BR), COUVE DE MURVILLE (FR), ANDREI GROMYKO (USSR), CHRISTIAN HERTER (USA).

group with East and West German advisors.

Garrison: The West insisted on keeping its Berlin garrison at its present level of 11,000. Russia demanded reduction of these to a "token" force of about 3500.

These were just details of the long fruitless sparring. The key issue remained Khrushchev's demand of November, 1958, that the Western powers evacuate Berlin and that both sides sign peace treaties with two separate German states. To grant the first demand, the West would have had to abandon its pledge to keep 2 million West Berliners free. In granting the second demand, the West would have had to acknowledge the permanent division

U.S. DELEGATE JAMES J. WADSWORTH (C. REAR) ATTENDS PAINFULLY SLOW BUT STEADY GENEVA NUCLEAR DISARMAMENT TALKS.

of Germany. Khrushchev's demand that both these moves be made within a time limit had turned the German issue into one of the major crises of the cold war.

Three other issues were involved in the Eisenhower-Khrushchev exchange. They were disarmament, nuclear tests and trade.

On disarmament the Western problem was how to trim forces and still be safe from Soviet attack. Khrushchev charged that the Allies sought to "encircle" the USSR with menacing bases. The Allied response was that the record of Soviet expansionism and Communist infiltration justified the bases. Khrushchev told President Eisenhower and other Western leaders that he would withdraw Soviet troops from East Germany, Poland and Hungary if the Western nations withdrew their troops from foreign countries. The West pointed out that its withdrawal would be greater geographically than that of the USSR, hence there was need of some international mechanism to police the withdrawal. Moscow refused such a mechanism.

On nuclear tests the issue, even after the Eisenhower-Khrushchev exchange, remained the same: an international policing organization to control a test suspension. The USSR had accepted this idea in principle but balked at the details after nearly a year of negotiations at Geneva. Both sides, however, seemed anxious to prevent any increase in the number of nuclear powers.

On trade, Khrushchev wanted expansion because Western goods and foreign exchange would aid him in fulfilling his seven-year economic development plan. The U.S. reply to this was that the Soviet Union uses trading as a state weapon and therefore is undependable. Besides, Moscow wants to sell what the U.S. does not need and refuses to buy what the U.S. wants to sell.

Behind the drama of the Eisenhower-Khrushchev exchange was a deep contest for high stakes. Khrushchev wanted nothing less than an agreement whereby the U.S. and the Soviet Union would divide the world into spheres of influence. This in turn would smash the NATO Alliance and open the way for Communism to promote what its party members say is inevitable—the fall of capitalism. Khrushchev's highly-publicized "invasion" of the U.S. also was a blow to the feelings of satellite peoples who looked on the U.S. as their chief champion in trying, eventually, to break loose from Soviet control.

President Eisenhower played for more modest stakes by agreeing to go to the Soviet Union. Yet these were momentous stakes. He sought a way of ending the combination of propaganda and threat that has enabled the USSR to spark one cold war threat after another. If he could break that chain there might be a basis for a solid peace.

Even before and during the Eisenhower exchange there was little to indicate a sincere Soviet retreat on the key issue of Berlin and Germany. The widespread publicity attending every move of the touring Big Two leaders did not mask the combination of friendly and hostile attitudes on both sides.

Important developments in Asia also tended to sour the circumstances of the Eisenhower-Khrushchev exchange. The Soviet Premier entered the U.S. with members of his family and a retinue of aides totaling approxi-

BIG CONCRETE MEMORIAL AT TEMPLEHOF AIRPORT COMMEMORATES ALLIED AIRMEN WHO DIED DURING BERLIN AIRLIFT A DECADE AGO.

mately 100 persons. Yet weeks before his arrival Communist forces, supported by North Vietnam Reds, attacked Laos. Red Chinese troops, who had conquered Tibet, also occupied parts of India's northern frontier. Khrushchev did not help his mission by issuing a stream of statements reiterating old Soviet positions on various issues. And the Soviet leader also announced that he would visit Peiping to see his old friend and colleague, Chinese Red leader Mao Tse-tung, immediately after he finished his U.S. tour. Meanwhile, he called on India and China to settle their dispute peacefully.

On the surface Khrushchev's visit to Peiping right after his talks with President Eisenhower seemed fair enough in the perilous East-West struggle. The U.S. leader had discussed mutual problems with his allies; the chunky Soviet leader would do the same with his main ally. Some observers thought Red belligerency in Laos and on India's borders was Mao's way of warning Khrushchev not to go too far toward "peaceful coexistence."

RED MISSIONARY Nikita Khrushchev promised separate peace treaty with East Germany when he arrived in Leipzig in March. With a bunch of flowers, he waves to crowd. He smiles (below) as Premier Otto Grotewohl makes a point. At left is Walter Ulbricht, known as the "German Lenin." Khrushchev announced "complete agreement" had been reached with the two local Reds on Berlin and German unity issues.

REFUGEES' FLIGHT WEAKENS ECONOMIC GAINS

THE EAST GERMAN government conceded in 1959 that it is the only country in the world with a steadily decreasing population.

Throughout this area, which the Communists call the German Democratic Republic, the people, who have given up hope that the two Germanys ever will be reunited, had the choice of resignation—or escape to the West.

More than three million had fled since 1949. They still were flowing into West Germany in 1959 at the rate of 10,000 monthly. West German Chancellor Konrad Adenauer himself had urged the East Germans to stay home as long as they could because the "land must be saved for Germans." But the refugees still poured westward. The vast majority were under 25, skilled workers, scientists, and teachers—men no country could afford to dispense with.

Economic reasons no longer were the main factor for the escapes, despite the fact that living standards were 30% below those of West Germany. Huge Soviet aid, some $400 million since the Berlin uprising of 1953, had helped make East Germany the most prosperous of Moscow's seven European satellites.

Shops were well stocked with consumer goods. Bread, potatoes, and coal were cheaper than in West Germany. Rents were low, clothing abundant. Many of the refugees fleeing to the west knew they would have to accept jobs for less money.

Refugees entering West Berlin during the year again cited the constant pressure to toe the Communist party line. Some examples:

In January, 87 East Germans were sentenced to prison or hard labor for "slandering" the state. Not long ago the Bitterfeld Construction Co., largest private construction firm in the GDR, was threatened with nationalization. So its entire management promptly went west. A shoemaker told how he left everything behind and fled to West Berlin because he feared arrest after he had refused to join a state-controlled "production cooperative."

Some diplomats felt that the general discontent and flight of refugees made East Germany a liability to Moscow. They argued that Walter Ulbricht, black-bearded Red party boss who still was a Soviet citizen, would be tossed out the moment the USSR withdrew its 22 divisions stationed in East Germany.

Others felt that the new 110,000-man East German army could put down any repetitions of the 1953 revolt. But whatever Moscow had in

RUSSIAN-FOSTERED TENSION over Berlin occurred while East Berlin workers were still removing World War II rubble such as the old Reichstag building *(c. background)*. The bunker *(l.)* was scene of Nazis' last stand, Hitler's death.

mind, there was no question of abandoning the Red regime.

A surprising fact was that, despite the exodus of skilled workers and the resentment of the people, East Germany was proving itself Russia's most valuable satellite. Its industries produced more than those of any other Communist-bloc nation except the USSR and Red China. East Ger-

many was Moscow's foremost trading partner, with a yearly trade of 3 billion rubles each way. East German chemicals were a vital factor in Soviet industry, and East German trade with underdeveloped countries played a key role in Soviet plans.

Soviet Premier Nikita Khrushchev, who had been threatening to sign a separate peace treaty with East Ger-

many, paid a visit in March. His official reason was to attend the Leipzig Fair, but he heaped scorn on the West in his attempt to get the Allies into a summit conference and to agree to making West Berlin a "free city," meaning one denuded of the protective presence of Allied soldiers. He made it clear the real Soviet aim was the absorption of all Germany.

FACTORY MILITIAMEN wearing blue uniforms are outfitted and trained to put down any anti-Red uprising in East Germany. They number 215,000, are in addition to 110,000-man army.

REFUGEES from East Germany, their few belongings beside them, wait for West Berlin airport bus and final journey to a new home in West Germany. Millions have fled Red rule.

49

KONRAD ADENAUER *(l.)*, West German Economics Minister Ludwig Erhard effect a truce. Tiff began when Adenauer decided to retain job as chancellor and not become president. Erhard wanted the job. Heinrich Luebke *(r.)* became president.

"SLY OLD FOX" DEFIES OPPONENTS

Konrad Adenauer survives ouster attempt

A RIFT in the ranks of the ruling Christian Democratic party was the major domestic event in West Germany in 1959.

Konrad Adenauer, the 83-year-old chancellor who guided his war-flattened nation back to top power and prosperity, announced in April that he would retire from the control post he had held since 1949, and run for the presidency, a prestige post but one without the power of the chancellorship.

The Germany that Adenauer built was now the key to the East-West battle in Europe. Its economic power was the base on which Western Europe was constructing a common market; and its army was getting U.S. nuclear arms. Fear of German power was one reason why the Kremlin spent years in plugging for a summit conference—in the hope of making a deal at the Germans' expense. So Adenauer's decision stunned both Germans and the Western allies.

Adenauer agreed to run for the presidency on the understanding that his party's rank and file would not contest his choice of successor—Finance Minister Franz Etzel—and that he would be permitted to keep a strong voice in the conduct of the country's affairs.

The party, however, concerned only with winning the 1961 national elections, voted for Dr. Ludwig Erhard, the Economics Minister and acknowledged wizard of German recovery.

In June, while Erhard was in the U.S., Adenauer reversed his decision, saying that "deterioration of the international situation" had led to his change of mind. An angered Erhard

50

"STAGGER SYSTEM" is used in new housing project in Munich. Each house gets full benefit of sun and owners get unimpeded view from each window.

"OLD FOX" Konrad Adenauer (second from r. in foreground) is flanked by cabinet ministers toasting him upon celebration of his 83rd birthday. This was in January, before summer dispute with Economics Minister Erhard (r.), who had expected to be new chancellor. Adenauer choice was man at his own right, Franz Etzel.

hastened home by plane from Washington, and the German press charged that Adenauer had dealt a blow to democracy. Erhard denounced what he called "current lies," stating that "I will fight the historical lie that I am less reliable than Dr. Adenauer in conducting international affairs."

For a time it seemed that some Christian Democrats would lead a revolt in parliament to try to oust Adenauer. The Chancellor himself admitted he had received some adverse mail. He said his favorite postcard contained only three words: "You old scoundrel." Yet Adenauer easily rode out the political storm. Dr. Heinrich Luebke, Agriculture Minister, was elected President, replacing Dr. Theodor Heuss, Sept. 15.

Germany's million Saarlanders regained their full rights as Germans in July for the first time since World War II. Reintegration of the small area was hailed as "removal of the last burden of French-German relations."

West German business continued to boom during the year, but there was anxiety over the steady Soviet efforts to isolate West Berlin.

WEST GERMAN SOLDIERS in camouflage dress set up U.S.-made "Honest John" rocket in firing position during training period at Eschweiler army base. First West German rocket battalion using tactical weapons became operational on April 1.

ATTENTIVE listeners to U N General Assembly debate are Sec'y-General Dag Hammarskjold, Assembly Pres. Malik.

WORLD BODY EXPANDS ITS ACTIVITIES

Behind shift of spotlight to U.S., Soviet chiefs, UN continues peace efforts, health and refugee programs

IN CONTRAST to the tense events of 1958, when the explosive Middle East situation resulted in the summoning of the third emergency special session in the U N 's history, 1959 seemed a relatively quiet year. The spotlight of international diplomacy had shifted to the meeting at Geneva and the reciprocal Khrushchev-Eisenhower visits. If the focus of attention seemed to have left the U N , its world-wide responsibilities remained, nevertheless, and its activities continued to expand in 1959.

Late in 1958, border troubles between Cambodia and Thailand led to a formal complaint being lodged by Cambodia and the dispatch, early in 1959, of Ambassador John Beck-Friis of Sweden as representative of the U N 's Secretary General. As a result of his visit and the accompanying negotiations, diplomatic relations between the two countries were renewed in February. Two months earlier, the U N Observation Group in Lebanon officially ceased operations when the last military observer left Beirut following the uneventful evacuation of U.S. troops from the area. The U N 's effort to find a solution to the problems of nearby Algeria, however, continued to be frustrated by the refusal of France to participate in discussions.

Various agencies and committees of the U N continued to investigate and report on problems ranging from census-taking methods (Statistical Commission) to the requiring of free consent to a marriage contract (Commission on the Status of Women). Under a program of major importance, over 55 million children and expectant or nursing mothers benefited in 1959 from the work of UNICEF (United Nations Children's Fund) in some 105 countries. UNICEF's largest financial allocation went into a vigorous anti-malaria campaign.

A U N expert was sent to Iceland to advise on methods for extracting salt from sea-water, while an expert on tourism was provided for Libya. Both were taking part in the U N 's vast technical assistance program, in which some 8,000 experts have served 140 countries in the ten years since the program's inception.

The difficulties of dealing with the problem of the world's refugees continued to engage much of the U N 's efforts. The number of refugees registered with UNRWA (United Nations Relief and Works Agency for Palestine Refugees in the Near East) was well over a million by May, and in Tunisia and Morocco some 180,000 refugees from Algeria were receiving emergency U N aid when the U N–sponsored World Refugee Year began in June.

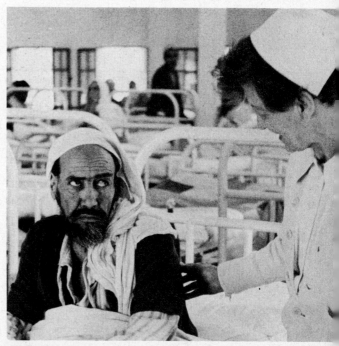

ENCOURAGEMENT is offered a patient at the UNRWA clinic in the Gaza Strip. UNRWA currently provides food, medical care and shelter to over one million refugees in this area.

FAR-FLUNG ACTIVITIES of the U N range from a committee chamber in its New York headquarters *(above)* to a primitive river valley in Cambodia *(below)*. In New York, Henry Cabot Lodge of the U.S. and Britain's Sir Pierson Dixon of the Committee on the Peaceful Uses of Outer Space sit next to the vacant seats of the Soviet and United Arab Republic delegations, who boycotted the May session with U S S R charging that too many "Westerners" were on committee. In Cambodia, members of an advisory board from the U N's technical assistance program survey a proposed dam site on lower Mekong river. Plans are underway to develop the river basin, where over 17 million people live, through irrigation, flood control, power and navigation projects.

REFUGEE PROBLEM continues to be a major concern of the U N and its agencies. The children *(above)* are part of a group of some 180,000 refugees from Algeria. In an attempt to concentrate international attention and effort on the problem of the world's refugees, the General Assembly of U N proclaimed World Refugee Year beginning June 1959, and adopted emblem *(below)* showing symbolic figure of a refugee protected by a pair of hands and encircled by the laurel wreath of the U N Recognition of an outstanding individual effort to aid refugees came to Belgium's Father George Pire *(inset above)*, whose crusade for refugees won him a Nobel Peace Prize.

BRITISH Paymaster-General Reginald Maudling *(r.)* and German economist Ludwig Erhard trade free trade ideas.

U.S. NATO PLANES QUIT FRANCE

stockpiling of nuclear arms;

Paris asks voice in

Britain helps form "outer seven" free trade area

NATO, the American-backed North Atlantic Treaty Organization, a defense shield for Western Europe, suffered a big political reverse in 1959. The western nations faced danger of rivalry and even a trade war.

NATO is the greatest peacetime coalition in history, embracing 450 million people inhabiting some 7.8 million square miles. Together, the fifteen member nations have 5.5 million men under arms, including 46 divisions allocated to NATO's joint military pool in three regional commands. They are pledged to regard an attack against one as against all.

French President Charles de Gaulle, in seeking to restore French "grandeur" and a place in the "nuclear club," told Gen. Lauris Norstad, Supreme Commander of the NATO forces in Europe, that he could not stockpile U.S. nuclear arms at U.S. bases in France unless France had a say in control of the weapons. So Norstad was forced to plan the transfer of planes to Britain and Germany.

Complications also loomed in 1959 for Europe's six-nation Common Market comprising France, West Germany, Italy, Belgium, the Netherlands and Luxembourg, with a combined population of 170 million. Britain, who rejected the customs union because of supernational and other features, helped organize an "Outer Seven" free-trade area of itself, Norway, Sweden, Denmark, Switzerland, Austria and Portugal. All hoped the two blocs would aid each other and not start a trade war.

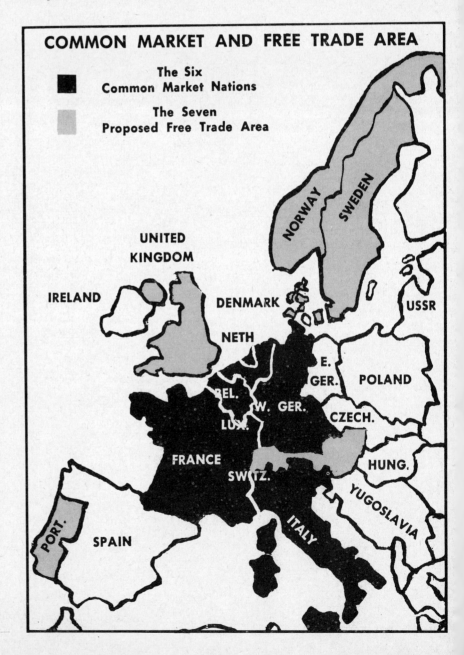

COMMON MARKET AND FREE TRADE AREA

The Six
Common Market Nations

The Seven
Proposed Free Trade Area

NORWAY · SWEDEN · UNITED KINGDOM · IRELAND · DENMARK · USSR · NETH · E. GER. · POLAND · BEL. · W. GER. · LUX. · CZECH. · FRANCE · SWITZ. · HUNG. · YUGOSLAVIA · ITALY · PORT. · SPAIN

TENTH ANNIVERSARY of NATO is spelled out in tribute by the crewmen of U.S. Navy carrier Franklin D. Roosevelt.

MARTIN MACE missile will replace Matador as newest weapon in NATO arsenal. France denied nuclear arms at U.S. bases unless it controlled the weapons.

GEN. LAURIS NORSTAD, Supreme Commander of Allied Forces in Europe, was unable to stockpile U.S. nuclear arms in France because of dispute with French.

COLD WAR THAW

**Khrushchev invited to U.S.
Eisenhower to USSR;
varied cultural exchanges
and successful soviet visit
by Vice-President Nixon
set stage for top level talks**

NIKITA KHRUSHCHEV, ebullient, outspoken and irrepressible boss of the Kremlin, achieved one of his major ambitions in August.

Simultaneous announcements in Moscow and Washington stated that the Soviet dictator would pay an official visit to the U.S. in September, and that this would be followed, before the end of the year, by a trip to the USSR by President Eisenhower.

The scheduled journey to the U.S. was undoubtedly a personal triumph for Khrushchev, who for years had been putting out diplomatic feelers for such an invitation.

The announcement came just after the end of Vice President Richard M. Nixon's own visit to the USSR (at the very moment that Nixon was being wildly cheered by crowds in Poland). In a sense it served as climax to the Nixon tour, during which Nixon stood up to the stocky Soviet premier in frank, blunt, no-holds-barred exchanges over the accomplishments and merits of the Free and the Communist systems. (Televised in the U.S., they not only advanced Nixon's political fortunes but brought Khrushchev to down-to-earth life for U.S. viewers.)

To the USSR's 200 million people Khrushchev pledged both a life of plenty and world supremacy.

TOP BRITON, Prime Minister Harold Macmillan, visited the Soviet Union in February and March on an "exploration" trip, trying to break the East-West impasse over the German problem. The fur-hatted British leader *(below)* inspects a Soviet guard of honor upon his arrival in Kiev from Moscow.

Soviet Premier Nikita Khrushchev *(r.)* also wears a fur hat. He was on hand to meet Macmillan when latter arrived at Moscow's Vnukovo airport. Khrushchev was cordial one moment with Macmillan and in the next made almost openly rude speeches attacking and ridiculing the West.

HUNGARIAN PATRIOTS, seething over Soviet crushing of the 1956 Hungarian freedom uprising, wait to greet Soviet Deputy Premier Anastas Mikoyan at New York's Idlewild airport Jan. 4 when he arrived for a two-week "informal" visit

to the U.S. They carried signs telling him to go back home, and saying "Remember Korea, Hungary!" The black-mustached, 63-year-old Mikoyan was heavily guarded by police *(above)* when he left Soviet headquarters to visit the U.N.

At the 21st Soviet Communist Party Congress in Moscow in February, largely a one-man show, the 65-year-old premier outlined this domestic program: a more rewarding life for all the people—after still harder work and sacrifice. Khrushchev specifically promised a 35-hour week in five years, a 40 per cent rise in real wages in seven years and a 70 per cent hike in farm output in the same period. The burly, energetic Premier offered: "good appetite, comrades . . . more sweet and less bitter." In this pie-in-the-sky future he said there would be better housing, no income taxes and less security police—except those used to hunt "imperialists."

The stocky Premier predicted Soviet industrial capacity exceeding all European nations by 1965, and surpassing the U.S. in per capita industrial output by 1970, figured at an annual 8.6 per cent growth compared with a current average of 1.5 per cent in the U.S.

In foreign policy Khrushchev demanded peace—but, as usual, only on Soviet terms. "Today, when we hold the advantage in rocket engineering," he said, "we again say (to the West), 'Let's ban for all time the testing, production, and use of nuclear and rocket weapons, and destroy all stockpiles.'" But Mr. Khrushchev made no mention of Western demands for effective disarmament controls. He repeated Moscow's determination to make West Berlin a "free" city, meaning a defenseless city by Western interpretation.

Western statesmen did not scoff at Khrushchev's industrial goals. Some warned that, unless the democracies worked harder, the Russians might surpass the West. And there was no denying that Khrushchev had ushered in a New Deal since Stalin died. Living standards had risen. Khrushchev's virgin lands program boosted grain production from 81 million metric tons in 1950 to 128 million in 1958; milk output was up from 67,000 to 1 million. Gov. LeRoy Collins of Florida, one of nine U.S. governors who toured the Soviet Union, commented: "The Russian people have never had it so good."

U.S. SEAMEN from the Navy radar picket ship Roy O. Hale *(in background)* maneuver in a small boat alongside the Soviet trawler Novorossisk, *(foreground)*, just before boarding vessel northeast of St. John's, Newfoundland, Feb. 26. Search party suspected fishermen might have caused some of 5 breaks in transatlantic cables. Search angered Moscow.

EXHIBITIONS were opened in Moscow and New York under U.S.-Soviet cultural agreement. The 200-ft. diameter gold-anodized Kaiser Aluminum dome, largest such structure to be built anywhere topped the U.S. National Exhibition in Moscow's Sokolniki Park. Although Moscow press attacked U.S. displays, thousands of Russians went to see it. Vice-President Nixon flew there to officiate at the opening and escorted Premier Khrushchev on exhibit tour. Cordiality of their meeting was mostly lost as each publicly accused other of making threats *(above r.)*. Soviet fair *(below, l.)* in New York's Coliseum shows statue of a Russian worker and a picture of Lenin, creator of the Communist state. On floor is a Sputnik nose cone. Soviet First Deputy Premier Frol Kozlov, who opened exhibit, toured toy plant for doll for daughter.

NEW HOUSING PROJECTS *(above)* are located in Krasnoyarsk Territory in Siberia. The apartments going up are being built for workers in a new metallurgical plant. The Soviet officials opened up a few "closed" cities in little-known Siberia to Vice-President Nixon and reporters on tour here.

TOPS IN HER CLASS is plaid-shirted Irina Gurova, who listens with other students to a lecture at the Moscow Aviation Institute. The second Russian woman to learn to fly a helicopter, she set a Soviet-claimed world's speed record in March, with a flying average of 108.96 miles per hour.

MAY DAY PARADE in Moscow shows Soviet tank crews passing in review beneath pictures of Karl Marx and Lenin. Such scenes and ceremonies no longer are limited to only a few western diplomats and newsmen. American and other foreign tourists now are familiar figures in Moscow streets.

TITO REMAINS THORN TO SOVIETS

Yugoslav president draws wrath of Moscow and Peiping; Red Satellites toe Moscow line

Marshall tito, dissident Red leader of Yugoslavia, remained in 1959 the biggest barb in the tough hide of Soviet Premier Nikita Khrushchev. The Yugoslav president traded insults with Soviet leaders and Chinese Reds who frequently attacked him as a "revisionist," one who refused the orthodox Moscow line.

The 67-year-old Tito made a three-month swing through Asia to keep himself and his country as an independent nation on display. He furiously denounced Soviet Vice Premier Anastas Mikoyan upon his return to Belgrade, because Mikoyan reportedly had remarked that Yugoslavia could be bought for $100 million.

Yugoslavia continued to get along well with the U.S. during the year, in contrast to its bitter relations with the Communist world. It received more than $150 million in aid from the U.S., which in 1958 had completed a military aid program costing nearly $1 billion.

Relations between the Communist satellites and the

"WELCOME COMRADE." Premier Nikita Khrushchev, whose Soviet tanks crushed the 1956 Hungarian revolt, is greeted by Red Hungarian premier, Muennich, on visit to Budapest.

Soviet Union had certainly changed since the days when Josef Stalin simply dictated the satellites' course. How much they had changed was anybody's guess and possibly the answer depended on the will and strength of each satellite's leaders to argue with Moscow. Walter Ulbricht, the East German Communist chief, was not known as a man who tried to argue with the Kremlin. Yet East Germany, the most advanced as well as the most docile politically among the satellites, was perhaps the key supplier for the Soviet seven-year economic plan.

Moscow received a damaging blow in East Germany during the year. Lt. Col. Siegfried Dombrowski, 43, deputy chief of Communist East Germany's military intelligence agency, deserted East Berlin for the freedom of West Germany. He turned over a master spy roster of the German Reds which contained 12,000 names.

Albania, Bulgaria, Czechoslovakia, East Germany, Hungary, Rumania, and Poland all remained fixed in the Soviet camp, and Khrushchev, beaming and voluble, continued to make good-will tours among them. Restive Poland retained greater freedom of expression—and contacts with the West—compared to the other satellites. Party leader Wladyslaw Gomulka parroted Moscow's line, but mapped his own economic course, including private farming, and held an uneasy truce with Roman Catholic Church, to which most Poles remained devoted.

YUGOSLAVIA'S itinerant dictator, President Tito, gets light from host, United Arab Republic chief Gamal Abdel Nasser, during his February visit to Cairo. Both are "neutralists."

ATOMIC REACTOR, first to be set up in Hungary, was placed in operation March 25. It was built with the aid of the Soviet Union in town of Csilleberg. Powerful experimental reactor will be used for research and the training of scientists.

CARDINAL Wyszynski, Roman Catholic primate of Poland, greets followers. His sermons criticizing Red regime were seized.

JANOS KADAR *(r.)* Hungary's Red party boss, mingles with Budapest crowds April 4 — anniversary of 1945 entry of Soviet troops.

ERICH KOCH, 64, former Hitler cabinet member, is held by Polish police after collapsing upon hearing himself sentenced to death for war-time atrocities. He was convicted of being responsible for the deaths of over 232,000 persons.

ANGRY ICELANDERS, estimated to number 15,000, gathered in Reykjavik, the country's capital, to protest against the presence of British warships in what were termed Icelandic fishing grounds. Icelandic coastguard patrol vessel *(r.)* Maria Julia heaves to near the British trawler Northern Foam, whose crew was fishing inside a 12-mile limit not recognized by the British. A British frigate protected the fishermen.

SCANDINAVIA ATTACKED BY KHRUSHCHEV

Nordic Bloc joins Britain in free trade area

SCANDINAVIAN leaders were castigated by Soviet Premier Nikita Khrushchev in 1959, but they did not seem to be unduly concerned. In fact, they showed relief at Khrushchev's decision to postpone a scheduled August tour of Denmark, Sweden and Norway.

Khrushchev complained of "insulting" remarks by the Scandinavian opposition leaders and press, and seemed particularly angry at Sweden, which is officially neutral in the East-West political struggle. Swedish Foreign Minister Osten Unden in June had rejected Khrushchev's proposal for a nuclear ban in the Baltic zone. He said Sweden was not interested in such talk since the USSR was the only nation in the area with nuclear weapons.

Sweden, observers believed, was moving slowly to a decision to manufacture her own tactical atomic weapons. Denmark and Norway, both NATO members, had refused to accept atomic arms because they did not wish to provoke Moscow. But Denmark, at least, reportedly was beginning to feel that refusal of arms cannot be insisted upon forever if the Atlantic Pact is to have meaning.

Finland, because of her proximity to Russia, did not have the same freedom of action as the other Scandinavian nations. Finnish President Urho Kekkonen early in the year visited Russia and talked with Khrushchev, then warned his countrymen

DISASTER occurred on a summer night on a little lake near Haderslev, Danish town near the German frontier. A picnic boat carrying 55 persons exploded suddenly, and resulted in the death of 40 persons. Although the craft was only 50 yards from the shore, rescuers were unable to save most of the passengers from the swiftly racing flames. The explosion was caused by a faulty gas pump in the boat.

ROCK 'N' ROLL KING of Scandinavia is Karl-Gerhard Lundkvist, or "Little Gerhard," 23, of Sweden. He defeated singers "Rockin' James" of Denmark and Per "Elvis" Granberg of Norway.

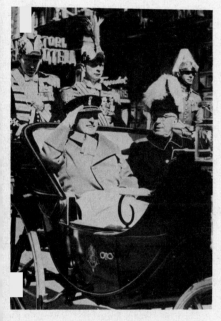

KING OLAV of Norway salutes a welcoming crowd in Stockholm on state visit. He is with Sweden's King Gustave (r).

DANISH Foreign Minister Jens Otto Krag (c.) discusses trade with German expert Ludwig Erhard in his Bonn visit.

FINLAND President Urho Kekkonen, who visited Soviet Premier Khrushchev, urged Finns to live with East, West.

to get along with both East and West.

An example of the comparative positions of Finland and her Nordic neighbors occurred in July when Sweden, Denmark and Norway joined with Great Britain, Switzerland, Austria and Portugal to create a second free trade area to supplement the European Common Market. Finland expressed interest but cited her "neutrality" as permitting a link to the group only through the members individually.

The free trade area embracing 90 million people was to become a tariff-free group by Jan. 1, 1970. It was to impose a 20% tariff cut by July 1, 1960, thus keeping pace with the six-nation European Common Market composed of France, West Germany, Italy, Belgium, the Netherlands and Luxembourg. The two groups advanced separately toward a single market concept, but some observers speculated fearfully that rivalry between them might cause a trade war.

BAUDOUIN VISITS THE U.S.

Bachelor king makes first state visit abroad; Prince Albert weds in Brussels

LITTLE BELGIUM was torn by strife at home and abroad in 1959, unlike the other two members of Benelux— Luxembourg and the Netherlands.

Luxembourg's 316,000 citizens have no territorial aspirations, no wish to add to their 999 square miles. The Netherlands still feels the loss of rich colonial revenues from Indonesia. Now Belgium is feeling the impact of Afro-Asian nationalism in

its huge African Congo territory, a source of much of the West's vital uranium ore. Riots swept Leopoldville, the Congo capital, early in the year. Seventy-one natives were killed and more than 260 were wounded. Unemployment, plus nationalism, was behind the rioting. King Baudouin's ministers offered a plan aimed to calm the natives. Baudouin launched the plan in a radio broadcast, saying "our firm resolution is to lead the Congolese people . . . without undue haste . . . to independence in prosperity and peace."

Later, the King, 28 years old and unmarried, made a visit to the U.S. on his first state visit abroad. The shy young sovereign received a warm welcome from President Eisenhower and other Americans during his tour in this country. In his absence the press suggested that Baudouin's father, ex-King Leopold, was meddling in state affairs. Leopold III abdicated under pressure in 1951 but had been living with his son in Laeken Palace. After much criticism, Leopold said he would move.

Another growing row was averted when the wedding of Baudouin's brother, Prince Albert, 25-year-old heir-presumptive, and Italian Princess Paola Ruffo di Calabria, was held in Brussels instead of the Vatican. Socialists had been quick to point out that Belgian law recognizes only civil marriages.

STRIKING Belgian coal miners demonstrate following the government decision to close some unproductive mines. More than 100,000 of them walked out, carrying such signs as "Deliver us from American Coal, Please." Government halted closures.

BAUDOUIN, bespectacled bachelor King of the Belgians, *(l.)* got warm, welcome in Brussels upon his return from three-week U.S. tour. Later, he held first formal press conference *(above)* at Royal Palace, to tell of American hospitality.

STAGGERED double decker buses are introduced in Southern Holland *(r.)*. Interior shows how passengers are accommodated on two levels. A single step leads between the backs of the lower seats. Thirty-five-foot-long bus holds 74 passengers.

FAIRY-TALE wedding of Belgian Prince and Italian Princess Dona Paola Ruffo di Calabria was in Brussels, July 2. Roman Catholic church ceremony followed civil rites at Palace.

JULIANA, Netherlands Queen, and husband, Prince Bernhard, talk with the Shah of Iran *(c.)*, Mohammed Reza Pahlevi. They met during the Shah's three-day official visit.

PRIME MINISTER Harold Macmillan, who led Britain's economic comeback, makes a point at Conservative party rally.

LABOR Party leader Hugh Gaitskell, in May Day speech, warns U.S. officials against any mixing in British politics.

BRITAIN'S ECONOMY COMES BACK

Macmillan visits Moscow, Washington

GREAT BRITAIN, under Prime Minister Harold Macmillan and his Conservative party, made the greatest economic recovery since World War II during 1959.

The nation relaxed curbs on imports that must be paid for in dollars. This enabled U.S. producers of scores of consumer items to compete in Britain on virtually an even basis with West Europe for the first time since the war. In the first six months of the year exports were higher than ever before in British history; the pound sterling was stronger in world markets than at any time since the war. Chancellor of the Exchequer Derick Heathcoat Amory said "We can see clearly before us the road to undreamed levels of achievement."

With an eye to remaining in office after the next general election, the Macmillan regime also cut more than a billion dollars from a back-breaking $15.3 billion tax bill. Income tax in 1959 was shaved $357.6 million, and the 1959-60 bill was cut back $641.2 million. This amounted to

roughly six to nine cents off each dollar previously paid. This made Macmillan and his men popular with the

masses, as attested by public opinion polls. It made Hugh Gaitskell, the Labor party leader, unhappy.

Gaitskell was having trouble in his own party. Frank Cousins, ambitious boss of the Transport Workers Union, the nation's biggest, threatened the unity of the entire Labor party by demanding immediate renunciation of the H-bomb. He also denounced Labor's backing of NATO on the ground that some NATO general might "plunge us into war." Gaitskell asserted his leadership, calling Cousins' attitude "escapist, myopic, and positively dangerous."

With business booming and dollar reserves growing, Britain announced plans to modernize its fleet, field a bigger regular army, make missiles and stress nuclear deterrents in its defense machine.

On the international stage, Macmillan visited Moscow in February to talk over with Soviet Premier Nikita Khrushchev the unending German question. Later he visited Washington to fill in U.S. leaders on the talks, which the French described as a "dialogue of the deaf."

Queen Elizabeth and Prince Philip, in Canada to open the St. Lawrence Seaway, got biggest ovation in Chicago, their only U.S. stopover.

A mid-summer announcement said that Queen Elizabeth expects the birth of her third child early in 1960.

RACE RIOTING is causing a great deal of trouble in Britain. Police are shown in the act of searching several rioters for hidden weapons in the Westbourne Park area of London. A big influx of West Indians led to post-war problems.

FIELD MARSHAL Viscount Montgomery, returning from trip to Moscow, apologizes quickly for earlier television remarks saying U.S. leaders were weak.

PACIFISTS try to prevent construction of missile-launching sites at U.S. bases in Britain. One demonstrator, with the inappropriate name of Will Warr, is dragged by police from the base near Swaffham. Police were compelled to use force to break up a demonstration sponsored by the "Committee Against Nuclear War."

"DEV" RETIRES TO PRESIDENCY

SEAN LEMASS was elected Prime Minister of the Irish Republic on June 23, replacing American-born politician Eamon de Valera.

EAMON DE VALERA, New York-born politician whose name is synonymous with Irish independence, finally relinquished his active grip on politics after four decades.

The 77-year-old leader, born of a Cuban father and Irish mother, was reared by a grandmother in County Limerick. He commanded a group of 50 in the Easter week rebellion against Britain in 1916, and was the only leader to survive it. After escaping from a British jail in 1919 he went to the U.S., where, as president of the Irish Republic, he raised over $5,000,000 for the revolution.

De Valera had dominated Irish politics down through the years. But in January, 1959, he decided to step down from the premiership and to run for the presidency. The Fianna Fail party leader was elected June 19, over Gen. Sean MacEoin, but got a smaller vote than expected. His political mantle went to Sean Lemass, new premier.

EAMON DE VALERA, 77, stormy petrel of Irish politics, casts his ballot in Ireland's general election. He was voted to presidency.

67

ROME RIOT police pin students against wall to control anti-Austrian outburst. Austria supported Alto Adige (South Tyrol) charge that Italy failed to give adequate minority rights. Italy acquired disputed German-speaking area after WW 1.

SILVIO MILAZZO, Red-backed politician who split with the Christian Democrats, kept control of the Sicilian government.

"MINORITY" CABINET RULES ITALY

But Segni's all-Christian Democrat regime retains coalition support; rebel Milazzo keeps power in Sicily

ANTONIO SEGNI, 68-year-old law professor, became the 20th Premier and Minister of Interior in post-fascist Italy in 1959 after fall of Amintore Fanfani's left-of-center regime. Fanfani's Christian Democratic and Democratic Socialist party coalition, which had been in power since July 2, 1958, fell when a split developed in Democratic Socialist ranks. Members of this party went over to Pietro Nenni's left-socialist group afer Nenni broke his alignment with the Communists.

Segni, a former premier, received a 333 to 248 vote of confidence in the Chamber of Deputies—largest since the

republic was founded in 1946. Yet his straight Christian Democratic cabinet was a minority regime, since it depended on Monarchists, Liberals and Neo-fascists for support. In mid-February, when Segni took office, he professed unhappiness over neo-fascist support, but he had halted, at least temporarily, the leftward list of recent coalition governments dominated by the Christian Democrats. Segni, who once was bitterly attacked as a "Communist" when he pushed through post-war land reforms, found immediate popular support in denying claims for greater autonomy among Italian Tyrol's German-speak-

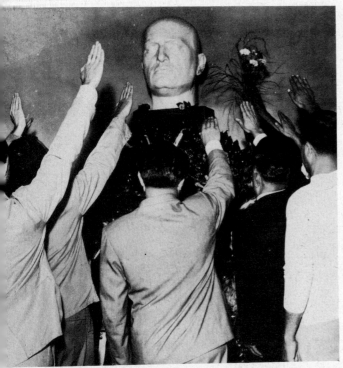

NEO-FASCISTS raise arms in salute before bust of Benito Mussolini at tomb in his birth place, Predappio. Body of executed dictator was turned over to his widow Rachele in 1957.

GIUSEPPE PELLA, new Italian foreign minister, *(l.)* shakes hands with President Giovanni Gronchi after being sworn into office in February under new Premier Segni *(r.)*.

GONDOLIERS hauled boats out of water at San Marco on Venice's Grand Canal in June to protest digging canal during summer tourist season. They claimed it hurt business.

CHARLES DE GAULLE visits with Italian President Giovanni Gronchi *(r.)* in an attempt to win Italian support for his plans to set up a French-led "Mediterranean bloc."

ing minority. On a wider front, the premier reaffirmed Italy's allegiance to the Western alliance and urged prompt integration into new European Common Market.

Domestically, Segni sought to rectify the dispute within Christian Democratic party which contributed to the fall of Fanfani. But Segni's party suffered a rebuff in Sicily's regional elections. Chubby Silvio Milazzo, 56, who had broken with the party, had formed a crazy-quilt coalition of Monarchists, Fascists, dissident Christian Democrats and Communists to gain assembly control of the regional assembly. Catholic Action groups worked

again Milazzo, but when the votes were counted the Christian Democrats got only 34 of the 90 Assembly seats, a loss of three.

The Communists won 22 seats and Nenni's Socialists 11, a gain of one each. Milazzo, however, captured nine pivotal seats with his rump Christian Social Union, and, after bitter wrangling, was re-elected regional head.

Italy announced that it would build an atomic submarine and that it hoped to get technical data from the U.S. The government also expected 2 million persons at the Rome summer Olympic games in 1960.

CHRIST, in the form of a massive statue, drew thousands of Roman Catholic faithful last May when the statue was unveiled officially. It stands on the south bank of the River

Tagus, looking toward Lisbon. The giant statue (in close-up, *l.*) is 91 feet high, stands on a 206-foot pedestal *(r.)*. It symbolizes nation's thanksgiving for World War II neutrality.

INFLATION, SUCCESSION TROUBLE SPAIN

Aging Franco devalues peseta, favors restoration of monarchy

GENERALISSIMO Francisco Franco, dictator of Spain for two decades, ran into deep economic troubles in 1959. Despite generous U.S. aid—close to $1 billion of non-military assistance since the 1953 defense agreement —Spain was forced onto an austerity road by a depleted treasury. (The nation was finally admitted to the Organization for European Economic Cooperation, the Western European trading community, and was pledged at least $375 million more in credits.) The peseta was devalued and the 66-year-old Franco promised drastic moves to halt inflation. Many observers believed that his ability to withstand the repercussions of politically unpalatable austerity might determine how much longer he would remain in power. No genuine threat arose in 1959; the masses had not yet begun to feel the pinch of the enforced austerity plans.

In April, Spain observed the 20th anniversary of the end of the disastrous 1936-39 civil war. The Spanish masses had known only rigid dictatorship and grinding poverty since the war in which a million persons died.

Franco, who showed no indication of wanting to retire, apparently still favored the restoration of Prince Don Juan, 45-year-old Count of Barcelona and claimant to the throne which Alfonso XIII gave up in 1931, upon his own death. He once favored Juan's son, Prince Juan Carlos, a cadet in the Spanish Air Academy. Don Juan, the father, still lived in exile in neighboring Portugal. There, another anniversary rolled around for Dr. An-

TRAGEDY struck the little Spanish village of Rivadelgado in January when a dam burst in Zamora province. A huge wall of water engulfed the village, killing more than 140 of its 500 inhabitants. Not a house was left intact. Survivors (above) clear away the rubble of their shattered homes.

PATRIARCH of Lisbon, Manuel Cardinal Cerejeira (l., front), and Admiral Americo Tomas, Portuguese Chief of State, lead a group of church officials and dignitaries toward the base of the Christ-king monument which was inaugurated May 17. Giant statue is in Almada, opposite Lisbon.

ANOTHER anniversary rolled around for Dr. Antonio de Oliveira Salazar April 27. He had been in office for 31 years, 25 of them as one-man ruler of Portugal. President Francisco Higino Craveira Lopes (l., offering anniversary congratulations) was fired later in year when he and Salazar disagreed.

PRINCE Juan Carlos, who may one day be King of Spain, took his first lesson in handling a plane May 30 at San Javier, where he is a Spanish Air Academy cadet. Generalissimo Franco once favored Juan Carlos to succeed him, but now inclines to his father, Prince Don Juan.

tonio de Oliveira Salazar on April 27—his 31st as premier and absolute ruler of the nation.

The former economics professor, 70 years old in 1959, had encountered little real opposition until 1958, when fiery Gen. Humberto Delgado ran for the figurehead presidency against Salazar's own candidate. Salazar let him run—and lose—and then "retired" him from the military. He vowed to continue fight from exile in Brazil.

MISSIONARY President Charles de Gaulle, in his attempt to settle the Algerian revolt and restore French "grandeur," made many visits outside France in 1959. Here he shakes hands with smiling young Moslem school girl in Algeria.

DRASTIC STEPS STABILIZE FRANCE

De Gaulle's reforms bring greatest administrative changes since days of Napoleon, but fail to halt Algerian war

FRANCE, in a year and a half under Charles de Gaulle, underwent its most drastic change since Napoleon.

In the spring of 1958 civil war loomed. The army and civilians revolted in Algeria. Mobs in Paris demanded that the general, a World War II hero and first post-war leader, emerge from retirement and rescue the nation from chaos, bitterness, and frustration largely stemming from the native revolt in Algeria.

A year later, President de Gaulle's reforming zeal had spread throughout French life. The army had been disciplined, civil servants stepped up their work, businessmen begrudgingly made more tax payments.

By February, 1959, soon after his decrees began taking effect, the nation had a hard-currency reserve of one billion dollars, with about $5 million still piling in daily. Industrial production rose at the phenomenal rate of ten per cent, and for the first time in years the nation was selling more than it was buying.

Foes still labeled de Gaulle a dictator, and parliamentary deputies writhed, but the vast changes were obvious.

Examples: A Fifth Republic which replaced the Fourth; a new constitution approved by 82.5% of the voters.

With a single stroke, the constitution all but wiped out the power of the National Assembly, which de Gaulle blamed for most of France's troubles; Communist party strength was cut from 143 deputies to ten; a new "truth and severity" economy which restored firmness to the long-buffeted franc; a new "French Community" of nations, replacing the former French African Empire and other overseas territories.

De Gaulle's moves to protect France's colonies from "independence fever" were accepted by every territory except Guinea.

Michel Debré, new French premier, declared: "France's internal rebirth can be achieved through administrative reform, through economic and financial severity . . ."

But de Gaulle's effort to restore French "grandeur" caused NATO to plan bases for nuclear-capable planes outside France. De Gaulle refused to allow nuclear arms solely under United States control to be based there.

NEWSMEN jammed press meetings held by de Gaulle to get his views on the Algerian conflict. Here during his first press conference, held in his Hotel Matignon office, he tells 300 French and foreign press members that a settlement of the Algerian question is not far away. National congress of the French Socialist party approved his "liberal tendency."

FRANCE, under de Gaulle, concentrated its efforts on an ancient enemy, Germany. In twelve months, de Gaulle and West German Chancellor Konrad Adenauer *(r.)* supplemented Franco-British alliance with a Franco-German entente. In March, the two leaders conferred on Soviet efforts to undermine Western allies' determination to hold rights in Berlin.

UNVEILED Algerian woman puts her ballot in box during one of three elections held since de Gaulle returned to power in the spring of 1958. Voters have smashed the once powerful FrenchCommunist party, reducing its National Assembly rep-

resentation from 143 to 10 deputies, given France a new constitution under a Fifth Republic, and all but wiped out the power of the National Assembly. In Algeria, where local politics used to be scant, most of the mayors now are Moslem.

THE ALGERIAN WAR, France's most acute problem, and the one that brought de Gaulle to power, sputtered on as before until September, when de Gaulle proposed a new peace plan which would give Algerian voters the chance to choose for themselves between independence, integration with France or home rule under France's wing.

Some peace hopes arose in January, when de Gaulle commuted the death sentences of 180 Algerian rebel prisoners to life imprisonment. Rebel prison terms were reduced by one-tenth, and about 7,000 rebel suspects in prison camps were freed outright.

But the most significant provision concerned four top leaders of the rebel National Liberation Front (FLN). Captured in 1956 when the French intercepted a plane carrying them from Morocco (where they had been King Mohammed V's guests) to Tunisia (where they were to be guests of President Habib Bourguiba), Ahmed Ben Bella and his lieutenants had been held as common criminals in Paris' Sante Prison. They were transferred to army jurisdiction, with virtual prisoner-of-war status long sought by the FLN as a basis for negotiations.

But no known negotiations occurred. Premier Debré, moving quickly to allay rightist suspicions, denied rumors of his dealing secretly with the "barbarians of rebellion."

Algeria, he said, would be "even more firmly welded to France." For its part, the FLN government repeated that there would be no cease-fire without political talks. The freed Ben Bella himself called de Gaulle's amnesty a "generous and courageous gesture." This led to hopes of new peace moves.

If negotiations do occur, Ben Bella, a moderate, may well be the key figure. He was the man who organized and led the Algerian revolt against the French until his capture. Even in prison he retained enormous influence.

De Gaulle himself predicted in May—a year after the army-civilian uprising had put him in power—that the end of war was "in sight." But this was interpreted as a very elastic term at best. Some reports persisted that de Gaulle is quite prepared to let the war drag on another five or six years if need be. In a sense he has put France on a war footing by his austerity moves, and French economy perhaps can withstand a long war better than can the rebels.

Part of de Gaulle's dispute with NATO stemmed from his effort to get NATO strategic planning extended to Africa, and to get open NATO backing for the French position in Algeria, where nearly 500,000 French troops were pinned down.

De Gaulle visited the Vatican in June and won the full support of Pope John XXIII and the Roman Catholic Church for his regime. The Pontiff praised France's peaceful aims and its "astonishing capacity of recovery in the face of danger." Italy remained cool, however, to de Gaulle's proposal of a special Mediterranean alliance, including Spain and Morocco.

De Gaulle's prestige was high among Moslem moderates. Rebel strength seemed to have weakened in the war. Moslem mayors, in three elections, won most of the offices in Algeria. De Gaulle's peace plan found strong support in many quarters, and raised cautious hopes that an end to the bloodshed might be near.

ARMY officers under Gen. Maurice Challe, the French Supreme Military Commander, had the political as well as the military job of trying to win a Gaullist peace in Algeria. Behind Challe is Major Gen. Jacques Massu, the paratrooper hero whose action in 1958 helped restore de Gaulle to power.

LARGEST SUSPENSION BRIDGE in Europe is shown below being completed. The 2,000-foot-long bridge spans the estuary of the Seine River, approximately 20 miles from Le Havre.

WAR LESSONS are taught to small groups in the 30,000 Algerian rebel Army of Liberation. These guerrilla fighters are getting instructions in the field on how to strip a light machinegun captured from the French. Picture was taken at a hideout for the Army deep in the Saharan Atlas Mountains of northwest Algeria.

SUDANESE Prime Minister, Gen. Ahmed Abboud (l.) talks with Ferhat Abbas, Premier of the rebel "Algerian Government in Exile", in May, during a dinner party in Khartoum, Sudan. given in Abbas' honor. Abbas' rebel movement seems to have lost some strength, although this is denied. It still demands full independence.

L'AFFAIRE LACAZE was scandal that held international attention. Key figure was Maurice Lacour (above) accused of hiring ex-paratrooper to murder Jean-Pierre Guillaume, adopted son of his client and amie Domenique Lacaze. Also involved was Jean Lacaze, brother of Domenique, and administrator of billion dollar Zellidja mines, which were at stake in confusing, intriguing case.

MINISTERS of Morocco met at Arab League foreign ministers' conference in Beirut in April. They are *(l. to r.):* Premier Abdullah Ibrahim; Abdel Khalek El Tarriss, ambassador to Cairo and Beirut; Under Secretary of Foreign Affairs Tayeb Ben Hami; and Si Futaimi, ambassador to Baghdad. Moroccan and Tunisian leaders have taken initiative in urging France to hold talks with Algerian rebels, but in vain.

MOROCCO GETS $40 MILLION U.S. AID

Both nations improve relations with France despite sympathy for Algerian rebels; both distrust intentions of Nasser

Morocco and Tunisia still feuded with the French in 1959 over the revolt in Algeria. But French relations with the two nations definitely improved under the leadership of Gen. Charles de Gaulle. Despite their open sympathy with the Moslem rebels in Algeria, Moroccan and Tunisian leaders had many problems of their own to solve. Both countries looked with distrust on Gamal Abdel Nasser, the Egyptian leader of the United Arab Republic of Syria and Egypt. He has been a main backer of the Algerian rebel regime, which has headquarters in Cairo. Nasser's initial ties with the Soviet Union and his attacks on Tunisian President Habib Bourguiba were not forgotten.

Spain, in months of negotiation, patched up relations with Morocco, where both Spain and France had protectorates until 1955. But ranking Spanish cabinet ministers voiced serious concern over reports of heavy Red infiltration in Morocco. Some Spanish intelligence reports said 210 persons were in the newly established Soviet Embassy in Rabat. Some were said to speak fluent Spanish and at least as many spoke fluent Arabic. Spanish leaders were in the habit of always raising Red scares, but their military chiefs seemed convinced that the U S S R was laying the groundwork for a pro-Soviet, anti-European movement in Morocco, the site of important U.S. air bases.

During the year, agreement was made on a $40 million U.S. aid program for Morocco. It was in the form of low-interest, long-term loans to be spent on irrigation, road building and modernization of agriculture. No strings of a political or military nature were attached. Moroccan Economic Minister Abderrahim Bouabid stressed that the U.S. had not shown any sign of "interference" in Moroccan domestic or foreign policy. It was the third straight year of U.S. aid. The U.S. lent $20 million in 1957 and $30 million in 1958. Bouabid said that no question was raised about the U.S. military bases in the negotiations for the new aid plan. He added that there has been no let-up in negotiations for the evacuation of the bases.

The strategic bases were established when the French and Spanish were in power in Morocco. Earlier U.S. had concluded a military agreement also giving it bases in Spain.

King Mohammed V's ministers have been talking with French leaders in an effort to settle the Algerian war. In a gesture of amity, the king flew to Corsica and Madagascar last February, visiting the scenes of his former exile. Tunisian president Bourguiba also urged the De Gaulle regime to talk with Algerian rebels, but his efforts were futile.

TUNISIAN President Habib Bourguiba (seated) wears an impassive expression as he listened to an orator during a constitution-signing ceremony in Tunis June 1. The ceremony marked the official emergence of the first constitution in the history of the new Tunisian Republic. Bourguiba has battled with the French, showing open sympathy with the Algerian rebels who are seeking complete independence from France. But he also fought against Gamal Abdel Nasser, a main backer of the rebels, because of Nasser's continuing flirtation with the Soviet Union.

ABD EL KRIM, leader of the Riff uprising against France and Spain more than 30 years ago, is a backer of the Algerian revolt. He is exiled in Cairo.

KING Mohammed V of Morocco (center), and Crown Prince Moulay Hassan (left in uniform), inspect paratrooper guard of honor on Poretta airfield near Bastia, Corsica, Feb. 21 before boarding their plane for Madagascar. The king visited both French areas, where he had been exiled before Morocco became free.

CYPRUS PACT HEALS NATO RIFT, SETS UP REPUBLIC

Greece, Turkey drop claims, Britain will keep only defense base

PEACE by compromise ended a five-year-old war in the British crown colony of Cyprus in 1959.

Britain had ruled the Mediterranean island, NATO partner Greece wanted it, and NATO partner Turkey wanted to split it.

In the long dispute bullets and explosions took more than 500 lives.

After long private huddles, Greek and Turkish Premiers Constantine Karamanlis and Adnan Menderes flew to neutral Switzerland and worked out a compromise based on a British blueprint.

As a result, Cyprus will become an independent republic in 1960. Its independence is guaranteed by international agreement barring either

partition or *enosis*, meaning union with Athens.

Cyprus will decide whether to stay in the British Commonwealth. A constitution will provide for a Greek Cypriot as president and a Turkish Cypriot as vice-president. A parliament's seats will be divided into about the same ratio as the population—70 Greek and 30 Turkish.

Thus Greece dropped its claims on the island; Turkey stopped talking of partition; and Britain, which once said that it would "never" grant independence to the colony, retained defense bases, approved compromise.

Archbishop Makarios, Greek Cypriot political leader who had been exiled, returned to a hero's welcome

surrounded with wild rejoicing by hundreds of amnestied Greek underground fighters.

Cyprus' destiny still was far from being secure. Russia's *Pravda* and the empire-minded London *Daily Express* joined incongruously in attack-

UNDERGROUND Greek Cypriot warriors, carrying personal belongings, celebrate their freedom after release from a Nicosia jail. The new amnesty came with plans for Cyprus independence.

MAKARIOS, Greek Orthodox Church Archbishop and Cypriot political leader whose activities touched off five-year revolt, was released February 24 from 13 months of exile in Seychelles Islands.

GREEK PREMIER Karamanlis greets Col. George Grivas (r.), Cypriot underground leader while his wife looks on.

ing the pact. Responsible members of both Cypriot communities have no illusions about the difficulties ahead.

The independence agreement provides an ingenious set of checks and balances, which is intended to permit the two groups to govern themselves. But violence in Cyprus has been commonplace for centuries.

Cyprus, also, is plagued by a skillfully-led Red-dominated leftist group and economic woes will face the islanders when most Britons leave.

Prospects of a durable peace offered many benefits. Greece and Turkey now could revive their Balkan pact with Yugoslavia, perhaps increasing freedom moves among Red satellites.

LONG WAR ended on Cyprus when Greek Premier Constantine Karamanlis agreed with Turks on a British freedom pact.

TURKISH PREMIER Adnan Menderes survived plane crash in Feb. and signed constitution for independent Cyprus.

FAZIL KUCUK, Turkish Cypriot minority leader, is hoisted by New York followers enroute to UN talks concerning Cyprus.

TEENAGE HOOLIGANS are paraded in Athens with signs "I am a jackass Teddy-Boy." Delinquency was on the increase.

QUEEN FREDERIKA of the Hellenes and Princess Sophie of Greece were guests of Mayor Robert F. Wagner in N. Y.

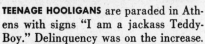

RED REBUFF

**Nasser attacks Communism,
signs U.S. technical pact
despite Soviet Aswan aid;
Iraq cools to Kremlin**

CHEERING CROWD FILLS A BAGHDAD STREET IN A

IN JULY, 1959, the Middle East marked the first anniversary of the revolution in Iraq, a revolt that destroyed a monarchy, threatened to spill over into nearby Lebanon and Jordan, and led to the landing of U.S. and British troops.

Hero of the 1958 revolution, Prem-ier Karim Kassem, was still the hero of the new republic, but the year had not been an easy one for him. Arab nationalists, anxious to see Iraq tied to Nasser's United Arab Republic, set off a revolt in Mosul early in March under Colonel Abdel Wahab Shawaf. In a few days it was all over; but an estimated 500 lay dead in Mosul, and Kassem had obtained his victory only at the cost of accepting more help from Iraq's Communists than seemed healthy.

Holding off pro-Nasserites with one hand, Kassem used the other to pull away from the West, announced

"GO HOME" SIGNS and an angry mob at Baghdad's airport greeted U.S. diplomat William Rountree on his arrival for talks with Premier Karim Kassem. Later, Rountree's car was the target for a barrage of eggs and stones, but he escaped injury.

MID-EAST EXPERT, U.S. Asst. Sec'y of State Rountree, had little luck in Iraq, which withdrew from Baghdad Pact.

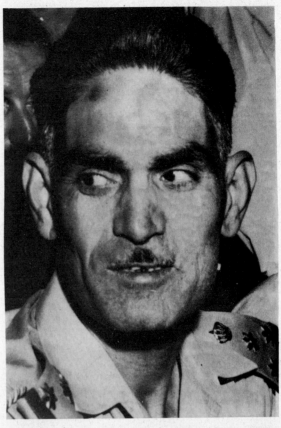

DEMONSTRATION OF IRAQI LOYALTY TO THE REGIME OF KASSEM

LEADER OF UNEASY IRAQ, PREMIER ABDUL KARIM KASSEM

the withdrawal of Iraq from the Baghdad Pact, and signed a $138 million loan pact with the U S S R

Although the months after the Mosul revolt saw Communists becoming increasingly powerful in Iraq's government, there were signs by midsummer that Kassem was trying to prevent his Red associates from taking over completely. Despite outraged howls from the Communists, he ordered an amnesty for political prisoners; fired Baghdad's party-lining police chief; ordered an end to the Popular Resistance Force, a Communist-backed civilian militia; decreed a halt in political party activity. In July, Kassem optimistically predicted that "by next Jan. 6 we shall celebrate the formation of political parties." also promised a new constitution, free elections in 1960.

Although some mid-east experts shared Kassem's optimism, others were not so sure. In Washington, C I A head Allen Dulles told a Senate subcommittee that the Iraq situation was one of the "most dangerous in the world today." In the confusing world of Arab politics, prediction was dangerous, too.

SURROUNDING THE COFFIN of Iraqi rebel Col. Mohamed Said Shehad, who died following an abortive revolt staged by pro-U A R Arab nationalists in Mosul, chief city of northern Iraq, Syrians protest communist influence in Arab world's affairs.

U.S. resumes aid to UAR as Nasser grows wary of Soviet aims

THE SAME MONTH that saw Iraq celebrating the first anniversary of its July revolution saw United Arab Republic's President Gamal Abdel Nasser leading a celebration of the seventh anniversary of the revolution he headed in Egypt. In those years, said Nasser, "we have only scratched the door of revolution." In the "radical change" he promised for the future, the U A R hopes to double its national income, eliminate strife between classes, provide equal opportunity for all.

To make a start, Nasser chose the March anniversary of the union of Syria and Egypt in the U A R as the time to begin the first distribution of 155,000 acres of land to peasants. He moved a step closer to making the Aswan High Dam project a reality by negotiating a pact with the U S S R for more than $1 million in financial, technical and material aid.

DEMONSTRATORS in Damascus protest Iraq's expulsion of U A R diplomats and reported air attack on Syrian town.

STILL STRONG man of the Arab world, U.A.R. Pres. Nasser *(below)* began to feel uneasy about Communist support.

WOMEN SOLDIERS parade before Nasser and his guest, Yugoslavia's Tito, celebrating the U A R's first anniversary.

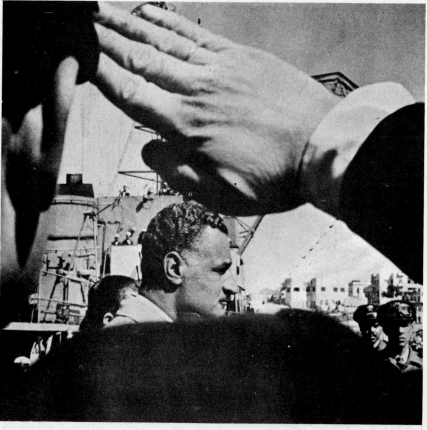

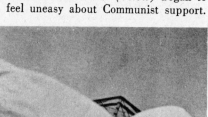

NILE RIVERBOAT, JAMMED WITH SOME 300 PASSENGERS, CARRIES OVER 100 PEOPLE TO A WATERY GRAVE AS IT SINKS NEAR CAIRO

Then, after watching the Mosul revolt in Iraq, which he was accused of fomenting, put down with the aid of increasingly powerful Iraq Communists, Nasser appeared to be having some second thoughts about his Kremlin ties. Momentarily abandoning his suspicion of Western influences, Nasser warned Moscow to keep its hands off Arab affairs, jailed some 100 Syrian Communists, beamed on Damascus demonstrators chanting "Neither internationalism nor Communism but Arab nationalism." Cairo radio, long a voice of anti-Western propaganda, began an active campaign against Communism.

Nearby Lebanon and Jordan continued to thrive, with Western financial aid, following the uneventful withdrawal of U.S. and British troops. Perhaps reassured by these circumstances, Nasser signed an agreement in July with the U.S. to resume the technical aid program for first time since the 1956 Suez crisis.

The total cost of the U.S. aid to the United Arab Republic is estimated to be $8 million, but even more significant than cost in the politics of the Arab world was the fact that Nasser had once again decided to accept assistance from the United States.

OFF-AGAIN, ON-AGAIN Aswan High Dam, a pet project of Nasser, was on again after U A R signed agreement *(below)* with U S S R for technical, financial aid.

Middle East Continued

EAST AND WEST met in a U.S. hotel room *(below)* where New York's Gov. Nelson Rockefeller called on visiting King Hussein of Jordan, and in the divided city of Jerusalem *(r.)* where a modern crane is being used in restoration work on the famed Omar Mosque, which stands on the site of Solomon's Temple. Hussein went happily back to Jordan, assured of the U.S. intention to continue its $50 million-a-year financial aid, and promptly named a new premier, Hazza el Majali, in May.

NEXT STORM CENTER of Arabia may be Kuwait, where popular discontent is increasing despite the many millions of dollars being spent for welfare and education. Sheik Abdulah Sabah *(left)*, ruler of the oil rich kingdom, put down some pro-Nasser demonstrations in February but the situation remained tense. Across the peninsula, in Yemen, Crown Prince Mohammed-al-Badr, the acting ruler, suppressed an army-led revolt, and then attempted to ease the unrest by giving Yemen the first representative government in its turbulent history.

KING SAUD *(l.)*, luxury-loving monarch of Saudi Arabia, who had hung onto his throne in 1958 only by turning over the direction of defense, finance and foreign affairs to Crown Prince Feisal, found the limitations on his power hard to bear. Under Feisal's stern control of spending (not a single Cadillac imported in the first six months of 1959), Saudi Arabian finances began to stabilize until Saud made a tour of his desert kingdom sheiks, passing out bank notes in the old royal manner, with Saud's overdraft reaching a reported $30 million. When Saud took another step toward resumption of absolute power by casually tossing a newspaper editor into jail, Feisal angrily resigned. A hastily called royal family council warned that if Feisal quit, the result might well be civil war, bankruptcy and ruin for the country. In June a compromise was reached: Feisal compensated for King's debts, and Saud promised to behave.

SHAH DEFIES USSR

Signs new military pact with U.S. despite Khrushchev threat, abusive Red broadcasts

IRAN, under Shah Mohammed Reza Pahlevi, signed a new military agreement March 5 with the U.S. despite Soviet threats of "dire consequences." Thus the West won the 1959 round in the continuing struggle for influence in the strategic land. Iran was still a Baghdad Pact member, despite the continuing menace of the glowering Khruschev.

Russia has coveted its oil-rich neighbor for centuries. A satellite Iran would give the USSR immediate access to the Middle East and would deny Iranian oil to the West.

But ever since 1953 the Shah has clung to the West, bolstered by U.S. aid programs.

Relations with Moscow worsened during the year, with Khruschev and other Soviet leaders attacking the Shah personally for the first time.

And ominous threats continued over Iran's northwest province, Azerbaijan, where a "people's republic" was set up after World War II under the protection of Soviet troops, who withdrew only after an ultimatum from President Truman.

Despite this, the prestige of the handsome, greying Shah, who still seemed to be yearning for his ex-wife, the beautiful Soraya, had reached an all-time high.

The 40-year-old Shah was fighting more than Red intrigues, however. He was battling for land reforms to ease peasant discontent in a country where the "thousand families" of wealthy landowners were absentee owners of 70% of the land.

The Shah himself distributed much of his own 2.5 million acres to those in need, but the "thousand families" failed to follow his lead.

PREMIER Manouchehr Eghbal leads thousands of his people in a demonstration of loyalty to the Shah in Teheran after Soviet attacks on the king.

POPULAR Shah of Iran, Mohammed Reza Pahlevi steps forward upon his arrival by plane May 23 at Paris' Le Bourget Airport. Iranian ambassador Nasraloah Eltezam (l.) and French official, Andre Negre, greet him.

ISRAEL SURVIVES TWO MORE CRISES, WOOS NEW INDUSTRY

Ben-Gurion resigns, remains at post

THE ISRAELI government, born in war and weaned on emergencies, survived two major crises in 1959.

The first—the $96 million cost of absorbing an anticipated influx of 80,000 immigrants suddenly "released" from Rumania—blew over as unexpectedly as it had developed. By mid-summer the Rumanian government, reportedly yielding to Arab pressures, had cut the flow down from a February high of 8000 refugees to an insignificant trickle.

Perennial Prime Minister David Ben-Gurion resigned July 5 (but consented to remain in a "caretaker" capacity) when ministers of the left-wing Mapam and Ahdut Avodah parties refused either to approve a contract to sell 250,000 grenade launchers to West Germany or to resign.

Although the dispute aroused a violent emotional storm, it was basically a political squabble. Ben-Gurion, who insisted the contract be honored, claimed the sale had originally been approved by the two parties.

The consensus was that the result of the November Knesset elections would be continuance in power of a coalition headed by Ben-Gurion's Mapai party.

Ben-Gurion's stand reflected the government's new drive to attract foreign currency by making Israeli goods competitive in the world market. New investment laws, which allowed liberal tax concessions, were designed to lure foreign capital.

Although industrial production had quadrupled since 1949, it did so with the help of $3 billion in foreign aid. But outside help—primarily from the U.S.—is expected to fall off in the next five years and German reparations, scheduled to total $822 million, will end in 1963. Unless the nation manages to cover this gap, it faces a severe reduction in living standards.

EXUDING CONFIDENCE even after his resignation, Ben-Gurion confers with President Izhak Ben Zvi *(r.)*. This is the fifth time he has resigned since taking office.

The need for world trade, hinged on access to port facilities, lent importance to the Suez blockade. Israeli vessels had been barred from the canal since 1948. However, in early 1959, the United Arab Republic intensified the blockade by seizing even neutral ships carrying Israeli cargo. The Israeli foreign ministry appealed to the UN to enforce a 1951 decision freeing canal passage. But the United Arab Republic remained adamant.

SUPER SHERMAN TANKS take part in 11th annual independence day parade. Defense budget of $108.5 million (with additional hidden expenses) is a strain on economy.

EXODUS FROM RUMANIA created economic crisis. Transportation of one immigrant plus temporary housing averages $1600. Cost of absorbing one family into economy is $3500.

FIRST REVIEW of the new 24-man Knesset Guard, organized to defend parliament, took place on Jan. 26. A plethora of political parties (nine) and a proportional voting system inevitably result in a coalition, so far always led by the Mapai.

ABBA EBAN resigned as Israeli Ambassador to U.S. and representative to UN in May to enter politics in Israel. He was expected to run for parliament as a Mapai candidate. Avraham Harman was his successor.

NEW IMMIGRANTS were sent to towns being developed in Galilee, Lachish and the Negev. Refugees (r.) had built their own homes. Ultra modern apartment projects have been built in Beersheba and in Ashkelon.

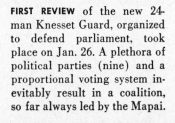

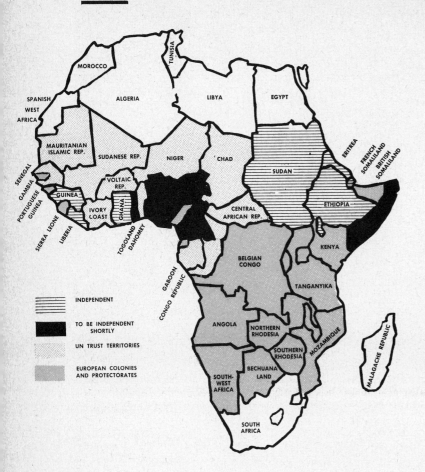

INDEPENDENT

TO BE INDEPENDENT SHORTLY

UN TRUST TERRITORIES

EUROPEAN COLONIES AND PROTECTORATES

CHANGING FACE of Africa shows independent states and those scheduled for self-rule. Campaign orator Helena "Fear Nobody" Mills harangues voters at Accra political rally. Ghana, first British African colony to achieve independence, was regarded as model by nationalists. Yet repressive laws were needed to protect infant nation from disunifying elements. Similar laws existed in white-dominated countries like Rhodesia.

EXPLOSION BELOW THE SAHARA

Black nationalist advance may prove to be too much too soon

AFRICA'S long-simmering nationalist movement came to a boil as the year opened. In Accra, capital of Ghana, leaders from every colony on the continent met at the first All-African People's Conference. The tone of the meeting was set by chairman Tom Mboya of Kenya, who demanded that Europeans "scram out of Africa."

This was no idle gesture. Violence swept the continent after the meeting. Suddenly the West realized the power that a handful of skilled orators could wield over 200 million semi-savage inhabitants of a land that was prehistoric less than a century ago.

African nationalists had a definite axe to grind. Wherever there was a European settlement, their people had been viciously exploited and humiliated. Yet many objective observers, European and African alike, were increasingly disturbed by the nationalists' often unreasonable demands.

For even in the face of outrageous injustices, the harsh fact remained that most African colonies were far from ready to assume the responsibilities that go with independence. Those countries which had achieved autonomy relied largely on European technical and administrative skill, not to mention capital. Their "neutralist" policies offered new opportunities for Soviet infiltration. Strong-arm rule, witchcraft and superstition all played important roles.

Yet the tidal wave of nationalism would not be stemmed, particularly in West Africa, where a brutal climate discouraged white setttlement. However, in the temperate highlands of East and Central Africa, European settlers had long established permanent roots, and many were grimly determined to retain the upper hand. Africans were prepared to oppose them, violently if need be.

The moderate, non-racial political groups were growing, but their chances were slim. Black nationalism appeared the almost sure winner— although it could simultaneously lose. Within a generation, Africa could consist entirely of independent nations. But would their people be free?

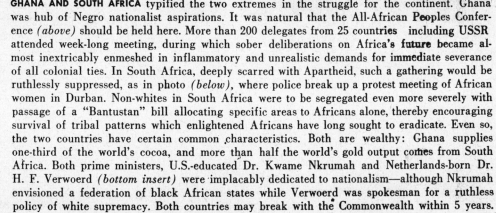

GHANA AND SOUTH AFRICA typified the two extremes in the struggle for the continent. Ghana was hub of Negro nationalist aspirations. It was natural that the All-African Peoples Conference (above) should be held here. More than 200 delegates from 25 countries including USSR attended week-long meeting, during which sober deliberations on Africa's future became almost inextricably enmeshed in inflammatory and unrealistic demands for immediate severance of all colonial ties. In South Africa, deeply scarred with Apartheid, such a gathering would be ruthlessly suppressed, as in photo (below), where police break up a protest meeting of African women in Durban. Non-whites in South Africa were to be segregated even more severely with passage of a "Bantustan" bill allocating specific areas to Africans alone, thereby encouraging survival of tribal patterns which enlightened Africans have long sought to eradicate. Even so, the two countries have certain common characteristics. Both are wealthy: Ghana supplies one-third of the world's cocoa, and more than half the world's gold output comes from South Africa. Both prime ministers, U.S.-educated Dr. Kwame Nkrumah and Netherlands-born Dr. H. F. Verwoerd (bottom insert) were implacably dedicated to nationalism—although Nkrumah envisioned a federation of black African states while Verwoerd was spokesman for a ruthless policy of white supremacy. Both countries may break with the Commonwealth within 5 years.

IMPETUS to African nationalist aspirations was furnished late in 1958 by France's President De Gaulle, when he offered French colonies choice between complete independence and new constitution providing autonomy within French Community. Referendums throughout continent gave overwhelming support to continued ties with France. De Gaulle and African leaders *(above)* meet at Elysee Palace in Paris. Present is Felix Houphouet-Boigny *(second from l.-front)*, Prime Minister of Ivory Coast and principal African spokesman for association with France. Only country to secede was Guinea, led by Houphouet's bitter political enemy, communist-trained Sekou Touré, *(l.)* in traditional Moslem *boubou*. Touré has set up strongman rule, recently conferred on Africa's future with Dr. Nkrumah and Liberia's President William V. Shadrach Tubman.

POLICE guard of honor is inspected by Duke of Gloucester during visit to Nigeria, which was scheduled for independence in 1960. Britain's largest colonial possession (one-and-one-half times size of Texas) already enjoyed internal self-rule, but observers anticipated serious problems with attainment of sovereign status. Nigeria was in 1959 federation of three states, each with its own prime minister and legislative council. Political and tribal rivalries were compounded by religious bitterness. Northern province, overwhelmingly Moslem, might be subjected to sharp Arab League pressures. Eastern and western states were led by two brilliant politicians who aspired to premiership of entire nation. Yet Nigeria was better prepared to conduct own affairs than most former colonies, due to trained civil service cadre. Country will be Ghana's chief African rival.

EMERGENCY OF DIFFERENT TYPE united Rhodesian Africans and Europeans in Spring in "Operation Noah," epic animal rescue project brought about by rising waters of Lake Kariba, which threatened thousands of head of wild game with drowning. Kariba, world's largest man-made lake, was formed by construction of Kariba Dam on the Zambesi River. Game Department wardens, scouts and rangers put their lives in daily peril as they manned small craft and carried or guided nearly every conceivable species of wild animal to safety. "Tranquilizer" bullets were used on lions and other more savage game.

WORST post-Accra outbreaks were in British Federation of Rhodesia and Nyasaland, experimental union of three territories. Permanent status was to go up for review in 1960. Riots bring troops to Nyasaland (police inspect looted store *below*), state of emergency in S. Rhodesia. Federation Prime Minister Sir Roy Welensky *(r.)* faces opposition from newly-formed, non-racial Central African Party urging African nationalism.

CENTRAL AFRICAN nationalist leaders were jailed as violence began. Nyasaland's Dr. Hastings Banda *(l.)* returned from lucrative medical practice in England, virtually demanded martyrdom. Belgian Congo, long considered model of colonial administration, also exploded with riots. Above, insurgent leader Joseph Kasabuvu *(l.)* goes to trial. On release he visited Belgium, which promised to hurry Congo independence.

EMERGENCY continued in Kenya although Mau Mau terrorism had been almost entirely suppressed. New secret society, K.K.M., specialized in poisoning victims, including hostile fellow-Africans. British soldier *(above)*, questions Kikuyu family. Nearly all Mau Mau and K.K.M. come from this tribe.

TWO SEAMEN of Royal East African Navy man anti-aircraft gun in maneuvers off Mombasa. Despite growing opposition to European domination, most of East African natives remained loyal to government. Easier franchise qualifications, more job opportunities helped hold nationalist fire-eaters at bay.

TOM MBOYA, Kenya labor leader, chats with David Dubinsky during 1959 U.S. tour. Hated but respected by Europeans, the Oxford-educated nationalist may be most powerful of all African politicians, including Nasser and Nkrumah. Brilliant, charming, Mboya demanded immediate self-government.

UGANDA nationalism was complicated by native kingdoms which sought to regain independence of pre-colonial days. Most troublesome was Buganda, ruled by Kabaka *(King)* Mutesa II, popularly known as King Freddie. He spent two years of exile in England for opposition to British "protection" treaty.

JULIUS NYERERE, political boss of Tanganyika, controlled party machine so well-organized that few African or European legislators could hold office without its support. A nationalist who advocated moderation, Nyerere would be first prime minister in unlikely event of territory's immediate self-rule.

MUSA AMALEMBA, Kenya's Minister of Housing, symbolizes emergence of moderate Africans who oppose nationalist demands, wish to work with whites toward liberal non-racialism. Though once on Mau Mau extermination list, labeled as stooge by extremists, he built 10,000 new homes in Kenya.

ETHIOPIA seemed due for powder-keg status in 1960, when neighboring Somalia, U.N. trust territory, becomes independent. Long-standing Somali border claims could touch off brush-fire war, alienate Egypt, which shares Moslem sympathies with Somali people. Meanwhile, Emperor Haile Selassie mends fences in visit of state with UAR President Nasser (above), who presents emperor with UAR top decoration.

SUDAN, independent since 1956, fell into category of African states under strong-man rule late in 1958, with military coup led by Gen. Ibrahim Abboud. Previously riddled with corruption, Sudan achieved greater measure of stability under Abboud's benevolent dictatorship and rigid adherence to neutralism in face of strong pro-Egyptian faction. Yet economy stayed shaky, disputes with Egypt over Nile could blow up.

93

PEKING CRUSHES TIBET

**Dalai Lama escapes to India,
accuses Red Chinese of mass murder, as Mao regime tramples
last embers of autonomy. Ruthless action
disillusions Indian neutralists, shocks rest of Free Asia**

TIBET, despite solemn pledges of complete self-rule, was ruthlessly and bloodily taken over by the Chinese Communists, although embers of rebellion flickered during the year.

The crushing of the Himalayan hermit nation, which shocked uncommitted Asia with its revelation of the iron fist beneath the velvet of Peiping's protestations of "peace," was, for another reason as well, less than an unqualified triumph.

The youthful Dalai Lama, sacrosanct civil and religious ruler as reincarnation of a Buddha, escaped to refuge in neutralist India, where he was given refuge in the lovely mountain resort of Mussoorie. With him, and following him, thousands of other Tibetans found haven.

The Dalai Lama's charge of bad faith, treaty breaking and genocide aroused world and Indian opinion.

They also stung the Chou-En-lai regime into blustering accusations that India, whose Prime Minister Jawaharlal Nehru has always seemed over-considerate of Peiping, actually had encouraged rebellion against China in Tibet, and that the city of Kalimpong, near the border, was "command center" of the revolt.

Actually, the rebellion, which the Chinese insisted was easily crushed, was caused by Peiping's violation of its 1951 pledges, and its insistence on destroying the Tibetan national and religious way of life, and replacing it with Chinese style collectivism.

It was precipitated when the hardy Khamba tribesmen on the China-Tibet border cut the new motor road to Lhasa, the capital, and engaged in some hard, bitter fighting.

Peiping replaced the Dalai Lama by his chief native rival, the Panchen Lama, also a youthful "incarnation," but a Red satrap held all power.

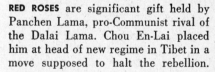

RED ROSES are significant gift held by Panchen Lama, pro-Communist rival of the Dalai Lama. Chou En-Lai placed him at head of new regime in Tibet in a move supposed to halt the rebellion.

HANDS UP, Tibetan fighters file out of fortress palace in Lhasa when Chinese Communist units moved in to halt flight of Nomads. Refugees arriving in India reported mass shootings to stop them.

"PEACE," HE SMILED. The 23-year-old Dalai Lama arrives in India, denouncing the Red Chinese leader for breaking a promise to let his people live in autonomy. This may mean end of his rule.

THE DALAI LAMA, once settled in his Indian refuge, broke centuries of precedent April 17 by holding a Western-style press conference.

He told the world—although Nehru might have been just as pleased had he spoken less bluntly—that the Chinese had killed at least 65,000 Tibetans and destroyed 1000 monasteries.

In India, where religion has always been deeply reverenced, press and public opinion erupted. Mass demonstrations were held in the major cities, demanding UN intervention and denouncing Peking.

For once, Nehru's cautious neutralism, which seemed to consist of going to almost any length to avoid offending Peking, was unpopular.

Parliament, more used to denunciations of the West, was the scene of bitter excoriations of Red China.

The repercussions of the Tibet "incident" further shook Nehru's leadership of the ruling Congress Party, which, while unchallenged externally, had become unwieldly and fat with office and showed very definite signs of an eventual disintegration.

RED TERROR is discussed by the Dalai Lama, leader-in-exile of Tibet. He told newsmen in Mussoorie, India, that China plans to smash the ancient culture of his people.

While the Chinese Reds were losing face and favor, India's homegrown Communists also were suffering a severe blow.

After months of agitation and disorders, including at least 15 deaths, the Delhi government suspended the Communist state government of Kerala, on the southwest tip of the Indian peninsula.

President Rajendra Prasad, on July 30, signed an order dismissing

JAN SANGH PARTY MEMBERS PROTEST OUTSIDE THE RED CHINESE EMBASSY, NEW DELHI, APPEALING FOR UN INTERVENTION IN TIBET

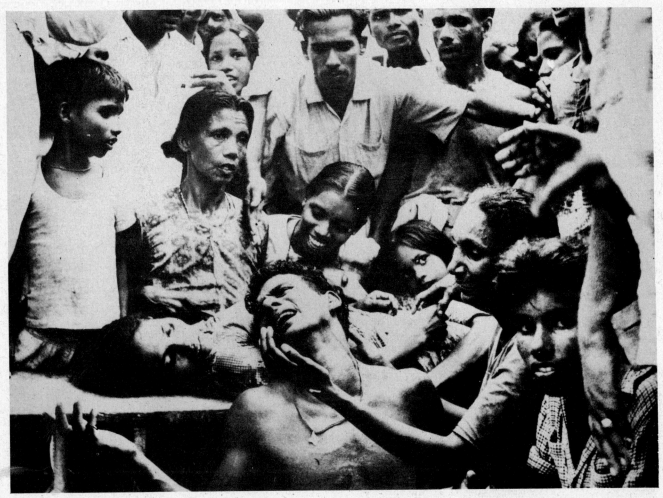

COMMUNIST POLICE bullets killed this mother of five children in Kerala. Her husband typified helplessness of demonstrators against Red-controlled gov't.

RED REGIME ENDS

New Delhi ousts Kerala's Commmunists

E. M. S. Nambudiripad, the state's Brahman but Red premier.

The decision, which was taken by the Nehru cabinet only after long hesitation, ended the world's only Communist regime ever set up by completely free elections.

The issue which overthrew Kerala's Communist government, which came into power in 1957, was its attempt to increase state—and hence Red— control of teachers and curricula of the 4000 private schools, mostly Roman Catholic. (Kerala is India's most Christian state.)

The Communist move against the church schools apparently aroused the majority of the population (the Communists in 1957 had polled

only 35% of the vote) and led to a traditional campaign of mass passive resistance and civil disobedience in the style used against the British Raj before independence.

Building entrances and bus and trolley routes were blocked by living bodies, and the state's public services faced paralysis when New Delhi finally acted.

Communism's fountainhead, the USSR, did, however, win a victory when a state-owned steel mill, built with Soviet funds and technical assistance went into operation in Madhya Pradesh. It was a substantial step, despite high costs and long delay, towards realizing Nehru's dream of democratic socialism for India.

DEFIANCE is expressed by E. M. S. Nambudiripad, Communist head of Indian State of Kerala. State was toe-hold on soft leg of pivotal, unstable Asia.

COUNTERPART to the Soviet-built plant—and symbolic of East-West rivalry for the allegiance of India's 400 million people—was the opening of a similar mill built with West German funds and help in Orissa state. Each had an annual capacity of 1 million tons. (Almost all of India's current output, estimated in 1958 at 1.3 million tons, came from the private mills of the great Tata complex.)

Each, too, was destined to play a part in India's ambitious second Five Year Plan, by which Nehru hoped to use British-style democratic socialism to lift the world's second largest nation by its own economic bootstrap —with billions in foreign help.

Foreign aid pledged for the plan included, by mid-year, a $200 million loan from the U.S. (added to existing aid programs) and a $350 million loan from the World Bank (mostly from the U.S.).

Half of the immense total was to be raised domestically, half abroad, and each half was to be raised in part from governments and in part from private business.

India, with an estimated 612,000 villages, was still an almost entirely agricultural country, and its leaders' hope was to attain a large measure of industrial self-sufficiency while increasing agricultural output enough to feed all Indians.

The population explosion, which is adding new Indians at the rate

NEHRU TURNS India's most important wheel: irrigation tap for wheat fields.

JAI PRAKASH NARAIN, once Nehru protege, emerged from political retirement to attack policies of Prime Minister.

of 7 million yearly, was the basic problem, since, even to begin to abate the nation's abysmal individual poverty, the economy had to advance even faster than the population. Imposition of ruthless controls was tempting, but could Nehru attempt to do so and remain consistent with his democratic ideals?

And if Nehru could not—or dared not—who could?

The question of a successor or replacement of the veteran leader, now 69, was the principal political question, as it had been almost since independence.

His hold seemed to be weakening over the Congress Party, as its hold seemed to be weakening over the nation in general.

The venerable Chakravarti Rajagopalachari, Free India's first chief executive, emerged from retirement to challenge both Nehru and Congress, denouncing "softness" toward the Reds in foreign policy and ineptness and corruption at home.

Another critic—and the man once regarded as Nehru's own choice as successor—was Jai Prakash Narain, who had broken with Congress to head the Socialists, and then withdrawn from the political arena.

But neither one was Nehru.

Meanwhile the threat from Red China, made actual by Tibet, and

ELDER STATESMAN Chakravarti Rajagopalachari, Indian Union's first chief of state, added voice to attacks on Nehru.

MODERN INDIA is epitomized by Indira Gandhi, daughter of Nehru and first woman president of Congress Party.

STRIKING NINE STORY BUILDING OF THE CHANDIGARH SECRETARIAT, DOMINATING THE NEW CITY IN THE PUNJAB, INDIA

PAKISTAN, INDIA DRAW CLOSER

Both endangered by Red agression

GEN. MOHAMMED AYUB KHAN, Commander of Pakistan Army, ends civil rule.

DISEASE, DEATH follow in wake of monsoon-born floods in Karachi, Pakistan.

prospects of agreement over division of the vital waters of the Indus watershed, had drawn together India and its Moslem twin, Pakistan.

Prime factor in the Indus negotiations was an American, President Eugene Black of the World Bank, who stated in May that both Nehru and Pakistan's military dictator, Maj. Gen. Ayub Khan, had accepted the "basis for negotiating a final settlement."

But this was hope for the future, and in 1959 West Pakistan was plagued by floods from the disputed rivers rather than drought.

And, while West Pakistan's wheat harvest was swept downstream, other raging waters played havoc with the rice and jute of East Pakistan, 1000 miles away on India's other side.

The Ayub Khan government, which had assumed office to end corruption and crush pro-Communism

threats, struck hard in carrying out its self-bestowed mission. Four important newspapers including the influential *Pakistan Times* were seized on charges of accepting "foreign"— meaning Communist—funds and directives. Military courts were busy.

99

IN HAPPIER DAYS, Red Premier Chou En-lai and India's Nehru met in New Delhi, before Tibetan revolt and brutal Chinese suppression campaign that shocked Indian people. After long indecision, Nehru criticized Reds, gave Tibetans asylum.

MOSCOW-TRAINED Liu Shao-chi *(l.)* took over as president of Red mainland in May. But Mao remained as leader of 13-million member Communist Party. Liu, long touted as Mao's successor, is dour one-time peasant who generally remains in background. He rose through Red ranks as hard-fisted labor organizer and now is regarded as his nation's leading theoretician.

RED CHINA: A BAD YEAR

Mao Tse-Tung's "Year of Big Leap" backfires as Tibetans revolt, workers' communes break down

COMMUNIST CHINA'S ambitious plans veered aground in 1959 on a reef of troubles.

Bloody revolt in Tibet and its even bloodier suppression brought the condemnation of the Free World on the Red regime. Even Asia's wavering neutrals—India and Burma—bitterly condemned Peiping.

Red China's bombastic war of words and bombs failed to dislodge Nationalist China from the off-shore islands of Quemoy and Matsu. Her threats of invasion melted away as the U.S. stood fast on its protection of the islands.

Internally, too, there was deep trouble. Red leader Mao Tse-tung's communes appeared headed for bitter failure. Crop yields fell short of targets and grumbling increased from overworked, hungry peasants.

Despite these failures, the world's largest nation celebrated with predictable enthusiasm its 10th anniversary October 1 with millions jamming Tien a Mien Square in Peiping for pep talks and parades.

Despite the celebration, rumbles of discontent were heard from Shanghai in the east to the walled city of Chengtu in the west. The exiled Nationalist regime on Formosa said it was only a matter of time before the Peiping government collapsed. Few Western diplomats agreed with Taipei, but all agreed—the Reds were in trouble.

Mao stepped down as chairman of People's Government in a surprise move. Moscow-trained Liu Shao-chi stepped into his shoes. But Mao retained the reins of power as boss of the Chinese Communist Party. Turning 65, Mao had dubbed 1959 as "The Year of the Big Leap."

His commune system fared badly. In the south, Red cadres loosened their hold by shortening working hours, allowing peasants more contacts with their families and boosting food allotments.

But it meant taking food from others. Shanghai suffered badly. Pork rations were cut to two ounces every 10 days.

Peiping acknowledged publicly that agricultural targets had fallen short of goals. The rice goal of 5 million tons fell short at least 25%.

Industrially, the nation faltered. Peiping's boast of doubling steel production by using backyard smelters hit a roadblock: the quality was so poor the steel was worthless.

Peiping's touted trade offensive proved empty. British traders who signed contracts for consumer goods reported the Reds were unable to fulfill promises. Only a few goods reached the outside and most were so poor they were returned.

"The Year of the Big Leap"—1959—backfired in the face of the Communist Chinese rulers.

WAITING ANXIOUSLY, women stand at border, hoping to enter British Hong Kong. Food shortages and ruthless Communist methods have sent thousands into exile from their homes. Many smuggle selves across lines, seeking better life. Reds favor emigration of cripples, women and children, but prevent able-bodied workers from leaving. Skilled labor is in short supply.

PEANUT HARVEST undergoes inspection in Hupeh Province by Red cadres. Although commune here reached quota, most rural cooperatives had difficult year. Hit by typhoons, floods and drought, nation suffered from periodic rice shortage. In June, devastating floods claimed hundreds of lives in rice-growing coastal provinces and sharply cut grain harvesting.

RISING STAR in Red hierarchy, Foreign Minister Chen Yi directs mainland's unbending anti-American policies. Western travelers returning from China report intense anti-U.S. propaganda is finding success with younger Chinese. A few Americans are still in China's jails.

PIGTAILED girls work alongside men in most factories. Despite Peiping's impressive statistics on production, Reds still suffer from shortages in virtually all goods. Unable to comply with trade contracts because of shortages, Reds lost much-needed foreign exchange during 1959. Foreigners who did buy mainland-made goods complained of inferior quality. Backyard steel furnaces turned out little usable steel and program was scrapped by year's end. China was forced to step up imports from Eastern European nations to make up for the lack.

SHOUTING and waving obsolete weapons these young Chinese farmers symbolize the huge militia that has been organized under Red regime. Estimated as high as 15 million, militia drills daily and prepares for so-called liberation of Formosa. Although Reds have slackened shelling of offshore islands in recent months, they maintain air strips with latest MIG jets within striking distance. Nationalist fliers downed five MIGs in swirling dogfight during summer over coast, returned with boast that Red pilots were badly trained and afraid to do battle.

WITHOUT U.S. aid, Nationalists would be sitting ducks for Communist invasion. During Quemoy crisis, U.S. vowed defense of the offshore islands, blocked Red invasion plans. In 1959, Formosan planes began rice and leaflet dropping missions over mainland as part of campaign to keep alive hopes of freedom.

PLEDGING Nationalists will return to mainland, Generalissimo Chiang Kai-shek addresses soldiers in Taipei. Government embarked on program weeding out old troops and replacing them with young Formosans during 1959. Draft and lack of political freedom on island set off sharp criticism of Chiang regime.

10 YEARS IN EXILE

CHINA'S exiled Nationalist government spent its 10th year on Formosa in 1959, far from reaching its goal of recapturing the Red mainland.

The island—a beacon of freedom for millions of Chinese scattered about Asia — suffered from natural disasters rather than from Communist guns.

Record rains in August killed almost 1000 and wiped out villages in Central Formosa. A few days later, violent earthquakes ripped the island,

killing scores, leaving many homeless.

Sporadic shellings of the off-shore islands by Red gun batteries were grim reminders of what exists between the Nationalists and the Communists. In June, U.S.-trained Nationalist pilots shot up five Red MIG-19s in an air battle over the Formosan Straits.

Formosan groups made demands for more political power in the ruling Kuomintang. President Chiang Kai-shek disclosed his plans to step down from presidency sometime in 1960.

RETURNING in June from one-year trip of steady travel, Madame Chiang Kai-shek holds out hand in greeting as crowds surround her at airport. Madame Chiang spent much of time attempting to win overseas goodwill for Nationalist cause. Despite sickness, Madame Chiang leads most of the women's organizations in Formosa in attempt to bolster morale. President Chiang welcomes wife on return.

MYSTERY surrounds shifting of Gen. Wang Shu-ming from chief of staff to advisory job. Wang, tough, able ex-air force boss, reportedly differs with Chiang Kai-shek over military policy.

HANDCLASP marks greeting between So. Korea's Syngman Rhee and visiting Gregory Cardinal Agagianian.

KOREA: COUNTRY DIVIDED

AMERICAN tank is unloaded at South Korean port of Inchon as U.S. continues military build-up. Communist North Korea is also bolstering army.

THE UNEASY KOREAN TRUCE erupted in violence a few times during 1959, but neither side made a move to shatter the six-year-old armistice that separates Communist North Korea from the free South.

In June, crackling gunfire shattered the peace momentarily and three Korean soldiers fell dead, two in the north of the 38th parallel and one on the south side. The news rated only a few paragraphs in American newspapers. Korea, for all practical purposes, is separated into two nations.

In the South, aging President Syngman Rhee indicated he plans to run for another term and pleaded with the U.S. for an opportunity to wage war against the north. The U.S., which supplies South Korea with all its military aid, told Rhee it would never approve force to be used as a unifying measure.

The North, meanwhile, waged a bitter propaganda campaign against the U.S., calling Washington the hub of "imperialism" among other things because of aid given to South Korea.

HUGE MOBS turn out frequently in both North and South Korea at beck of government bosses. They hail train (above) carrying No. Korea's Premier Kim Il Sung and support anti-Red parade (r.).

ATTIRED in ancient robes *(above)*, Crown Prince Akihito and pretty Michiko Shoda pose stiffly just before their wedding rites. After the private 11-minute ceremony, royal couple stood outside their Tokyo palace *(r.)* to receive their guests. Millions lined streets to cheer Akihito and his bride.

A PRINCE
MARRIES
A COMMONER

FOR THE FIRST TIME in Japanese history, a commoner married the heir to the age-old throne of the Land of the Rising Sun. In April, 1959, Crown Prince Akihito wed lovely young Michiko Shoda, daughter of a prosperous flour merchant.

PRO-AMERICAN Prime Minister Nobusuke Kishi spent much of 1959 touring foreign areas in attempt to boost trade.

Although carried out with strict Shinto ritual handed down from the ancestors of the Imperial House, the wedding, said to be a love match, shattered centuries of tradition. The heir has always previously married a girl from the inner circle of the high court nobility.

But Japan, while it was growing away from tradition in Imperial marriages, was resuming its key role, this time as champion of the free world, in turbulent Southeast Asia. Under the dynamic leadership of its Prime Minister, Nobusuke Kishi, Japan emerged as the leading nation in the Far East. In a trade battle with Communist China, it easily emerged the victor, temporarily, at least. Kishi, despite sharp political opposition, stood firm on his policy of non-recognition of the Peiping government.

But storm clouds darkened during the year over Japan's widening trade relations with the U.S. and European nations. The tuna and salmon industries cried out loudly for import restrictions. European and South American textile manufacturers placed limits on Japanese imports. Kishi, disturbed by the growing outcry, undertook in July a long tour of Europe and Latin America in an attempt to create goodwill for Japan by discussing policies and problems.

At home, Japanese manufacturers began limiting exports. They also introduced rigorous export standards.

Militarily, Japan remained a minor factor in the balance of power. The country's total defense budget for 1959 was $377 million, a fraction of pre-World War II expenditures.

U.S.-Japan relations remained healthy despite a March decision from a Japanese court that the presence of U.S. troops in Japan violated the new, MacArthur-inspired constitution.

The decision was regarded as a legal technicality. There was no expectation that the Kishi regime would initiate steps toward implementing this court ruling.

SELF RULE FOR SINGAPORE

Reds resume Laos attack, demand U.S. withdraw military aid; Malaya welds unity

T HE NEW independent state of Singapore was born during 1959. It
came into being in an area torn by
rebellions and facing the threats of
Chinese Communist domination.

Southeast Asia, during 1959, was
a vast area of contradictions. In Laos,
the Red-dominated Pathet Lao, dor-
mant for two years, revived its civil
war with the Royal Government.

Other new nations such as Cambodia and South Vietnam made
steady progress toward strengthening
their free governments.

Singapore, long a British bastion
in the Far East, became a self-gov-
erning state June 3 and Lee Kuan
Yew was named prime minister.
There were fears that Lee's leftwing
People's Action Party might lead the
crowded island toward Red control,
but Lee denied Communist leanings.

GOODWILL visit sees India's President
Rajendra Prasad (r.) greeted by Tuan-
ku Abdul Rahman, Malaya's chief ruler. Both are in British Commonwealth.

DEMANDING release of Huk rebel who
sought asylum, rioters stone Indonesian
embassy, Manila. Huk threat is fading.

INFLATION and corruption are major
problems facing Philippine President
Carlos P. Garcia, shown here with wife.

To the north, Malaya's free government moved to wipe out the Communist threat, seized 190 on Red subversion charges and pressed its grim
war against Reds in jungle hideouts.
Prime Minister Tengku Abdul Rahman resigned temporarily to solidify
his multi-racial anti-Communist alliance—a union of leading Malay,
Chinese and Indian parties. The result was a smashing victory for the
alliance and the West—and a blow to
Red hopes—in the Aug. 17 elections.

In South Vietnam, a bomb thrown
by Red rebels killed two U.S. aid officers watching a motion picture, a
grim reminder of the tense "peace"
that separates the free South from
the Communist North. This was one
of many daily bombings and assassi-
nations by Red agents that harrassed
South Vietnam during the year. In
May, President Ngo Dinh Diem ordered martial law in an attempt to

put a halt to the rampant lawlessness.

In neighboring Cambodia, border
troubles kept jazz-loving Premier
Prince Norodom Sihanouk busy
during the year. The prince accused
both Thailand and South Vietnam of
border violations threatening peace.

A brief revolt in February was put
down quickly. Soon afterward, the
bullet-riddled body of Dap Chhun,
sought as rebel leader, was found at
Siem Reap.

The major 1959 threat came in
little Laos, where the Pathet Lao resumed its civil war in the northern
provinces. Hours later, Red China
warned the U.S. to pull its military
aid teams out of Laos. Washington
dismissed the blast as propaganda,
but recalled the warnings had a ring
like those nine years ago preceding
Chinese intervention in Korean War.

Burma's military government made
phenomenal progress during 1959 in

CLAPPING students march in parade observing birthday of aging HoChi Minh, Red boss of North Vietnam. Ho, 69, led revolution against French that ended in partition of country into two blocs.

FATE OF Singapore lies largely in hands of Lee Kuan Yew, who took over as prime minister in June after Britain gave island independence. Lee's People's Action Party is regarded as left-wing.

putting the nation's affairs in order. Gen. Ne Win virtually wiped out a long-standing rebel threat and cut the cost of living 25 per cent. As defense measure, he rammed a military conscription measure through the Chamber of Deputies and took steps to move away from ties with Soviet-bloc nations.

Thailand's Field Marshal Sarit Thanarat, who seized power in late 1958, consolidated his power and confined to jail dozens of alleged Communist sympathizers in first test of sweeping anti-Communism acts.

SUPERMARKET, first in Asia, opened during year in Singapore. Owners, who named it "Donald Duck," reported booming business on opening days, expected to gross two million annually.

OVERCROWDED street is typical sight in Singapore, where more than one million people are crowded. Diverse nationalities have led to race riots. Even greater fear is Communist subversion.

SUMATRAN rebel leader, Lt. Col. Hasanuddin (*on bench*), addresses troops at his jungle headquarters. North Sumatra rebels agreed to end rebellion for increased autonomy.

INCIDENTS between Russian embassy and newsmen prompted Burmese reporters to picket Soviet legation in Rangoon in May. During year, Burma turned increasingly toward United States, accepted $30 million for economic construction and military aid. Action was reversal of past neutralist policy. Border incidents with Red Chinese and revulsion by Communist brutality in Tibet apparently brought about policy switch.

DESPITE appearance of friendliness, relations between U.S. and Indonesia had rough moments during year. Sukarno and Ambassador Howard P. Jones (*above*) enjoy a laugh. In June, Sukarno dissolved national assembly, took over as head of "guided democracy" and named 10-member cabinet to help him run country. Communists were left out, and Army chief took many top posts. Critics called it dictatorship.

POPULATION TOPS 10 MILLION

PERIPATETIC Prime Minister Menzies *(l.)* toured U.S., Canada, West Europe, Pakistan, India after election victory. External Affairs Minister Casey *(r.)* retained post.

Menzies government reelected; relations with USSR resumed

MELBOURNE'S venerable Catholic archbishop, Dr. Mannix, stirred up election storm by raising pro-Communism issue.

AUSTRALIA began 1959 with Prime Minister Robert G. Menzies' coalition government more firmly in power than ever after a late Fall election marked by a serious below-the-surface split in the opposition Labor Party.

The government won 75 seats in the House of Representatives (Liberals 58, Country Party 17) to Labor's 45. In the Senate, chosen by proportional representation, the government won a 32-28 majority.

Highlight of the campaign was the charge of "softness" toward Communism hurled by the dean of Australia's Roman Catholic hierarchy, the 84-year-old Archbishop of Melbourne, Msgr. Daniel Mannix, against the dominant Labor faction headed by Dr. Herbert Evatt.

Dr. Evatt, opposition leader in Parliament and former President of the UN General Assembly, is Australia's best known diplomatic figure next to Menzies himself.

Since Catholics make up a large part of the Labor Party, the charge cost it many votes, even though many influential Catholics, including other ranking prelates, hastened to Evatt's defense.

But, for most Australians, memories of the election were quickly overshadowed by the fact that, on March 10, the young nation's population passed the 10 million mark. It was an increase of 2 million in 10 years, and to a large extent the result of the more liberal post-World War II immigration policy.

Also in March, Australia resumed diplomatic relations with the USSR, broken by Moscow in 1954 after a Royal Commission investigated an espionage ring linked with the Soviet Embassy in Canberra.

Among visitors was Indonesian Foreign Minister Subandrio, but his friendly reception did not change Australia's firm support of Netherlands sovereignty over West New Guinea, which Indonesia claims. (Australia rules East New Guinea.)

Evidence of economic advance was a 1958-59 budget deficit of only $66 million. Forecast was $250 million.

WOOL is staple of Australian exports. Industry, hard hit in 1958, recovered rapidly in 1959 as demand, prices rose.

YEAR FULL OF WORRIES FOR SOUTH AMERICA

**Economic instability still
plagues most Latin nations;
Argentina's first
post–Peron regime
faces grave crisis**

FOR MOST OF SOUTH AMERICA, 1959 was a troublesome year, full of economic and political harassments.

Probably the brightest spot on the scene was the election, in Venezuela, of Rómulo Betancourt as the first president to succeed dictator Marcos Pérez Jiménez.

Betancourt, a staunchly anti-Communist liberal, had kept his Democratic Action party alive underground during the 11 years of Pérez Jiménez' dictatorship, while he himself lived in exile in the U.S. In the free elections of December, 1958, it swamped its opponents at the polls.

Adm. Wolfgang Larrazabal, who had headed the na-

ADDING TO WOES of economically and politically harried Argentianians, floods hit Buenos Aires in April. (Shopkeeper, *l.*, carries girl across knee-deep street.)

NEW CABINET was appointed by Argentine Pres. Frondizi *(r.)* in June when pressure from military leaders forced governmental shakeup. Key man was Minister of Economy and Labor Alvaro Alsogaray *(below)*, an energetic advocate of free enterprise who had polled only 60,000 votes as a Presidential candidate in 1958 national elections. He set out to win cooperation of labor and business in fight to halt Argentina's wage-price spiral.

tion's interim government, ran against Betancourt for the presidency, but the prestige that attached to him as a leader of the 1958 revolution was not enough to outweigh the popularity of Betancourt and Democratic Action— and the fears aroused by the enthusiastic endorsement he got from the Communists, although not one himself.

Larrazabal acknowledged his defeat generously, calmed down his supporters, who might have run wild and kept Betancourt from assuming office, and did all he could to help the new president get on with his job.

At the other end of the continent, another post-revolutionary regime, that of Arturo Frondizi in Argentina, was running into rough sailing.

The stiff austerity program he had imposed to get the nation back on its feet after the economic orgies of dictator Juan Perón led to a wave of strikes, which in turn got the all-powerful Argentine army so worried that the beleaguered president replaced his entire cabinet.

The army, which could probably have deposed Frondizi as easily as it had Peron, made it clear that it was giving him one more chance to win back popular support.

Chile got a new president, conservative Jorge Allessandri, in a bitterly fought but orderly election that marked the nation's 27th revolution-free year.

His biggest job, like that of his predecessor, Carlos Ibañez del Campo, was fighting Chile's endemic inflation.

In May, 1959, delegates of the 20 Latin American nations and the U.S. met in Buenos Aires to talk economics.

Virtually every one of the 20 was worried about inflation, debts, trade deficits and/or low living standards, and wanted more aid from the U.S., which had poured $736 million into Latin American economic development in 1958.

It was agreed to set up a new Inter-American Development Bank, with initial capitalization of $1 billion, but the U.S. also strongly urged its southern neighbors to start offering more inducements to private investment.

BRAZILIAN ECONOMY was beset by foreign debts, inflation, and a $300 million trade deficit. Coffee plantations, *(above)*, provided a major export asset. Kubitschek government asked International Monetary Fund for fourth major loan since 1953. But giant nation also made strides in industrial development.

ARGENTINE PRESIDENT Arturo Frondizi fought a losing battle against inflation all year, got $300 million loan from U.S. (Eugene Black, head of International Bank for Reconstruction and Development, *above r.*, takes leave of Pres. Frondizi, *l.*, and Economy Minister Donato after Feb. conference.)

111

ANGRY CROWDS rioted for days in Bolivian cities after appearance of *Time* Magazine article quoting U.S. embassy official there as saying that the small Andean nation should be "abolished." Demonstrators in the capital, La Paz (*r.*), stoned U.S. Embassy and Information Service office, burned copies of the magazine in the streets. Pres. Siles Zuazo appealed for calm while U.S., Bolivian and *Time* officials each apologized.

RIOTING IN LIMA, Peru, began when 32 leaders of the Left-of-center Popular Action Party were arrested for defiance of the conservative government of Pres. Manuel Prado Ugarteche. Constitutional guarantees, including that of public assembly, had been suspended during wave of strikes, and Popular Action high command had scheduled a mass rally in spite of ban. After arrests, leaflets urged people to "come outside."

ROMULO BETANCOURT was the victor in Venezuela's first free presidential elections after 1958 overthrow of dictator Marcos Pérez Jiménez. He defeated Wolfgang Larrazabal, head of the nation's post-revolutionary provisional government. Betancourt had held presidency before Jiménez took power, and had spent 11 years in exile in the U.S.

U.S. TOURISTS were just beginning to discover South America. Continent still lagged far behind Europe and the Caribbean in popularity, but airlines, government tourist agencies were starting active publicity campaigns, emphasizing such off-beat attractions as skiing in Venezuela (*l.*), fishing in the Andes.

HERO'S ENTRANCE into Havana after victory march across Cuba was climax of Castro's triumph. He had fled Cuba soon after July 26 student uprising began anti-Batista resistance in 1953, gathered small band of exiles in Mexico and returned, landing off a yacht in eastern Cuba, in 1957 to take up guerrilla war against Batista regime in Sierra Maestra mountains.

CASTRO TRIUMPHS

Rebels oust Batista after two years of guerilla war

FIDEL CASTRO and his army of bearded revolutionaries came down out of the mountains on January 1, 1959, as heroes of Cuba.

After two long years of guerilla warfare, the dictatorship of Fulgencio Batista had collapsed overnight. Batista was on his way to refuge in the Dominican Republic. The regular Cuban army was going through the motions of setting up a provisional government, but in reality, the nation belonged to Castro.

As the Castro forces moved westward toward Havana, crowds lined every mile of the road to catch a glimpse of their almost lengendary heroes. Every city the rebels entered went wild with joy.

It took the ragged, jubilant Castro four days to reach Havana, although the first elements of his army entered the capital on Jan. 2. (600 of the rebel soldiers took over the elegant ballroom of the Havana Hilton hotel for a barracks.)

He stopped off in Santiago de Cuba to proclaim Dr. Manuel Urrutia—a widely respected, non-controversial middle class liberal who had belonged to the anti-Batista resistance although not to Castro's own 26th of July movement—as provisional president of the nation.

Castro himself was as picturesque, likeable and puzzling a figure as had appeared on the international scene in some time.

Even after he had entered Havana and settled down in a hotel suite, he refused to discard his khakis or shave his beard. He loved the roaring crowds that swallowed him up wherever he went. His energy seemed inexhaustible—at least to the reporters who attended his midnight press conferences. But nobody had a very clear idea of what he planned for Cuba.

"WAR CRIMES" TRIALS of about 400 Batista supporters began in mid-January. In Havana, trials were held before frenzied crowds of thousands in Sports City Stadium. Parades of witnesses came forward to testify to army officers' "murder" of civilians, burning of homes. (María Gálvez, *above, l.,* testified against Maj. Jesús Sosa Blanco, *above, r.,* one of many condemned to firing squad.) Trials were widely criticized, especially in the U.S., for their "Roman Circus" atmosphere.

Aftermath of revolution brings new problems, tensions

His "utopian radical" ideas of politics and economics soon began to worry most outside observers—and many Cubans. A drastic land reform program, which called for distribution of more arable land than there actually is in Cuba, was especially disturbing to the U.S. and Cuban owners of the giant sugar plantations that form the basis of the Cuban economy.

Dr. Urrutia's first cabinet broke up early in February, and Castro, who had steadily disclaimed any wish to hold political office, became Prime Minister on Feb. 14.

As the year went on, the new government's road grew rockier and rockier. At times, it seemed to be veering dangerously toward the Left, although there was little reason to believe that Castro himself was a Communist. Land reform was opposed, economic woes multiplied.

In July, Castro resigned as Prime Minister in what seemed to be a grandstand play for renewal of his popular mandate. He got it—and also forced the resignation of Urrutia, who had turned out to be too much of a moderate for revolutionary tastes.

On July 26, the sixth anniversary of the tragic student revolt against Batista from which his movement had taken its name, he let a cheering "We Want Castro" rally of machete-swinging peasants in Havana's biggest stadium persuade him to return to his job.

In August, the never-a-dull-moment leader uncovered and crushed a counter-revolutionary plot, hatched, he claimed, by the Dominican Republic's dictator, Gen. Rafael Trujillo, with whom he had been trading accusations all year.

Castro was learning to run his country the hard way, and he baffled his friends as often as he confounded his enemies. But most of Cuba still had high hopes for him.

HAVANA CASINOS were closed until Feb. 19. Castro would have liked to keep them closed, but their contribution to Cuban economy was too important. Under the new laws, gambling was allowed for tourists and for Cubans earning over $20,000 a year. Hundreds of U.S. visitors were in Havana on New Year's Day when revolution struck, but all left safely.

CASTRO WAS A HIT on April visit to New York, but drove police half frantic by refusing to stay out of crowds. (In Penn. Station, *above*, policeman tries to stop his address to cheering throngs.)

ANTI-CASTRO PICKETS paraded in front of Cuban's Washington, D.C., hotel during his U.S. visit. Most were probably from the Dominican Republic. Castro regime had issued blanket condemnation of remaining Latin American dictatorships as soon as it took over, soon severed diplomatic relations with Dominican Republic where dictator Trujillo held sway. Tension between two nations mounted steadily all year.

IN EARLY DAYS of revolution, Urrutia shared Castro's popularity. (Havana crowds, celebrating on Jan. 2, *above*, carry sign proclaiming, "Long Live the Revolutionary Government—Urrutia Pres.")

URRUTIA GOVERNMENT was, in fact, extremely short-lived. In July, Castro quarreled with his first choice and Osvaldo Dórticos *(above)* took over presidency.

115

WAVE OF REVOLTS STRIKES CENTRAL AMERICA

Inspired by Cuba's Castro, rebels try their luck in four nations; all fail, but unrest lingers in Trujillo's Dominican Republic

NOT-SO-COMIC OPERA regime of Gen. Rafael Trujillo in Dominican Republic appeared to be heading for real trouble.

CARIBBEAN would-be revolutionaries declared themselves an open season on governments in 1959.

In the wake of Fidel Castro's successful Cuban revolt came a series of outbreaks in Panama, Nicaragua, the Dominican Republic and Honduras, each more unsuccessful than the last.

Late in April, a boatload of 87 adventurers landed on the Panamanian coast and marched inland to the village of Nombre de Dios. Finding that nobody was inclined to rise up in arms and join them (the Panamanian government, headed by Ernesto de la Guardia, was by and large

conscientious and democratic), they surrendered on May 1 to an investigating committee sent in by the Organization of American States.

The invasion force was mostly Cuban, although one Puerto Rican and a few Panamanians came along. However, it was repudiated by Cuban Premier Castro.

The invasion of Nicaragua, early in June, was airborne and at least had as its object the overthrow of a bona fide dictatorship, that of Luis Somoza.

After Somoza's well trained National Guard had hunted down the invaders (it took them two weeks), the government imposed a tight curb on civil rights. It was broadly hinted that this attempt at revolution, too, had originated in Cuba.

Late in June, three revolutionary landing parties came ashore in the Dominican Republic.

All were quickly crushed by the forces of the veteran Dominican dictator, Gen. Rafael Trujillo.

However, it appeared that unrest in the small island nation was increasing, and that more serious trouble lay ahead for the 30-year-old Trujillo regime.

There was no doubt that these invaders were Dominican exiles, but Trujillo promptly accused both Cuba and Venezuela of having aided them.

SMALL BAND of Nicaraguan rebels voted (46 to 16) to surrender when surrounded by Somoza forces. Nicaraguan dictator pointed to invaders' uniforms, resembling those of Castro's army, and beards, when he cited "foreign" instigation of brief revolt.

HAITIANS IN HAVANA protested against broadcasts from Cuba attacking government of Pres. Francois Duvalier. Haiti was hard pressed throughout year by near-bankruptcy, church-state strife and political intrigue.

The Honduras revolts, in February and July, were directed against the shaky two-year-old regime of Ramón Villeda Morales. Their leader was a political exile, Col. Armando Velásquez. The July rebellion was put down only after hard fighting, and brought rifle, machinegun and mortar fire to the streets of Tegucigalpa, the Honduran capital.

On July 13, the OAS decided that enough was enough, and called a foreign ministers' meeting of the 21 American nations to deal with the Caribbean crisis.

The week-long conference, held in Santiago, Chile, in August, resulted in a strong reaffirmation of the OAS' traditional principle of non-intervention in the affairs of any nation by any other, emphasizing that dictatorships were just as entitled to this courtesy as democracies.

Fidel Castro, who frankly favored international cooperation in dictator-ousting, and who had already received a reprimand from the OAS for his apparent willingness to let Cuba be jumping-off point for revolutionaries, termed meeting a "farce."

MEXICO enjoyed another year of political stability and economic growth. Tourism helped boost national income as former sleepy fishing villages like Mazatlán (r.) turned into popular resorts.

INTERNATIONAL INTEREST was added to Panamanian revolt by arrest on suspicion of revolutionary activity of Great Britain's leading ballerina, Dame Margot Fonteyn. Dame Margot's husband, Robert Arias, was known to be enemy of de la Guardia regime, but denied link to revolt. She was released, and couple were reunited (above) in Brazil.

RENEWED RED agitation, rumored invasion fleets from Castro's Cuba, complicated economic woes beset Guatemala's conservative president, Miguel Ydigoras Fuentes.

ELIZABETH II WELCOMED IN CANADA

Opening of seaway, royal tour are highlights of 1959

FIRST SHIP to enter the St. Lawrence Seaway was icebreaker Ernest Lapointe, at St. Lambert lock on April 16. Nine days later, opening was informally celebrated when d'Iberville led parade of cargo ships upstream to the Great Lakes. All Seaway's (r.) channels and locks have minimum depth of 27 ft.

A ROYAL VISIT and opening of the St. Lawrence Seaway were the two great events of the year in Canada.

Queen Elizabeth II and Prince Philip were greeted by jubilant crowds in St. John's, Newfoundland, on June 18. The main event of the royal couple's six-week Canadian tour was to be the official dedication of the Seaway, on June 26 in Montreal.

However, the new water route to the Great Lakes had actually been open since April 16, and its completion had been "unofficially" celebrated on April 25, when the Canadian icebreaker d'Iberville led a parade of ships upstream from Montreal.

The procession of deep draft ocean vessels—the first ever to sail the St. Lawrence—and small canal boats, veterans of the river's old 14-foot waterways, was noisily saluted by ships at their moorings and given enthusiastic civic welcomes at practically every Great Lakes port on both the U.S. and Canadian sides of the border.

The 182-mile Seaway had cost the U.S. and Canada $471 million, and was expected to bring tremendous commercial expansion to the entire Great Lakes area.

Canada had built five locks, beginning at St. Lambert, 1000 miles from the ocean, and miles of canals to bypass the turbulent St. Lawrence rapids between Montreal and Lake Ontario. The U.S. contributed two giant locks and 10 miles of canals in the area near Massena, N.Y.

A $65 million dam and hydroelectric power station, financed by the province of Ontario and the state of N.Y., were an important by-product of the Seaway project.

The official dedication ceremonies were as colorful as flag-draped Montreal could make them.

President Dwight D. Eisenhower arrived to represent the U.S. and share the speech-making with Queen Elizabeth, and thousands of visitors, including notables from Canada, the U.S. and other nations, were on hand.

After the dedication services, Elizabeth and Philip, President and Mrs. Eisenhower and Prime Minister and Mrs. John C. Diefenbaker of Canada boarded the royal yacht, Britannia, for a cruise up the Seaway and a review in which Canadian, British and U.S. ships took part.

The rest of Elizabeth and Philip's trip took them west to Vancouver, north to Yellowknife in the Northwest Territories and Whitehorse in the Yukon. They visited 132 towns, cities and hamlets in 44 days, and met Canadians from every walk of life — which included a delegation of Montganais-Naskapi Indian chiefs in Labrador.

AS QUEEN OF CANADA, Elizabeth II was welcomed with delight wherever she went in her biggest Dominion. Most Canadians are staunch royalists—partly, perhaps, because the Queen is "something we have that the Americans don't." Elizabeth had frequent bouts with illness during her 44-day tour, but kept up arduous schedule of public appearances. (Seaway opening celebration brought meetings with Pres. Eisenhower, *above, l.,* and, in ceremonies at Cornwall, Ont., *l.,* with Vice Pres. Nixon.) News that she was expecting her third child was kept secret until party returned to England.

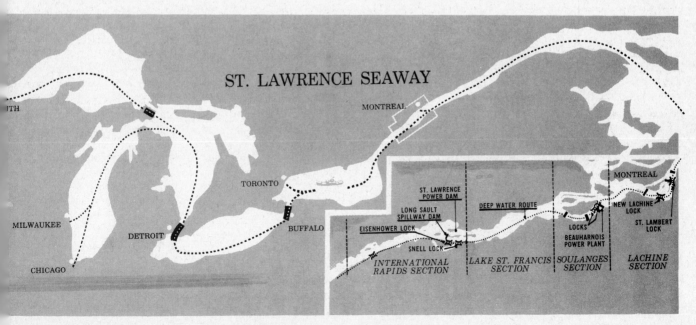

ST. LAWRENCE SEAWAY

MONTREAL

TORONTO

BUFFALO

MILWAUKEE

DETROIT

CHICAGO

MONTREAL

ST. LAWRENCE POWER DAM

LONG SAULT SPILLWAY DAM

DEEP WATER ROUTE

NEW LACHINE LOCK

EISENHOWER LOCK

LOCKS

ST. LAMBERT LOCK

SNELL LOCK

BEAUHARNOIS POWER PLANT

INTERNATIONAL RAPIDS SECTION

LAKE ST. FRANCIS SECTION

SOULANGES SECTION

LACHINE SECTION

CANADA AND THE U.S. strengthened their alliance for hemisphere defense during the year.

In February, operational control of the vitally important DEW (Distant Early Warning) Line passed from the U.S. Air Force to the Royal Canadian Air Force.

A Canada-U.S. nuclear defense agreement, signed May 22, authorized exchange of classified information on military reactors, atomic and anti-atomic weapons.

Negotiations on U.S. missiles and a nuclear warhead stockpile for Canada got under way.

Defense was the biggest single items in the record-breaking Canadian budget for the fiscal year 1960, getting $1.7 billion appropriation out of a $5.7 billion total.

The Canadian defense industry received a severe setback, however, when the $400 million development program for the Avro Arrow fighter was abandoned. The 1500-mph plane would not have been operational until 1962, and it was decided that, by then, it would have been pushed into obsolescence by ICBMs. Cancellation of the Avro Arrow program threw 14,000 men out of work, and was bitterly attacked by the opposition Liberal Party.

Canadian trade with Red China ($12 million worth in 1958) caused some resentment south of the border, and U.S. "dumping" of surplus wheat in Canadian export markets was equally irritating to Canadians, but relations between the defense partners were generally good.

CANADA'S FAMED "MOUNTIES" (on parade, *below*) got a new chief in March. Comm. L. H. Nicholson (*r.*), resigned, was succeeded by Charles Edward Rivett-Carnac (*l.*). Cause of resignation was bitter dispute over Newfoundland loggers' strike that had begun Dec. 31, grown increasingly violent. Newfoundland Premier Joseph R. Smallwood had won passage of bill outlawing striking union, the International Woodworkers of America. Violence increased, policeman was wounded in clash with strikers, and Royal Canadian Mounted Police asked for reinforcements. Federal government refused, and Comm. Nicholson resigned to dramatize force's inability to handle the situation without reinforcements.

CANADA'S COMMONWEALTH TIES were strengthened by March visit of Prime Minister Macmillan. In May, new coordinating Canadian-British Space Research Committee was formed.

PREMIER SMALLWOOD of Newfoundland sued Federal government twice—for "breach of contract" in Mounties case, and for $15 million a year in economic assistance for province.

INDIAN CHIEFS in Ontario revolted against government, declared themselves rulers of Six Nations reservation, sent request to Eisenhower for "treaties between our nations."

NEW U.S. AMBASSADOR to Canada was Richard B. Wigglesworth, previously a Republican Congressman from Massachusetts, appointed in October, 1958, to succeed Merchant.

NEW POPE BEGINS REIGN BY CALL FOR CHRISTIAN UNITY

John XIII, despite great age, combines warm personality, strong leadership

FAVORITE PET, tiny chaffinch, perches on the finger of Pope Pius XII, who kept several birds in cages at Castel Gandolfo, his summer residence. Among the Pope's many interests were animals.

IN 1959 a new, firm—and different —hand controlled the destinies of world's largest organized religious body, the half billion members of the Roman Catholic Church.

Where his predecessor, Pope Pius XII, who died Oct. 9, 1958, had stressed international relations, the new Supreme Pontiff, John XXIII, born Angelo Giuseppe Roncalli, regarded himself first of all as pastor.

He opened his reign and the new year of 1959 by an action which showed he considered the whole world his flock. He summoned an Ecumenical Council of the whole church, the first since 1870, to work for restoring unity of Christianity.

The new Pope showed in numerous other ways that, despite his 77 years, his leadership would be vigorous and bold, his reign no stopgap.

John, the name he chose upon election Oct. 25, 1958, by the College of Cardinals after 11 ballots, had not been used by a Pope since 1334.

He filled the high posts in the Papal Curia, administrative center of the world-wide church which Pius had left vacant.

He made himself much more easily available to subordinates. He drop-

ped the custom of dining always alone. He visited prisons, took part in processions. He submitted, good-humoredly, to press conference questioning. He blessed a helicopter.

Without compromising intrinsic dignity, he retained the warm personality, the concern for individuals, he had displayed as Patriarch of Venice, Nuncio to France (where his diplomatic dinners were noted) and for 19 years as Vatican representative in the Balkans and Middle East.

He told U.S. visitors he was learning English, to match his Bulgarian, Russian, French and Italian.

Significantly, he did not give princely titles to his relatives.

CARVED ANGELS hover above the body of late Holy Father as it lies in state in St. Peter's Basilica. Members of Noble Guard stand at sides of bier. Pope was buried in crypt underneath St. Peter's.

CONTRAST to age-old solemnity of the Vatican is U.S.-made "helicopterum" being blessed by new Pope, John XXIII, after landing on courtyard. It was first aircraft ever to land in the Vatican.

BARE FEET of newly ordained priests are humbly kissed by Pope John during Holy Thursday rites in St. John's Lateran, the Pope's Cathedral as Bishop of Rome. The new pontiff is much more personally active both in ceremonies and administration than was Pope Pius. He has created 23 new cardinals (two from the U.S.), bringing the total to 74, highest ever.

NEW "triple crown" for Pope was gift of government and people of Bergamo, North Italian province which is Roncalli family home. Pope John was born in village near Bergamo Nov. 25, 1881, and after ordination in 1904 became secretary to Bergamo's bishop. After many years as Vatican representative in Balkans, he became Papal Nuncio to France where he won wide esteem, and cardinal and Patriarch of Venice in 1953.

KNEELING PRISONERS applaud as Pope John XXIII visits the Regina Coeli (Queen of Heaven) prison, Rome's largest, on a goodwill trip. This revived a custom of Pope Pius IX who visited the prisoners every Christmas during his pontificate from 1846 to 1878. Pope John spent an hour and ten minutes with the 1300 male prisoners in the jail, carrying hope and a message of faith into the bleak cells. The new Pope is already known for his friendly personality that brings a touch of the modern to his traditional post as leader of Catholics over the world. His departure from precedent was dramatically shown during his coronation when he read a short homily. The Papal coronation was first ever televised.

POPE JOHN XXIII, borne on traditional "seda gestatorialis"—portable Papal throne—blesses the congregation in St. Peter's as berobed and mitred archbisops, bishops and other high prelates gathered from every quarter of the globe watch attentively. The new Pontiff, while delivering his homily in Latin during the ceremony, asked the prayers of "pious and fervent souls throughout the world" to help him reach "perfection in meekness and humility" in his pastorate.

AMERICAN SCENE -- 1959

Optimistic nation hopes for peace, plans for space, enjoys record prosperity

THE U.S. seemed a supremely satisfied nation in 1959, and the mass of Americans, more prosperous than any large group of human beings ever had been before, were unshaken either by the steel strike or the *debacle* of the New York Yankees which ended a baseball era.

The national economy, moving irresistibly and inexorably forward after the slight (in retrospect) 1957-58 setback, approached an annual Gross National Product (total of all goods and services) of $500 billion, an unimaginably huge magnitude usually reserved to express distances in outer space.

It was appropriate, however, both because it expressed national wealth never before attained on earth and because, in 1959, the U.S. was poised on the space frontiers.

Seven men, the pick of the Armed Services in know-how, brains and physique, were in actual space voyage training. And in the almost immediate future, one of them was to be sent into first manned space flight.

While these were the most exotic jobs, others were available to virtually all Americans who wanted to work. Employment, in mid-Summer, passed 67.5 million, the highest in Labor Department records.

A prosperity-mellowed U.S. viewing the world and the future through spectacles tinged with the rosy hope that nothing would upset the economic applecart, was prepared to regard even the Soviet world with friendly curiosity. After all, the USSR was reported growing rich too.

Along with stiff-as-usual diplomatic notes, the U.S. and the USSR were exchanging everything from senior statesmen to dance troupes.

"Exchange" was the fashion, all the way from the Eisenhower-Khrushchev, Nixon-Kuzlov-Mikoyan level to exhibits in New York and Moscow which vied in demonstrating art, appliances and automated kitchens. (Both fairs played to packed houses.)

Following announcement of the Khrushchev visit, every section—and, it seemed, every city and town—vied in offering to show the burly, balding boss of the Soviet Union the genuine "American way of life."

Moscow, Idaho, claimed priority because of its name; Texans were convinced even Khrushchev would be impressed by Texas; Iowa wanted to welcome a comrade corn grower; and the rest had equally valid claims.

In fashion itself, the chemise, the sack and other man-

NATIONAL GAME IN THE SPACE AGE

displeasing modes disappeared from the scene completely, to be exchanged for frankly female curves. In keeping, the European Bikini was bared on almost every beach. And, perhaps a reflection of the vogue for things Russian, earnest young women wore black ballet leotards everywhere, even under skirts on the street.

In sports, the do-it-yourself trend grew ever stronger, with millions of Americans taking to the boats in summer and the bowling alleys in winter.

Perhaps it was just as well; the U.S. lost the Davis Cup to Australia in a surprise upset, and, for the first time since 1932, the world's heavyweight championship moved abroad.

Meanwhile, 10,000 U.S. tourists poured into the USSR, and these were but the highwater mark of a travel tide which saw 1.5 million Americans spend $2.3 billion abroad and 24 million families take 40 million vacation trips within the nation's borders.

Most spectacular theatrical event, in a year not distinguished for new offerings, was the victory of free Shakespeare in New York's Central Park over the mighty Robert Moses, monarch of the city's and state's park and public power systems, to name jobs at random. He had tried to compel the sponsors to charge admission.

Motion picture attendance continued to decline as TV reached the saturation point, with sets in almost 90% of U.S. homes.

Chief literary event was Federal Judge Frederick Van Pelt Bryan's decision releasing the unexpurgated text of D. H. Lawrence's *Lady Chatterley's Lover* from a Post Office ban. He reaffirmed the doctrine that a serious work must be judged as a whole, and not by isolated passages and single words torn from their context.

The nation learned its utter dependence on electricity when power was cut off from mid-Manhattan in the midst of a sweltering heat wave. For many hours in the paralyzed area lights were dark, elevators motionless, and, momentarily worst of all, air conditioners useless.

But public discipline obviated crime or serious harm.

Educators decided U.S. methods were pretty good after all, despite Sputnik; integration made further quiet gains, establishing a token beachhead even in Faubus-haunted Little Rock.

1959's United States was rich and easy-going.

HIGHEST EMPLOYMENT LEVEL, HIGHEST AVERAGE INCOME ON RECORD BROUGHT U.S. PEOPLE UNPRECEDENTED PROSPERITY IN 1959

U.S. PENETRATES SPACE FRONTIERS

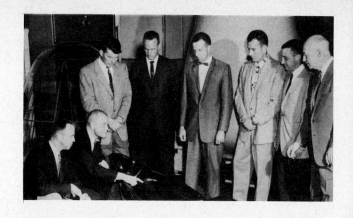

Astronauts trained for first manned voyage; satellites map radiation

IN SCIENCE, 1959 was pre-eminently the year of mice, monkeys and men—seven men, four mice and two monkeys.

In the step-by-step U.S. plan to explore the black, chartless seas of outer space, laboratory animals were preceding the first human voyagers. Not since the Soviet Sputnik flashed through the skies in 1957 had so many strange and varied craft been launched. Some of them are shown on these pages: the successful rocket ride of monkeys Able and Baker; the four hardy black mice sent up from

the new U.S. spaceport on the West Coast; the "talking satellite" that opened a new era in communications; and the "Weather Eye" satellite which boosted hopes that one day man could predict earthly weather with assurance.

Nor were the Soviet scientists idle. The Year III of the space age opened with a bold Russian attempt to hit the moon with a rocket carrying the USSR coat-of-arms. The vehicle, dubbed "Lunik," missed the moon and went into orbit around the sun, but Lunik II, fired in September,

reached its target successfully.

Although the feat of Lunik I was duplicated by the smaller U.S. Pioneer IV, it was another demonstration of Red rocket power. The Russians also boasted they would beat the U.S. in the field where interest is understandably greatest: the pioneering flight of the first Astronaut. Undoubtedly, there were Russians in training for space flight somewhere in the Soviet Union. In the U.S., seven superbly qualified military test pilots, the pick of U.S. manhood, were tapped for the Mercury (Man-into-Space) program set up by the newly-formed National Aeronautics and Space Administration. Sometime in 1961, if all goes according to plan, one of the seven will be strapped into the Mercury vehicle's contour couch and be boosted up 300 miles high for from three to 15 earth-circling orbits before splashing back down into the South Atlantic. The ride in the capsule will require a pilot's skill, NASA emphasizes, but the typical Astronaut need not be a "Superman."

One of the first Astronaut's jobs will be to report his findings, which no monkey or mouse can do. Already, thanks to a hard-working physicist from the State University of Iowa, one of the unknowns of space flight has been plotted. In one of the major findings of the century, U.S. Army Explorer satellites, instrumented by Prof. James Van Allen, detected two lethal bands of radiation girding the earth. The extent and shape of these "Van Allen Belts" was precisely determined when the U.S. detonated three atomic-tipped rockets high over the South Atlantic. Radiation was trapped in the earth's magnetic field.

MERCURY Astronaut Leroy G. Cooper Jr., an Air Force Captain, undergoes training in a special centrifuge for pioneering space flight. At 32, he is the youngest of the seven Astronauts, whose average age is 34.4. All are married with average of 2.1 children. Critics questioned backgrounds for a dangerous mission.

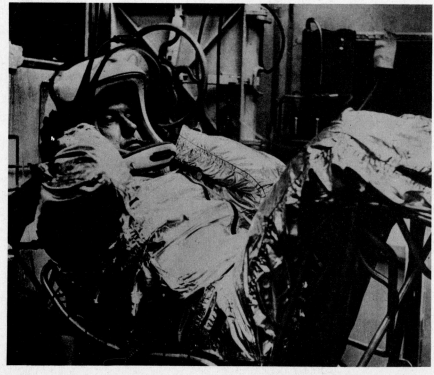

SEVEN ASTRONAUTS picked to ride in Mercury examine moldings used to make its contour couch. Bell-shaped ship, about the size of small car, is being custom-built for the average Astronaut: 164 pounds, 68 inches. NASA official is at right.

IOWA PHYSICIST James Van Allen holds model of Jupiter-C rocket used to push Explorer satellites into orbit. He designed instruments carried aboard the Explorers. They uncovered bands of radiation from 600 to 40,000 miles high.

MONKEY ABLE, a seven-pound Rhesus and the larger of two female simians sent rocketing 1700 miles over the Atlantic from Cape Canaveral, sits astride her instrument-jammed space cabin after flight. She later died during an operation.

ROARING UP from its husky steel-and-concrete pad with all three rocket motors straining mightily, powerful Atlas ICBM takes off on a Christmastime mission: a tape recorder aboard broadcast President Eisenhower's "Peace on Earth, Good Will Toward Men" message to the entire world.

FOUR BLACK MICE, of a strain known for its hardiness, were blasted into space from the West Coast aboard the first of the animal-carrying Discoverer satellites. This unfortunate quartet perished, but many others were readied to follow.

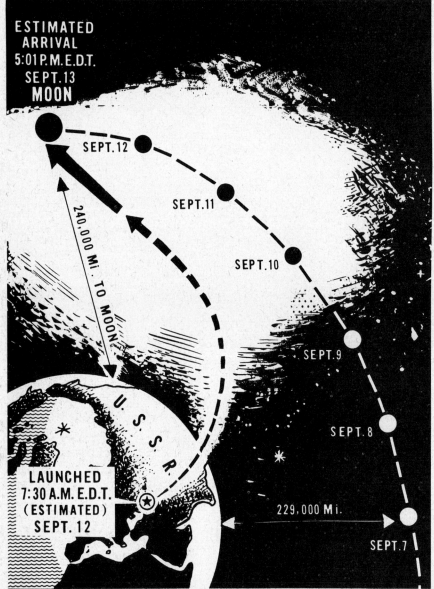

ESTIMATED
ARRIVAL
5:01 P.M. E.D.T.
SEPT. 13
MOON

SEPT. 12

SEPT. 11

SEPT. 10

240,000 Mi. TO MOON

SEPT. 9

SEPT. 8

U.S.S.R.

LAUNCHED
7:30 A.M. E.D.T.
(ESTIMATED)
SEPT. 12

229,000 Mi.

SEPT. 7

PHYSICAL OBJECT originating on earth reached another celestial body for first time in history Sept. 13 when Soviet rocket was shot to moon. Khrushchev carried replica of rocket's metal pennants to U.S. as gift to President Eisenhower, called them "symbol of our appeal for the concerted effort of Soviet and American scientists . . . for peace."

AFTER EONS of looking up at the sky and trying to guess what next day's weather would be, man has succeeded in putting up a satellite eye to scan the atmospheric cauldron where weather is brewed. Two special photo-electric cells placed in a Vanguard satellite (dark aperature shows eye) record variations in light intensity from cloud cover, land and sea, radio back findings to earth where the signals are then reconverted.

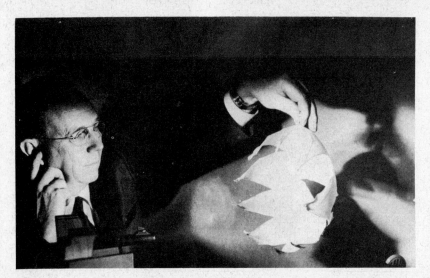

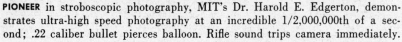

PIONEER in stroboscopic photography, MIT's Dr. Harold E. Edgerton, demonstrates ultra-high speed photography at an incredible 1/2,000,000th of a second; .22 caliber bullet pierces balloon. Rifle sound trips camera immediately.

SYMBOLIC of spirit of science are two masked technicians *(r.)* engaged in sterilizing first U.S. moon rocket lest it contaminate lunar surface with earthly germs. The sterilizing squad acts for science rather than sentimentality: a pristine, uncontaminated moon is a better prize for first explorers to study. Exploring the atom, a world as remote heretofore as the moon, now is possible through the ion microscope invented by Dr. Edwin Mueller *(below)*. The Pennsylvania State University physicist stands in front of an atomic model, in this case of a tungsten crystal. A secret of another sort is being tracked by Harvard's Dr. Carroll M. Williams *(l.)*, who has isolated in moths a "juvenile hormone" that slows down aging.

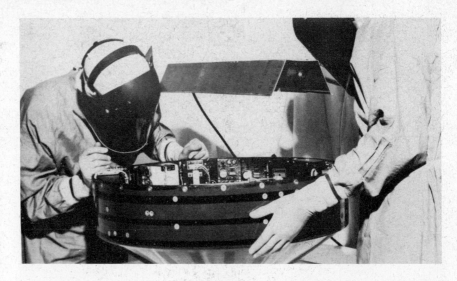

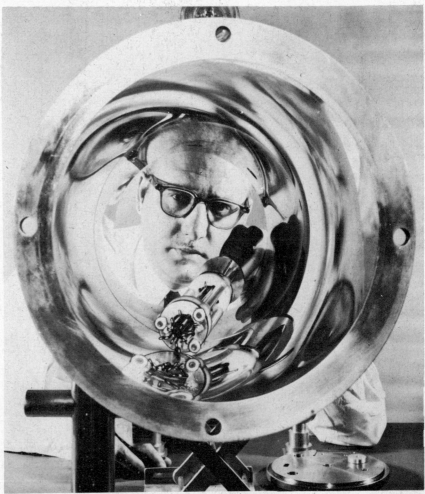

ATOMIC CLOCK, so accurate that it will neither gain nor lose a single second in 1000 years, is being developed for use in an orbiting satellite by Hughes Aircraft Co. Invented by Dr. Harold Lyons *(above)*, it will give Einstein's General Theory of Relativity the best practical check it has ever had. If Einstein was right, the clock, running in a different gravitational field above the earth, will seemingly run fast compared to a clock on the ground. The experiment will also recheck Einstein's famous "twin paradox," long a source of fascination to science fiction writers as well as scientists. If the orbited clock comes back "younger" than its counterpart on earth, it will follow that the same phenomenon would affect human space travelers—and that a man traveling in space at close to the speed of light for 20 years would find the earth millions of years older when he returned from flight.

MEDICAL RESEARCH SEEKS END TO DISEASE

Probes health problems on land, below sea, in space

RUSSIAN DOUBLE-HEADER coexisted 30 days. Head, forepaws of puppy, grafted by Dr. Vladimir Demikhov onto full-grown German Shepherd, were nourished by larger dog's body. After a month, successful amputation of the transplant was performed.

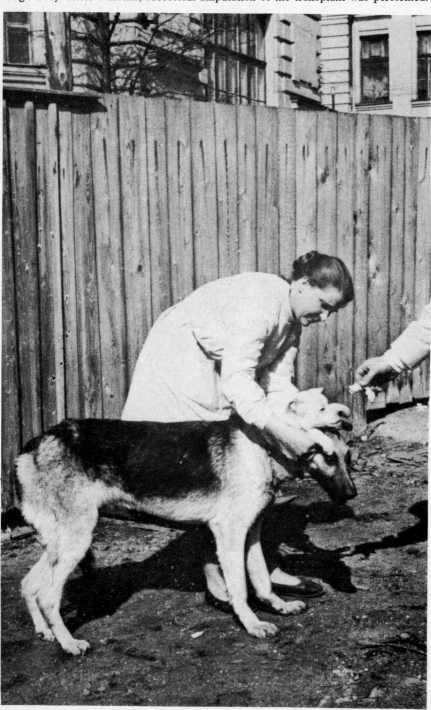

BELIEF of the American people in medical research during 1959 was indicated by the $484 million appropriation voted by the Senate—five times the 1947 sum. The "Health for Peace" bill was further evidence of the popular attitude. This proposed a new program of international medical research, with headquarters at the National Institute of Health in Bethesda, Md.

Nuclear medical research was highlighted by the Atomic Energy Commission's new center at the Brookhaven National Laboratory on Long Island. Here the first nuclear reactor specifically for medical use was set up for radiation therapy and the sprouting field of radio-isotope research, diagnosis and treatment.

Supplied by U.S. "isotope farms," some 2000 doctors and medical institutions have now been licensed to conduct "radio-isotope medicine."

Dr. Sidney Farber, of the Harvard Medical School, stated before the Senate that, due to research programs, the cure rate of cancer has risen in the last three years from one in four to one in three. He listed three areas of great promise: (1) chemotherapy; (2) search for fast, accurate, inexpensive diagnostic tests suitable for all; (3) studies of the causation of cancer that may lead to its prevention.

In the field of heart disease, doctors still debate the correlation between the fatty substance, cholesterol, and heart disorders. Already, food and drug firms have marketed several cholesterol-lowering products.

Dr. Michael E. DeBakey, noted pioneer heart surgeon, received the 1959 American Medical Association Distinguished Service Medal. He discovered that 40% of blood vessel blockages occur outside the brain and are amenable to surgery. Plastic replacements for blocked artery seg-

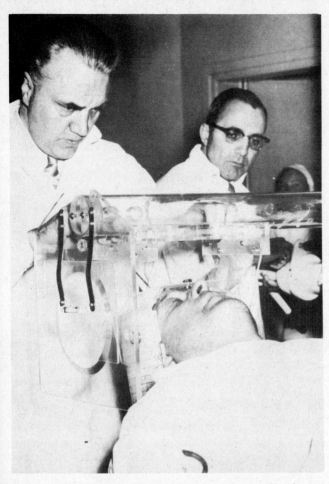

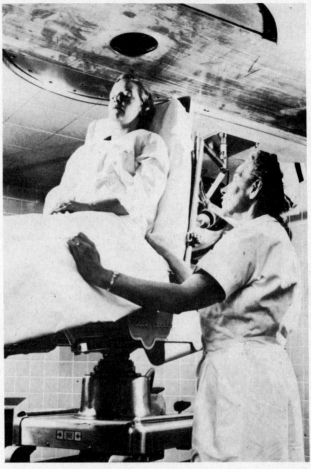

ATOMIC SCALPEL performed the first operation on the brain itself without an opening of the skull. At the Univ. of Uppsala, Sweden, Prof. Lars Leskell, seen *(above l.)* in an earlier experiment, severed two nerve tracts inside the brain, using proton beam technique developed at Univ. of Calif., Berkeley.

NUCLEAR CANCER THERAPY has steadily improved its direct attack by radiation from reactors, and diagnosis and treatment by radioisotopes. Research, training facilities have been expanded and refined. Dry-run training *(above)* at MIT, shows model positioned under irradiation opening to reactor core.

ments, he reported, were extremely effective.

As polio climbed in the U.S. above 1958 levels, over 90 million still lacked the basic three Salk shots. Most of these were in the lower income and below five years age brackets.

At this critical time, the World Health Organization received favorable reports on 20 field studies of mass immunization of millions in Africa, Asia, Europe, Latin America and the USSR. The oral, live-virus vaccines used had been developed separately in the U.S. by University of Cincinnati's Dr. Albert Sabin; Lederle's Dr. Herald Cox; and Dr. Hilary Koprowski, Wistar Institute.

Low cost, ease of oral administration and possible one-dose immunization of the newborn were reported advantages. Also, the immunizing viruses tended to spread from the vaccinated to others in a community.

Anticipating acceptance by the U.S. Public Health Service of the new vaccines at least by 1960, Lederle and other drug firms started preparations for large-scale production.

In the meantime, the Health Service has strongly urged a fourth "booster" shot of the Salk vaccine.

Following favorable long-run test results from the live-strain tuberculosis vaccine, BCG, Dr. Gardner Middlebrook reported experiments at Denver's National Jewish Hospital in spray BCG vaccination against TB. He maintained that it would be easy to immunize an entire theater full of children.

Dr. John F. Enders, Nobel Prize winner for past work on polio virus, reported a successful test on children of a live-virus measles vaccine. All children developed antibodies as "good as if they had had the measles itself."

In antibiotics, simultaneous announcements were made in the U.S. and Great Britain of methods for creating innumerable variations of man-made penicillin. The discoveries promised more effective attacks on drug-resistant, disease-causing microbes and reduction of increasingly harmful side effects.

Anti-diabetic pills remained a source of controversy. Orinase, taken by 500,000 of the known 1,500,000 U.S. diabetics and believed the safest, has been successful mostly at adult level. Serious side effects have so far plagued stronger drugs designed to decrease further, or eliminate, diabetic reliance on insulin and diet control.

Extensive research will continue.

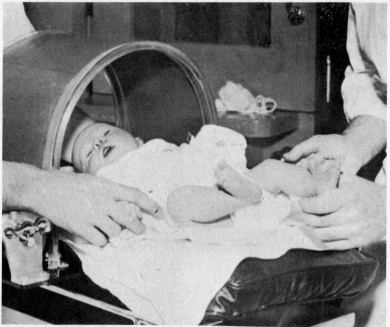

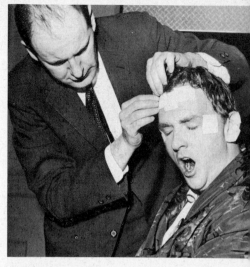

200 HOURS AWAKE was record set by disc jockey Peter Tripp, shown after first night's sleep. March of Dimes and research benefited.

NOT A BOMB SHELTER, device *(above)* was perfected by Drs. Sydney S. Gellis and John J. Gorman of the Boston Univ. School of Medicine to measure the vision of newborn infants. Tests, based on optical reactions to varying line patterns, promise early detection of eye abnormalties. Absence of vision in one or both eyes is immediately apparent.

HYPNOSIS AS MEDICAL AID has now been sanctioned by the A.M.A. In the Quincy, Mass., City Hospital, Dr. N. L. Simon has hypnotised patient *(r.).* Dr. W. P. Ridder is performing an arm operation with no anaesthetic but the hypnotic trance. The A.M.A. endorsed the use of hypnosis by trained physicians and dentists—not for entertainment.

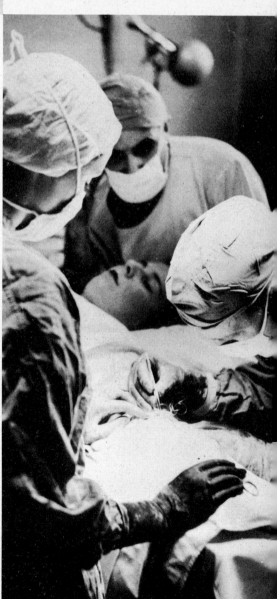

MEDICAL RESEARCH REACTOR at Brookhaven National Laboratory, Upton, L. I., is the first reactor in the world designed specifically for medical use. The new $6.5 million research center was constructed by the A.E.C. to provide direct irradiation and radioisotope treatment of ailing humans, and to expedite nuclear research experiments on animals.

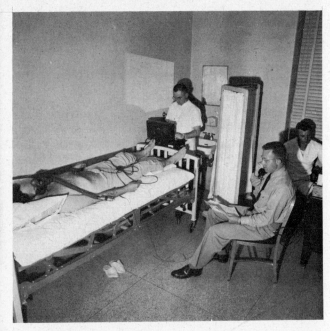

HEART DIAGNOSIS BY TELEMETER was conducted *(above)* on patient in Bethesda, Md., Naval Hospital by doctors 1,000 miles away. Naval Capt. Norman L. Barr, developer of the technique, later directed 4,000-mile radio transmission of electrocardiagram readings from Bethesda to ship off Greece.

SEALED SAFETY CAPSULE *(r.)* is to protect airmen downed at sea from long exposure to the elements. Testing is directed by Col. John P. Stapp, chief of the Wright Air Development Center Aeromedical Laboratory. Airman emerging with cigar in mouth spent 72 smoke-less hours in all-metal capsule.

TUBE STEAKS FOR SPACE MENUS have been devised by U.S. Army QM's Food and Container Institute in Chicago. Airman in space gear *(below)* sips a liquid meat meal. Semi-solid ham, chicken and steak can be squeezed from a collapsible metal tube. Zero gravity makes solids more difficult to swallow.

LIVE-VIRUS POLIO VACCINE, developed by Dr. Albert Sabin *(below)* of Univ. of Cincinnati, has been widely hailed after successful field trials immunizing, among others, over 6 million Russians. Dr. Sabin believes its safety and effectiveness should be proven for general use by end of 1959.

133

CHOICE OF U.S.-TO-MOSCOW ART ASSAILED

A Rubens brings record price; Picasso outpoints customs "critics"

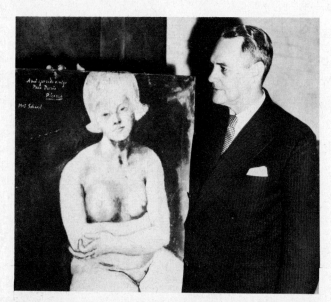

SERENE-LOOKING "La Belle Hollandaise," by famous artist Pablo Picasso, was bought for the Queensland Art Gallery, Australia, for $154,000. Painting, whose title means "The Beautiful Dutch Woman," is held by D. J. Muir, agent-general for the gallery. Bid is highest for work of living artist.

AMERICAN art for Russian eyes was the center of a bitter debate in 1959 as amateur painter Dwight D. Eisenhower and art critics tangled over the paintings and sculpture selected for the U.S. Exhibition in Moscow.

The selections, made by a jury of art experts chosen by the State Department, were attacked by Rep. Francis Walter (D-Penn.), chairman of the House Committee on Un-American Activities, and Wheeler Williams, sculptor and president of American Artists Professional League.

Walter asserted that many of the artists whose works were chosen had "connections with Communist fronts and causes."

Williams called the paintings and sculpture "childish doodles" and said most of them were a "discredit" to the nation.

President Eisenhower expressed distaste for the selections, calling one picture a "lampoon," and said that art selected to be shown abroad should include "what America likes." He refused, however, to censor the selections, despite charges of Communist affiliations. The President's contention drew strong support from eminent art leaders. It was later decided to include traditional works alongside of the criticized modern selections.

STRIKING MURAL, "The Wall of the Moon," exemplifies modern design of the newly-opened UNESCO Palace in Paris. The ceramic mural, by Spanish artists Joán Miró and Josep Llorens-Artigas, won the $10,000 first prize in the Harry F. Guggenheim round-the-world search for new paintings. The mural stands in the gardens in front of the palace in which UNESCO held its 10th general conference. The building, the permanent headquarters of the UN's Cultural and Educational Division, was officially opened by then French President René Coty. Dr. Luther Evans of the U.S., former UNESCO director-general, also attended the ceremony. The present director-general is Dr. Vittorino Veronese of Italy.

FAMED Renaissance masterpiece, "Adoration of the Magi," by Flemish painter Peter Paul Rubens, looms in the background as London art dealer Leonard Koetzer stands by after bidding 275,000 pounds for it. The price, equivalent to $770,000, was a public art auction record. Koetzer was acting for a client whose name he refused to reveal. The painting was part of the collection of the late Duke of Westminster, whose wife was selling some of the family treasures to help pay off high death duties on his estate. The sale took place at Sotheby's famous London Gallery on June 24.

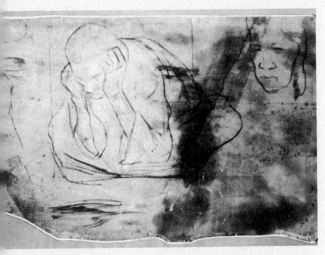

NEWLY-DISCOVERED panel of three drawings by Paul Gauguin, French artist who died in poverty in Tahiti, is on display at the Chicago Art Institute. It was found on the back of a charcoal drawing entitled "Standing Tahitian Nude (Eve)," the outline of which may be seen running at right angles.

LOST MASTERPIECE by Benvenuto Cellini, 16th century Florentine artist, is bust of Cosimo de' Medici. The Renaissance treasure was purchased for the M.H. de Young Memorial Museum by Roscoe F. Oakes, an art patron. The bust was the object of a two-year search by art expert Dr. Walter Heil, director of the museum. For years the portrait sculpture of the powerful Renaissance Duke had been gathering dust unnoticed on the premises of small art dealers. It was valued by Dr. Heil at more than half a million dollars.

Much novel 1959 sculpture started out as cast-off household items and was rescued from the junkyard to be banged, welded, or twisted into art. Steel, bronze, phosphor and chrome emerged into elegant patterns and puzzling intricacies. Many of these designs claimed to reflect the confusion and chaos of modern times.

The restoration of paintings attracted much attention. X-rays, tracings and other means of detection helped art "detectives" regain such painted-over pictures as a portrait of Thomas Jefferson, done by Gilbert Stuart in 1800. Careful work repaired many ancient paintings.

U.S. Customs inspectors who called a Picasso mosaic "bits of glass on stone" and classified an Alberto Burri collage as a vegetable fiber product, and taxed them both accordingly, drew howls from art lovers who claimed that as original works, they should be duty-free. Art won.

PRESIDENT'S GRANDSON is shown following in golfing footsteps of his famous grandfather in this painting, "David Eisenhower, by Granddad." Painting was one of several by the President shown at Ligonier bi-centennial celebration in Pennsylvania. Eisenhower came under attack by director of the Whitney Museum of American Art, Lloyd Goodrich, when he took a stand against censoring the art chosen for the United States Exhibition in Moscow, which opened July 25. Goodrich was a member of the four-man jury that selected the U.S. collection. He said experts should have last say on choice. Other influential art leaders backed Eisenhower.

EIGHT-FOOT, two-ton statue of former Prime Minister of Great Britain, Sir Winston Churchill, is worked on by sculptor David McFall in his London studio. The statue was commissioned by Churchill's constituents in Woodford district, which he represents in parliament. Although it was intended as a monument to Churchill, critics of the statue doubt that it will be installed. They claim statue is a "caricature," and that it makes him look "gorilla-like." Last hassle over the representation of Churchill was four years ago, when critics attacked portrait painted on his 80th birthday.

TINY CELL of Benedictine Monk Father Ambrogio Fumagalli is crowded with traditional and modernistic art in Rome's Santa Maria In Ara Coeli Monastery. The 43-year-old monk is noted for his skill in restoring such ancient paintings as a representation of "The Last Supper". Father Fumagalli is even more noted for his own art. He is shown at work on his modernistic "Christ." The cubist canvas (r.) is another of his paintings. Fumagalli held his first one-man show in Milan in 1944. His work has since been shown in many top art galleries in the United States and Europe.

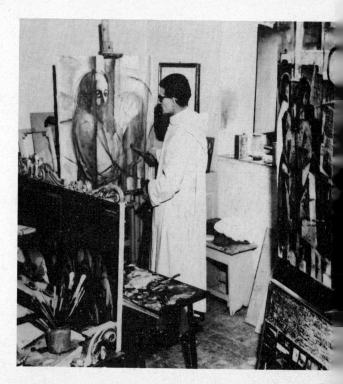

"LOLITA" LEADS LIST OF BEST SELLERS

Court decision kills postal ban on "Lady Chatterley's Lover"

DOCTOR ZHIVAGO by Russia's Boris Pasternak *(above)* was widely hailed as a novel and, to many Westerners, a deeply moving indictment of the Soviet Revolution and its effect on the individual.

NATIONAL BOOK AWARDS went to Theodore Roethke's *Words for the Wind* (poetry), *Mistress to an Age—A Life of Madame de Stael*, J. C. Herold (non-fiction), *The Magic Barrel*, B. Malamud (fiction).

SHOCKED readers, disgusted readers and delighted readers combined to shoot Vladimir Nabokov's *Lolita* to the top of the best-seller list early in 1959. By mid-summer, the story of a middle-aged European's affair with a 12-year-old American "nymphet" had sold 250,000 copies.

Probably the three most talked-about books of the year were *Lolita*, Boris Pasternak's *Doctor Zhivago* and *Lady Chatterley's Lover*, the 31-year-old D. H. Lawrence classic, published in unexpurgated form for the first time in the U.S.

Among other top fiction successes were *Exodus*, by Leon Uris, *The Ugly American*, by William J. Lederer and Eugene Burdick, and Paul Gallico's *Mrs. 'Arris Goes to Paris*.

The Light Infantry Ball, by Hamilton Basso, a civil war tale laid in the Georgia town created in the author's 1954 best-seller, *A View From Pompey's Head*, began a rapid climb up the best-seller list in July.

Veteran novelist John O'Hara had a new book—*From The Terrace*, a lengthy chronicle of sex and status in small-town Pennsylvania, New

York and Washington. Most reviewers thought it one of his worst, but it sold briskly throughout the year.

James Jones' third novel, *The Pistol*, was short, carefully written and a pleasant surprise to most of the critics.

Two of the year's best-received first novels were John Updike's *The Poorhouse Fair* and Herbert Mitgang's *The Return*.

On the non-fiction side, James Thurber wrote lovingly of the *New Yorker* and its founder in *The Years With Ross*.

Richard Rovere looked backward in a different mood in *Senator Joe McCarthy*.

And Vance Packard followed up *The Hidden Persuaders* with another witty dissection of contemporary U.S. society, *The Status Seekers*.

The year's most popular historical biography was Elizabeth Jenkins' *Elizabeth The Great*.

Other non-fiction best-sellers ranged from the scholarly (*The House of the Intellect*, by Jacques Barzun) to the homespun (*Only In America*, by Harry Golden) to the inspirational (*Mine Enemy Grows Older*, by Alexander King).

Paperback books—especially "quality" ones, representing the best in contemporary and classic fiction and non-fiction — continued to blossom. About 6000 titles were available in paper covers, and close to half a million volumes were sold.

Formation of two new publishing firms during the year was another sign of the industry's vitality.

Simon Michael Bessie, Editor of Harper & Bros., Hiram Haydn, Editor in Chief of Random House, and Alfred Knopf, Jr., vice president of Alfred A. Knopf, joined forces in March to form their own house, The Atheneum Press.

And Star Press Books, with a group of TV, motion picture and magazine industry backers that included Art Linkletter and Groucho Marx, went into business in the fall.

SURPRISE WINNER of Pulitzer Prize for Fiction was Robt. Lewis Taylor, author of *The Travels of Jamie McPheeters*.

POET ROBERT FROST celebrated his 85th birthday in 1959, still wrote, lectured, enjoyed holding forth to interviewers.

The Post Office ban forbids us to tell you where you can buy a copy of *that* book.

GROVE PRESS

THAT BOOK was unexpurgated *Lady Chatterley's Lover*, which stirred up legal storm when Grove Press published it in spring. U.S. Post Office sought to ban it from mails, on grounds of its graphic sexual language, won first round of court battle. Publisher promptly applied for injunction, meanwhile began sending books out by truck, and had sold over 100,000 copies by middle of July. Then, late in July, a federal court decision upset ban, and book was legal.

EUGENE O'NEILL won his fourth Pulitzer Prize, the first ever awarded posthumously, for play, *Long Day's Journey Into Night*, a 1958-59 production.

AMERICANS IN PARIS still flocked to sidewalk cafes *(above)* as had the expatriates of the '20s. Those who wanted a nostalgic view of "Lost Generation" could visit an exhibition in the U.S. Embassy's new Left Bank cultural center, "The Twenties: American Writers in Paris and Their Friends." Photos, letters, avant garde magazines like *Transition*, scribbled drawings and notes to and from Ernest Hemingway, Gertrude Stein, Ezra Pound and others of the group came from the private collection of Sylvia Beach, whose Shakespeare and Co. bookshop had been the expatriates' literary clubhouse for years.

F. SCOTT FITZGERALD, chronicler of the 20s on this side of the Atlantic, was the subject of a successful biography, *Beloved Infidel*, by Sheilah Graham, *(above)* and a not-too-successful Broadway play, *The Disenchanted*. Scribner's began reissuing his short stories, hitherto little known to general reading public in comparison with modern classic novels like *Great Gatsby*.

U.S. WELCOMES SOVIET'S BOLSHOI BALLET

Musicians honor a great composer; dancers leap into headlines

TWENTIETH CENTURY musical names — Bernstein, Cliburn, Rubinstein, Callas — were joined in the news by that of an eighteenth century composer, as musicians paid their respects to George Friedrich Handel on the 200th anniversary of his death. Musical organizations, amateur and professional, gave special attention to Handel's works, ranging from the familiar *Messiah* to a wide variety of rarely performed oratorios, operas and instrumental works. The City of New York entered into the spirit of the occasion by proclaiming a Handel Festival which was climaxed in May when The Little Orchestra Society presented an open-air performance of the *Water Music* and *Music for the Royal Fireworks* in Central Park.

Music's sister art, the dance, which won front-page headlines with the arrival of the USSR's Bolshoi ballet in April, made another kind of news in March when *Les Ballets Africains* opened in New York. The troupe of native dancers from Guinea had won rave notices all over Europe, delighted critics and audiences in Boston and Philadelphia. But in sophisticated New York, License Commissioner Bernard O'Connell, unimpressed by pleas to preserve the authenticity of the performance, took a shocked look at the native African dress and insisted on the addition of brassieres to some costumes. There was no question about the authenticity of the interest aroused.

"Bolshoi" means "big" in Russian, and so big was the demand for tickets to performances of the Bolshoi ballet

TRIUMPHANT CLIMAX to 35 years of effort by impresario Sol Hurok *(l.)* came in April when Moscow's famed Bolshoi Ballet arrived in the U.S. for an eight-week tour under Hurok management. Having sparked the fiercest ticket race in recent music history, the Bolshoi opened its U.S. tour at the Metropolitan Opera House before a celebrity-studded audience that gave the dancers a standing ovation at the conclusion of Sergei Prokofiev's *Romeo and Juliet*. Highlighting the 3½ hour performance was the sensitive portrayal of Juliet by the 49-year-old prima ballerina Galina Ulanova *(above)*, hailed by critics as "true wonder of her time."

that scalpers were reportedly receiving up to $150 for a single seat. The U.S. tour of the USSR's most famous cultural organization was part of the cultural exchange program between the two countries, and a personal triumph for impresario Sol Hurok, who managed the group's U.S. appearance. Audiences were wildly enthusiastic, and the critics generally agreed. Praise was unanimous for the muscular leaps of the male dancers and the

REHEARSING for their opening night in New York, dancers from the Bolshoi's 110-member company try out the stage of the Metropolitan Opera (one-third smaller than their Moscow stage). Members of the conservative, tradition-oriented Bolshoi had a look at some contemporary trends in the dance at New York's City Center and in a Broadway musical *(West Side Story)*, but confined themselves largely to the classic repertoire in their performances. On hand to help celebrate the Bolshoi's opening-night success was Soviet Ambassador Mikhail Menshikov *(above r. with ballerina Ulanova).*

TEMPERAMENTAL DIVA, Maria Meneghini Callas, added the Metropolitan to the growing list of opera houses with which she has parted company. Rudolf Bing, general manager of the Met, announced the cancellation of her contract after a dispute over the soprano's refusal to appear in *La Traviata* between performances of *Macbeth*. Only N.Y. appearance of Madame Callas took place in Carnegie Hall in *Il Pirata*.

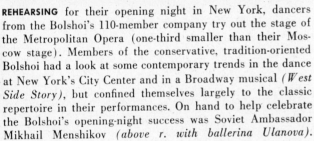

artistry of prima ballerina Galina Ulanova.

But a few voices pointed out that the technique and style of the Bolshoi, long isolated from outside influences, had remained frozen in the Victorian-era tradition, untouched by modern trends in the dance.

The Russians scored another hit with the U.S. debut of mezzo-soprano Zara Doloukhanova, the first Soviet singer to be heard in the U.S. since World War II. Madame Doloukhanova, who is noted for a repertoire of 500 works in five different languages (including English), won *bravas* following her Town Hall debut in March. Another noteworthy debut was that of Viennese soprano Leonie Rysanek, who took over the role of Lady Macbeth left vacant at the Metropolitan Opera when Maria Callas departed amid verbal fireworks.

For hi-fi addicts, the big news of 1959 was the boom in stereophonic home-listening equipment and records. At the beginning of the year, stereo disks (which usually cost $1 more than a comparable monophonic issue) were accounting for about 10% of total LP sales; but record manufacturers predicted that stereo sales would represent a third of total at year's end. Meanwhile, U.S. housewives rearranged furniture to make room for another speaker.

NEW HOME for the New York Philharmonic will be Philharmonic Hall (artist's rendering *above*), the first building under construction in the planned Lincoln Center for the Performing Arts. President Eisenhower officiated at the May 14 ground-breaking ceremonies for the $9.8 million hall, which is scheduled for completion in 1961. Also to be included in the Center are a new Metropolitan Opera House, Repertory Theater, Chamber Music and Recital Hall, Dance and Operetta Theater, Library-Museum of the Performing Arts and several Juilliard School of Music buildings. Conducting, talking, playing the piano and harpsichord, Leonard Bernstein led the N.Y. Philharmonic through its most successful season in recent years. Bernstein's campaign to bring new life to the Philharmonic season included some thoughtful programming and the introduction of informal "preview" concerts. Critics cheered, and booming business at the Carnegie Hall box office spoke for the city's many concert-goers.

SUCCESSFUL SEASON of New York City Ballet included first U.S. production of Kurt Weill's *The Seven Deadly Sins*, starring Lotte Lenya (Weill's widow), Allegra Kent in split role of heroine, with male quartet representing her smug family.

ITALIAN influence, long felt in the motion picture and fashion worlds, infiltrated the popular music field in the person of Domenico Modugno *(above)*, the Milanese crooner-composer, whose *Volare (Nel Blu Dipinto Di Blu)* was a juke-box sensation. Most phenomenal pop record success in years was won by a bit of clamorous nonsense called *The Chipmunk Song*, brainchild of song-writer Ross Bagdasarian, who saw his squeaky disk reach sales of 3.5 million copies in five weeks. Generally, however, the pop field continued to be dominated by rock and roll, which flooded the country with hypnotic, unvarying rhythm (and occasionally a startling lyric), to the delight of millions of rabid teen-age fans.

LONG JOURNEY from its origins on the wrong side of the tracks has been made by jazz, sometimes hailed as the only native U.S. art form. Concert-hall performances by various jazz groups have become increasingly common in recent years, and even churches are opening their doors in welcome. Here the Rev. Anthony P. Treasure, rector of St. Paul's Episcopal Church in Norwalk, Conn., serves communion to his parishioners to the accompaniment of a four-piece jazz combo. Music for the "Jazz Mass" was the *Twentieth Century Folk Mass*, written some years ago by a British rector in an attempt to frame words of the liturgy in a modern setting.

METROPOLITAN OPERA won critical acclaim for its first production of Alban Berg's *Wozzeck*, with baritone Hermann Uhde in the title role and soprano Eleanor Steber as Marie *(above)*. Long considered a milestone in music, *Wozzeck's* atonal music, sordid, bitter plot and half-spoken singing style have made it an opera more discussed than produced.

A SERIOUS SEASON

Broadway audiences find littl

EUGENE O'NEILL'S drama, *A Touch of the Poet*, gave veteran actress Helen Hayes her best role in years. It contributed a choice bit of gossip when actress Kim Stanley resigned her role and named co-star Eric Portman as the main reason.

TOP TONY AWARDS, presented by the American Theater Wing, went to *(l. to r.)* Jason Robards Jr. as the top male dramatic actor (in *The Disenchanted*), and Gwen Verdon, Richard Kiley as best actress and actor in a musical *(Redhead)*.

DRAMA CRITICS CIRCLE named *A Raisin in the Sun*, starring Sidney Poitier and Claudia McNeil *(below)*, as best American play. *Raisin*, a first effort by playwright Lorraine Hans-

berry, narrowly nosed out Tennessee Williams' *Sweet Bird of Youth* and Archibald MacLeish's *J.B.* for the honor, became the first play by a Negro writer to earn the award.

of the light touch in a year of thoughtful drama

IT WAS a year for seriousness on the Broadway stage. A theater-goer could take his choice from the sordid and the sentimental, the exotic and the earthy, the spiritual and the shocking among the new dramas; but there was a surprising dearth of first-class new offerings in the fields of comedy and the musical.

The state of affairs was underlined when the award-giving time rolled around in late spring. The Drama Critics Circle first debated the possibility of not giving any award at all for a musical, finally cast its vote for *La Plume de ma Tante*, a French import. The Antoinette Perry Award in the musical category went to *Redhead*, which had received raves for the performance of star Gwen Ver-

don, but impressed no one with its creaky plot. The season's entry by Rodgers and Hammerstein, *Flower Drum Song*, was vaguely reminiscent of the pair's *South Pacific*, but not in the same quality-league. Best reviews of the season went to *Gypsy*, which brought Ethel Merman back to Broadway in top form. Based on a book by ex-stripper Gypsy Rose Lee, *Gypsy* opened too late to be in the running for the season's awards.

Serious drama fared better. A new

playwright, Lorraine Hansberry, made an impressive debut with her warm and moving *A Raisin in the Sun*. Veteran playwright Tennessee Williams continued his exploration of the seamier side of life in *Sweet Bird of Youth*, illuminated by the impressive performance of Geraldine Page and Paul Newman. Other noteworthy productions of the season included the prize-winning *J.B.*, the Japanese-based *Rashomon*, and the late Eugene O'Neill's drama, *A Touch of the Poet*.

WINNER of both the Pulitzer Prize and the Tony award as the best dramatic offering of the year was *J.B.*, a modern re-telling of the story of Job by poet Archibald MacLeish *(below)*. Title role in the drama was created by actor Pat Hingle *(r.)*, who won critical acclaim for what Brooks Atkinson termed "an almost unbearably moving performance," then met personal tragedy when a fall down an elevator shaft resulted in serious injury. Hingle's acting assignment was taken by James Daly.

FANCY LAMB cuddles close to Ethel Merman as two pose during a rehearsal of "Gypsy," Broadway musical based on the memoirs of Gypsy Rose Lee. "Gypsy," which opened at the Broadway Theatre, featured Karen Moore portraying young Gypsy and Jacqueline Mayro as her baby sister, June Havoc. Among other outstanding musicals of the season were "Destry Rides Again," starring Andy Griffith as a singing-shooting sheriff, and "Flower Drum Song," presenting Pat Suzuki singing in the Rodgers and Hammerstein musical.

THEATRE-IN-THE-ROUND designed by noted architect Edward D. Stone is shown here *(above)*. The outdoor, arena-style structure opened during the summer at the Wollman Skating Rink in New York's Central Park. The project, known as the Hudson Celebration Theatre-in-the-Park, featured concerts and songfests by well-known performers. Stone, designer of the American Pavilion at the Brussels World's Fair, is currently working on new 10-story Gallery of Modern Art which will soon be erected in New York City.

FREE SHAKESPEARE in Central Park returned with *Julius Caesar* when producer Papp *(above)* triumphed over Park Commissioner Robt. Moses' ban. Latter wanted admission charge.

STARRING in first American ice show to play in Russia, Arnold Shoda does act without skates on Moscow street. Watching him are "Skateniks" who also appear in "Holiday on Ice."

ACTRESS Gertrude Berg was named for a Tony as top dramatic actress for her performance in *A Majority of One*, which co-starred Sir Cedric Hardwicke *(c.)* and gave veteran motion-picture maker Dore Schary *(far r.)* his first directing job in the Broadway theater. *Majority* cast Miss Berg, long familiar as radio and TV's Molly Goldberg, in the role of a plump Jewish widow from Brooklyn involved in an East-meets-West romance with a Shintoist Japanese. Result: a "kosher sukiyaki" dish.

HILARIOUS French musical revue *La Plume de ma Tante* won the accolade of the Drama Critics Circle as the best musical of the season, received a special Tony award presented to the entire cast of fourteen, first time such a collective prize has been awarded in 12-year history of the Tonys. Critics Circle award was also unique, representing the first time the honor has ever been given to a revue. Language barrier was no obstacle to enjoyment of musical.

DURABLE favorite, *Our Town*, Thornton Wilder's tale of life, love and death in a small town, was a Broadway hit of the Thirties. In 1959 it was a hit again, this time at the off-Broadway Circle in the Square theater, where a fine production directed by Jose Quintero was delighting theater-goers. Featured in the cast were Jane McArthur and Clinton Kimbrough *(r.)* with John Beal. In another off-Broadway success, young actor Hal Holbrook won acclaim for his brilliant portrayal in *Mark Twain Tonight!*

NIPPED, DIPPED AND HIPPED

1959 fashions bring curves back into style again. Soft feminine clothes are once more in favor

THE FEMININE FIGURE was whipped back into shape again in 1959. The Empire line, which rose from the ashes of the chemise to dominate the early scene, shyly reinstated a high under-bosom waistline. And, by midwinter, designers were no longer hinting at women's curves —they were exploiting them.

Necklines dipped, hiplines curved and waistlines were snugly belted. Skirts swelled out and sleeves belled out, while shoulders curved wide. Topping everything were oversized collars—caped, tiered or pleated.

No one silhouette dominated the spring shows in Paris. The big news out of France was a name rather than a design. Jules Francois Crahay, a 41-year-old Belgian, designed a collection for couturiere Nina Ricci that catapulted both him and the house of Ricci from quiet obscurity to the top of the fashion heap.

Crahay's clothes, called the epitome of everything that was soft and feminine in all the collections, were also distinguished by outstanding craftsmanship.

In the U.S. highest honors, the Coty American Fashion Critic's award, or

"Winnie," went to an even younger man, 27-year-old Arnold Scassi, evening dress and fur designer.

Coats, like everything else, were softer and rounder. Fall suit significance lay in the hip sheathing length of the tunic jacket—part of the belted, hippy look credited to Crahay.

Sportswear reached new lengths— both extreme. Long-johns of stretch nylon (waist-to-toe leotards) showed up under skirts even on city streets. Bathing suits, on the other hand, shrank to nothing. The European bikini—cut to the razor's edge of decency—finally took firm hold on U.S. beaches.

Heading the frivolous fads department were wigs—hairdressers fortunate enough to own wig blocks reported "full houses"—"glue-it-yourself" eyelashes and an inexplicable vogue for white cosmetics, which if not skillfully applied had a mortuary pallor.

SENSATION of Crahay's show for Ricci was tunic suit *(above)* with belted bush jacket, patch pockets and bell bottom skirt built out over buckram. Copies later flooded U.S. stores. Most sensational Crahay design was black cocktail dress *(photo r.)* with huge bertha and plunging neckline worn by model *(l.)* at Paris fashion party. Decolletage was so low, model, shown with the Duc de Brissac *(c.)* and mannequin *(r.)* wearing more conservative dress by Jean Desses, confessed she was afraid to move or walk about in the dress.

"HOLLYWOOD WRAP" from George Carmel was handled in beige-white tweed. Oversized collar typified 1959 coats.

ON-AGAIN, OFF-AGAIN ease of wigs, especially after a swim, added to their appeal. Some women owned several styles.

USSR GLAMOUR GIRLS fascinate guard at the $1 million fur display *(above)* at Soviet trade exhibition in N.Y. Coliseum. Four Soviet designers and six models brought over 200 fashions (half of which were in synthetic fabrics). Modern textile designs are examined *(below)* at House of Fontana, Italian couturier, whose styles modeled in background reflect abstract influence. Italian shows attracted many U.S. buyers, often rivaled French.

"WINNIE" RECIPIENT Arnold Scassi designed satin gown *(above)*. Sportswear designer Donald Brooks and coat manufacturer Ben Zuckerman won other Coty awards. Late Claire McCardell was named to "Hall of Fame." Brevity of bikinis like Rose Marie Reid model *(below)* shocked U.S. women when introduced in 1946. Increase of private swimming pools and exposure through European travel explained acceptance.

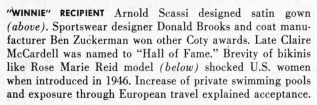

FIRST FRENCH INVASION of USSR fashion world was spearheaded in June by House of Dior. Models, arriving at Moscow airport *(above)*, brought Dior's most ·conservative styles. Event was swamped by 13,000 Russians. Leotards like the model from Capezio *(r.)* swept the U.S. A Detroit store sold 1000 the first week, a Boston store stocked them on all seven floors. They were worn for work, sports and leisure.

PLENTITUDE OF PLEATS lent soft, feminine note to short evening dress by House of Dior's Yves Saint-Laurent. Huge cape collar and tunic-type skirt were newsworthy details.

DEMURE LINES of this black chiffon empire dress by Herbert Sondheim was typical of the transitional period between the shapeless chemise and the new curvey-feminine fashions.

SCHOOLS SEEK HIGHER STANDARDS WITHIN U.S. TRADITION

For educators, the 1958-59 year was a time for taking stock of current teaching trends. The first panic about the deficiencies of U.S. education, brought on by the USSR's 1957 triumphs in the race to outer space, had faded. There was still deep concern about the soundness of academic training in the nation's high schools, but there was concern, too, about preserving the traditional democracy of the public school system and avoiding the establishment of an "intellectual elite."

PERHAPS the most important contribution to the educational debate was former Harvard president James B. Conant's *The American High School Today*.

A moderate book, *American High School* heartily endorsed the U.S. system of control by local school boards, rejected the idea of secondary education as stratified as that of Western Europe (and the USSR),

but maintained that superior students in U.S. high schools were not working hard enough, or getting a sufficiently balanced academic curriculum.

It advocated, for college-bound students, a minimum program of four years of English, three of social studies, four of mathematics, three of science, four of one foreign language.

All over the country, experimental programs for bright students, includ-

ing language study in grade school and plans for early admission to college, were introduced.

However, it was apparent that the upgrading of U.S. education would be a long, slow business.

In the meantime, the chronic problems of overcrowded classrooms and underpaid teachers were still there to be reckoned with, and, especially in the cities, threatened to make the upgrading process an even more difficult one.

The drama of Southern integration remained the hardy perennial of the September headlines.

The opening of the 1958-59 school year saw small numbers of Negro students entering previously all-white

schools in towns throughout the border states, sometimes with flareups of violence, often quite peacefully.

In Virginia, however, Governor J. Lindsay Almond brought down the full force of the state's carefully prepared "massive resistance" laws when a small number of Negroes were admitted to classes in Norfolk, Charlottesville and Front Royal, and closed the schools.

For the entire first semester of the year, 13,000 white students attended makeshift classes in private homes—or no classes at all. Most of them, and their parents, decided as the winter wore on that they wanted their public school system back, integrated if it had to be.

In January, two separate decisions—from the Virginia Supreme Court of Appeals and a Federal District Court — ruled "massive resistance" unconstitutional. The schools quietly reopened, with Negro students in class.

The whole theory of "massive resistance" seemed to have collapsed in its first real trial. But the states of the deep South, still preserving total segregation in their schools, planned to try similar tactics whenever integration orders came.

Schools in Atlanta, Ga. were expected to be the 1959-60 testing ground.

In Little Rock, Ark., scene of 1957's greatest integration battle, Gov. Orval E. Faubus closed four high schools for the entire year, after a plan for transferring them to a private corporation to keep them segregated was ruled out by the courts.

It seemed likely, however, that they would reopen with "token integration" for the 1959-60 school year.

EXPERIMENTAL chemistry class in Monroe, La., high school is taught by Lon Colburn, who taught 34 years in Pittsburgh, Pa., came out of retirement to help Monroe launch the special project. He offers college level work to carefully selected students, gives them two hours of homework a night. Students are reported to be highly enthusiastic.

CORPORAL PUNISHMENT received legal endorsement in Memphis, Tenn., when Sessions Judge Willard Dixon (*l., at desk*) refused to issue assault warrant against John Barnes (*second from r.*), principal of Bartlett High, who had paddled 14 students. Irate mothers had demanded warrant. In N.Y., State Assembly passed bill authorizing "hickory stick" treatment for pupils, but new Gov. Nelson A. Rockefeller vetoed it.

JAMES BRYANT CONANT, author of widely read *American High School Today*, announced in May plans for a follow-up survey of seventh and eighth grades. Entire project was financed by Carnegie Corp. of N.Y., which gave him an extra $85,000 for junior high school study. Dr. Conant also planned "a final report . . . which I hope may assist the lay citizens to understand some of problems facing those in charge of our schools."

REPORTER GEORGE N. ALLEN of the N.Y. World Telegram & Sun spent a month teaching at John Marshall Junior H.S. in Brooklyn slum, wrote eye-witness account of "blackboard jungle" conditions he found there. His series confirmed what most New Yorkers already knew — that it was physically dangerous to teach or even try to maintain discipline, and almost impossible to learn, in worst of city's public schools. N.Y. Board of Education indignantly declared that Allen's masquerade "seriously violated the moral and ethical standards of the teaching profession." But they had to admit that his rather frightening report was accurate.

NEW YORK CITY TEACHERS voted on April 10 to stage one-day walkout in protest against low salaries, poor working conditions. More than 3800 teachers attended mass rally at St. Nicholas Arena. Walkout was called off, however, when Board of Education renewed its threats and pleas. Earlier, in February, city's night school teachers actually did go out on strike, closing 16 schools with a total enrollment of 30,000. Five temporary night schools were set up, staffed with substitute teachers during emergency. Teachers were protesting their pay of $12 per night, only $2 more than the 1932 figure. Strike won them a raise of about $6.

PARADOXICALLY, University of Chicago chose 1959, year of search for higher academic standards, to scrap famous undergraduate plan. System introduced by former dean Robert Hutchins had allowed two years for "general education," then sent students into graduate work. Reorganization restored traditional four-year course. New dean, Dr. Allan Simpson *(above)*, said: "We have asked ourselves if beauty and brawn do not deserve a place on our campus as well as brains... the ordinary American boy who will only make a million later in life, the ordinary girl who wants a husband as well as a diploma, are as welcome here as the Quiz Kid." Most students regretted the change.

FIRST DAY OF SCHOOL at Granby High, Norfolk, Virginia, came in February instead of September. One Negro student, Betty Jean Reed *(above)*, enrolled; 16 others began classes in previously all-white schools elsewhere in the city. Integration in Virginia began quietly; most students, especially seniors, worried about college admissions, were simply glad to be back after semester-long "vacation" imposed by school closings. For 1959-60, Gov. J. Lindsay Almond planned a course of "passive" rather than "massive" resistance: compulsory school attendance laws were revoked, state grants were made available for private schooling.

ATLANTA HOUSEWIVES, Mrs. Thomas M. Breeden, Jr.*(l.)* and Mrs. Hamilton Lokey, were among founders of Georgia's "HELP" *(Help our Public Education)*, an organization formed to fight threatened public school closings. Although opposition to integration was strong, especially in rural areas, few parents wanted to see Georgia schools close as had those in Virginia.

UNITY CALL STIRS CHURCHES

But Protestants warn reunion must be "mutual"

NEWEST U.S. CARDINALS are Richard J. Cushing, Archbishop of Boston *(l.)*, John O'Hara, Archbishop of Philadelphia. Their elevation brings U.S. number to four. Total of 23 prelates received Red Hat, including Bishop of Berlin.

BEARDED ARCHBISHOP JAMES, born Demetrios Coucouzis, was enthroned May 1 as Primate of Greek Orthodox Church in Western Hemisphere. The 48-year-old prelate, a U.S. citizen, previously served as Metropolitan of the island of Malta.

A CALL by the Pope, John XXIII, for an ecumenical council to establish formal unity of all Christian communions set the religious tone of 1959.

Primary purpose of summons, it was believed, was to heal the centuries-old schism between Rome and the major Eastern Orthodox churches (several of smaller Eastern groups have always remained within Pope's jurisdiction).

Such a reunion would have major consequences for East-West relations, since bulk of Orthodox Christians live in the USSR or its satellites. Prospects of success seemed fair; only minor doctrinal differences separate Rome and Eastern churches.

But major differences, both in belief and in acceptance of the Papal supremacy, to Catholics an essential condition of reunion, continued to keep apart Roman Catholics and Protestants.

Representatives of 60-odd U.S. Protestant denominations and their 80 million adherents were cautious in attitude. The Rev. Dr. Edwin T. Dahlberg, President of the National Council of Churches, said that steps toward unity would have to be a "mutual coming together, not under conditions laid down by one church for the others."

Episcopalian unity was strengthened when a U.S. bishop, the Rt. Rev. Stephen F. Bayne, Jr., of Washington, became Executive Officer of world-wide churches in communion with the Church of England.

A Gaelic-speaking, Dublin-born rabbi, Dr. Theodore Lewis, accepted a call to the Western Hemisphere's oldest Jewish congregation, Touro Synagogue in Newport, R.I.

WASHINGTON'S NATIONAL cathedral was scene of consecration of Rt. Rev. Arthur Lichtenberger, shown here with wife. Former Bishop of Missouri was installed as Presiding Bishop of U.S. Protestant Episcopal Church. He declared his prime aim and goal would be the restoration of Christian unity.

OLD TIME RELIGION came to Australia with evangelist Billy Graham shown resting in Hawaii with wife. Preacher also visited United Kingdom, Soviet Union during year.

NEW AGA KHAN watches from gilded throne burial rites of his grandfather, who chose him as successor over father, Ali Khan. Ismaili head was June Harvard graduate.

LEADERS of three faiths join hands with New York City officials to lay cornerstone of Beth Israel Hospital nurses' residence. Clergymen are (l. to r.) Rabbi L. Jung, Msgr. J. Voight, and the Rev. J. Coleman.

157

JET AGE TRAVEL SOARS

1.5 million U.S. tourists=$2.3 billion

A T 8:09 A.M. Oct 4, 1958 the earth shrank. The first British Overseas Airways Corp. jet left London for New York and the Atlantic became only six-and-one-half hours wide. Pan American launched its trans-Atlantic jet service just three weeks later. Domestic airlines followed suit within months, shrinking the U.S. itself to four-and-one-half hours.

In the new jet-contracted world more Americans—1.5 million—spent more money—$2.3 billion—on international travel (an increase of 10%—five times that of domestic travel) than ever before in history. An all-time high of 637,000 U.S. tourists spent $560 million in Europe alone. The greatest number, 381,000, visited France, but the most money was spent in Italy, which was richer by $100 million U.S. travel dollars.

Hawaii and Alaska, riding on the wave of statehood, had record breaking seasons. Hawaii's visitors increased at least one-third; Alaska counted on another gold rush, a 100% increase to 87,000 visitors spending $49 million.

Although Canada (not included in international figures)

JET BOOM was economic as well as audible. Payloads on flights like this Pan American one increased to more than 90%. For first time more tourists went by plane than by ship.

ARCHEOLOGICAL RUINS like Hall of Monoliths helped build record tourist year for Mexico. Deluxe hotels in Mexico City and Acapulco drew 625,000 Americans to spend $320 million.

was still the favorite vacation spot of more Americans—7.5 million—than any other country in the world, volume dropped 5% reflecting recession effect on border cities.

In the U.S. 24 million families took 40 million trips. Bargain prices and air conditioning helped Florida resorts enjoy an off-season summer bloom. The Cumberland Gap National Historic Park—nation's newest—opened in Kentucky. The Shakespeare Festival in Connecticut and the Berkshire Music Festival in Massachusetts attracted thousands who wanted culture with their suntans.

NEW LUXURY HOTELS like San Juan Intercontinental helped make tourism Puerto Rico's third largest industry. Most spectacular opening was that of Laurance Rockefeller's $10 million Dorado Beach Hotel. Despite new construction there still were not enough rooms for 248,000 visitors. Entire Caribbean except politically disturbed Cuba and Haiti profited.

FAR EAST was fastest expanding tourist area in the world. U.S. expenditures increased 20% to $65 million. 180,000 travelers visited Japan alone, creating severe hotel shortage. Jet service is expected to increase influx. 104 weekly flights and 21 luxury liners carried 65,000 U.S. tourists beyond Hawaii. Visitors to Hong Kong doubled in past five years.

SOVIET OFFICIAL *(l.)* welcomes U.S. governors who toured USSR. Group of nine included *(l. to r.)* LeRoy Collins, Fla.; Cecil Underwood, W. Va.; William Stratton, Ill.; and Luther Hodges, N. C. 10,000 Americans (100% increase) ventured beyond Iron Curtain. Easing of visa restrictions helped.

WINE STORAGE VAT in Heidelberg Castle was one of many tourist attractions in Germany. Average overseas traveler was 46 years old. 72% had incomes of $10,000 or more. Average air traveler stayed abroad 41 days, spent $1440. Average sea traveler stayed 68 days, spent $1710. 1/3 went on business.

STRIKE SHUTS DOWN NEW YORK

N.Y. "Trib" gets new edito

C RISES, elections, revolutions, conferences and rumors of conferences kept newsmen busy and presses rolling throughout the year.

But for 19 days, New Yorkers were put on a starvation diet.

A deliverymen's strike closed down the city's nine major dailies (combined circulation, 5.7 million).

Empty-handed railroad and subway commuters stared uncomfortably at hastily prepared car cards and flyers advertising pre-Christmas wares.

Circulation of the city's myriad foreign language newspapers, some of which began including English sections, hit an all-time high. Copies of the *Wall Street Journal*, whose de-

NEWS-STARVED NEW YORKERS crowded around store windows *(below)* during December newspaper deliverers' strike to catch latest wire service bulletins from tie-in machines placed throughout the city by the Teleprompter Corp.

N. Y. HERALD TRIBUNE got a new editor and publisher, Robert M. White, 2nd (above, *r.*, with Trib owner John Hay Whitney), in July. The Republican Trib's new boss was a Missouri Democrat, a third generation newspaperman

NEWSPAPERS

liverymen stayed on the job, were stolen from subscribers' mailboxes.

Radio and TV coverage was expanded, often brilliant, but nothing could take the place of newsprint.

After the strike ended, the *Times* published two special issues containing a two-page edition for each of the 19 days.

N. Y. *Herald Tribune* editor and publisher Ogden Reid waited until the strike was over to announce his resignation, expected since mid-1958, when control of the paper had passed from the Reid family to John Hay Whitney, multimillionaire U.S. Ambassador to Great Britain.

The biggest editorial shakeup in the magazine world came when Otis Wiese resigned as editor and publisher of thriving *McCall's* and Herbert Mayes, editor of a top competitor, *Good Housekeeping*, moved in.

On the Washington scene, newsmen scored a partial victory in the battle with the State Department over travel to Red China—a few passports for reporters were issued. However, the Peking government turned the tables and refused to let them in.

PULITZER PRIZE for editorial writing went to Ralph McGill of Atlanta *Constitution*, cited his "long, courageous and effective editorial leadership" in school integration controversy. Moderate McGill strongly advocated keeping schools open, with limited integration if necessary, and attacked school and synagogue bombings. Photo prize went to William Seaman of Minneapolis *Star (l.)*, for a shot of doctor walking away from child killed in traffic accident. Other Pulitzer journalism awards: to Joseph Martin and Philip Santora of N. Y. *Daily News* for a series on brutality in Cuba under then-dictator Bulgencio Batista; to Mary Lou Werner of the Washington, D. C. *Evening Star* for year-long coverage of the school integration crisis in the state of Virginia.

CHILLY WEATHER greeted picketers in front of N. Y. *Daily News (l.)* and other newspaper offices on Dec. 10, first day of deliverymen's strike. Night before, union had voted 877 to 772 to reject proposed contract with city's nine major dailies. Other employes stayed on the job till papers stopped publishing.

NEW ARRIVAL on the magazine publishing scene was *Horizon*, a hard-cover bimonthly put out by American Heritage. Billed as "the most beautiful magazine in the world," it carried no advertising, sold by subscription at $18 a year, in bookstores at $3.95 a copy. It ran lavishly illustrated articles on arts and letters, history, ideas and the contemporary scene. By mid-1959, it had over 170,000 well-heeled subscribers.

161

JUBILANT PORGY (Sidney Poitier, *c.*) returns from jailhouse poker game with gifts for Maria (Pearl Bailey) and his Catfish Row friends in happy finale to Samuel Goldwyn's $7 million movie, *Porgy and Bess.* Memorable George Gershwin melodies distinguished the celebrated American folk opera. Cast included Dorothy Dandridge, Sammy Davis Jr.

1959 YEAR OF QUALITY FILMS

Producers resort to "blockbusting" in tough competition with TV

DAVID NIVEN (*Separate Tables*), Susan Hayward (*I Want to Live*) won Acting "Oscars." *Gigi* received nine awards.

STILL HARASSED by mediocre showings at the box office, Hollywood decided to reduce its usual 300-350 films per year, then concentrate on fewer but bigger pictures with big budgets — high quality "blockbusters." Producers intended to entice patrons by making theater-going an "event," showing quality spectacles at reserved-seat prices ($3-$4 top). MGM spent $15 million on a re-make of *Ben Hur*, largest amount ever spent on a U.S. film, and multitudes of exhibitors and merchandisers hopped on the *Ben-Hur* chariot to cash in on the expected bonanza. Samuel Goldwyn's *Porgy and Bess* cost $7 million; and 20th's *Diary of Anne Frank*, Warner Bros.' *The Nun's Story*, and Otto Preminger's *Anatomy of a Murder* between $4-$6

million each. By summer's end, all but *Diary* promised handsome profit.

Meanwhile, several inexpensive but well-made films hit the jackpot. Disney's *Shaggy Dog* (cost, $550,000) headed for an $8.5 million domestic gross. *Al Capone* and *House on Haunted Hill* (cost, $450,000 each) grossed millions, put Allied Artists strongly in the black. *Imitation of Life* ($1.5 million) was certain to outgross all U-I films. The public showed it was relatively hungry for good pictures, whatever the cost.

With so encouraging an outlook, studios perked up, dusted off the "happy days" sign, and stepped up activity. Even though much of their effort was, ironically, for TV production, it was good to be busy— and good to know it was for profit.

LOEB-LEOPOLD MURDER case *(1924)* was basis of high-powered drama, *Compulsion*. Stars *(l. to r.)* Dean Stockwell, Bradford Dillman, Orson Welles won 2 joint awards for performances.

MASQUERADING AS A FLAPPER to escape gangland pursuers, Tony Curtis *(l.)* joins an all-girl band, whose vocalist is Marilyn Monroe *(r.)* in *Some Like It Hot*, satire on the 20's.

MOST EXPENSIVE FILM ever made, MGM's *Ben-Hur* cost $15 million, was based on Gen. Lew Wallace's classic 1880 novel *(later a 1900 stage play, 1926 silent film)*. Filmed in Italy

with a tremendous cast by Director William Wyler, the religious spectacle's climax was harrowing chariot race with Charlton Heston *(Ben Hur)*, Stephen Boyd, Jack Hawkins.

TAKING REFUGE from the Nazis in a spice factory-warehouse attic in Amsterdam, the Frank and Van Daan families wait out a tense moment in *The Diary of Anne Frank*. Directed by George Stevens, the emotional drama starred *(l. to r.)* Diane Baker, Gusti Huber, Millie Perkins *(Anne)*, Joseph Schildkraut (from the stage cast), Shelly Winters, and Lou Jacobi.

"THE NUN'S STORY" starred winsome Audrey Hepburn as Sister Luke, nursing nun of Belgian Congo who endures a personal tug-of-war between her rebellious spirit and her wish to respect discipline of the order. Zinneman directed.

ROOM AT THE TOP, called "Best Film" by the British Film Academy, treated physical love in adult, sophisticated

His TRUE, SHOCKING Story... Filmed With BULLET FORCE!

CHICAGO HOOD Al Capone *(Rod Steiger)* was subject of well-made, socio-dramatic study triggering cycle of gangster films.

SENTIMENTAL BIOGRAPHY of Dixieland jazz cornetist "Red" Nichols was tailor-made vehicle for Danny Kaye *(r.)*, star-ring with Louis "Satchmo" Armstrong *(l.)* in *The Five Pennies*. Nostalgic story of the '20's had strong family appeal.

manner. It told of a scheming young man *(Laurence Harvey)* who has tempestuous affair with an older woman.

MAY-DECEMBER romance between a young divorcée secretary *(Kim Novak)* and her middle-aged widower employer *(Fredric March)* was the delicate problem of *Middle of the Night*, based on the play written by Paddy Chayevsky.

PATTERSON BEATEN IN YEAR'S BIGGEST UPSET

Right hand ends champion's reign as Johansson takes title to Sweden

BIGGEST BOXING upset occurred on a wet night in June when Ingemar Johansson of Sweden stopped Floyd Patterson in 2:03 minutes of the third round to win the heavyweight championship of the world. It was the first time the title had left the U.S. since Max Schmeling of Germany beat Jack Sharkey in 1930. The punch that started Patterson on the road to oblivion *(r.)* was a right-hand wallop to the face which Floyd' never even saw. Before Ruby Goldstein, the referee, stopped the fight Patterson was knocked down seven times by the Slugging Swede. The big question before the bout was—does Ingemar have a right? Patterson and the boxing world found out in the third round. Another champion, Hogan (Kid) Bassey, lost his featherweight crown to Davey Moore *(r. below)*. The fight was halted in the 13th round. Moore's quick hands had cut Bassey's eyes and the Kid's manager threw in the towel "because my boy can't see." The aging Archie Moore, (age unknown—at least 43) was one champion who held his crown. Archie, who may be the oldest champ on record, successfully defended his light heavyweight title by knocking out Canada's Yvon Durelle.

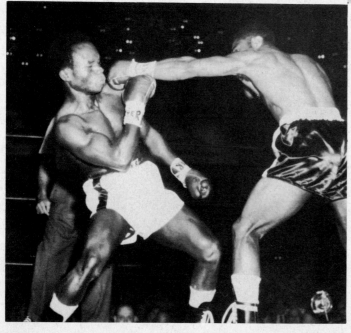

MONTREAL CANADIENS (who else?) won the Stanley Cup for the fourth straight year. The champions finished first in the regular season and defeated Toronto *(above)* in the playoffs. Jacques Plante *(dark shirt on ice)* made many great plays to spark victory. Andy Bathgate of the N.Y. Rangers was voted Most Valuable Player. Rangers and Detroit failed to make playoffs.

DEANE BEMAN, 21-year-old Maryland College student, *(above)*, catapulted to golf fame when he won the British Amateur title by defeating another American, Bill Hyndman of Philadelphia, 3-2. The names of Ben Hogan and Sammy Snead were fading from the headlines as Art Wall, Jr. *(l.)* who won the Masters, and Billy Casper, victor in the National Open, became the new golf heroes.

SOUTH AMERICA TAKE IT AWAY was the theme of London's classic Wimbledon championships. Alex Olmedo *(below)* of Peru, a student at the University of Southern California, won the men's title and Maria Bueno of Brazil took the women's. Maria beat Darlene Hard of California. It was the first time since 1938 that an American failed to win the women's crown. The U.S. beat Australia 3-2 for the 1958 Davis Cup, with Olmedo pacing the victory with his fast game.

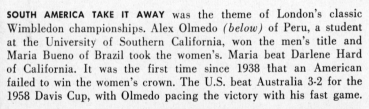

CANADA'S Tom Gayford, who won top individual honors at the National Horse Show, holds the bit of his mount, Blue Beau *(above)*. Mrs. W. Joshua Barney Jr. *(r.)* presented the trophy to Gayford. West German riders performed notably in show.

167

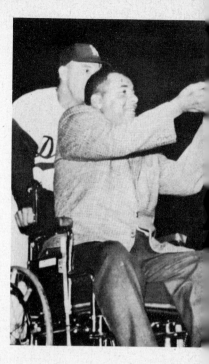

NEW YORK YANKEES, perennial champions, hit rock-bottom in the American League—last place—on May 20 when the Detroit Tigers clawed them at Yankee Stadium. It was the Yanks' first trip to the basement in 19 years. Yogi Berra leads the unhappy procession to the showers after the game. Team later made bid for recovery.

HARVEY HADDIX, (r.), Pittsburgh Pirate lefthander, proved a pitcher can be perfect—and lose. Haddix pitched 12 perfect innings against Braves in Milwaukee but, in the 13th inning, the home team got one hit, a double by Joe Adcock, and won the game. Fantastic but true, it probably will never happen again.

TED WILLIAMS, (below), Boston's aging pride, smashed out his 2500th hit in May in game against Kansas City. The game was halted to hand him the ball. Another great hitter, Stan Musial, who has made more than 3,000 hits, banged out 652nd double against Pittsburgh to top Honus Wagner's National League record.

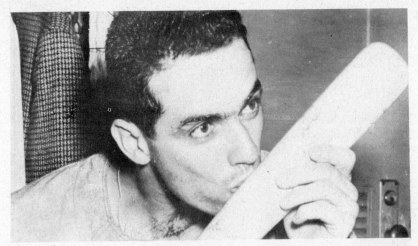

ROCKY COLAVITO (*above*), kisses bat he used to wallop four home runs in game at Baltimore. The young Cleveland slugger became eighth major leaguer to turn the trick. The last to do it was Joe Adcock of the Braves. He did it in the 1954 season. Rocky walked in the first inning and then homered in the third, fifth, sixth, and the ninth innings to bring the Indians to victory.

THE ANNOUNCER SAID "Roy Campanella" and 93,103 fans in the Los Angeles Coliseum jumped to their feet and roared a welcome to Campy that he would never forget. Pee Wee Reese wheeled his former teammate to the pitcher's mound, where Roy tossed the baseball, basketball style, to Johnny Podres, and the Dodger-Yankee game in his honor got underway. It was the largest crowd ever to see a game in the U.S., and it was all for the Dodgers' Campanella.

THERE SHE GOES! Gil McDougald hits 10th-inning homer off Warren Spahn, who turns to watch flight of ball. Homer gave N.Y. 4-3 win over Milwaukee, evened 1958 series at three-all. Yanks won last game for their 18th world championship and 7th under Casey Stengel. Bob Turley, relieving Don Larsen, bested Lew Burdette. Bill Skowron's three-run homer in eighth inning wrapped up the game. The Yankees, who ran away with the AL flag, trailed the Braves, three games to one. Yankees finished 10 games ahead of Chicago White Sox with Boston and Cleveland rounding out the first division. In the National League, Pittsburgh finished second with San Francisco third and Cincinnati fourth. In the individual races, Ernie Banks of Chicago and Jackie Jensen of Boston were voted the Most Valuable Players. Ted Williams led AL hitters with .328 mark and Richie Ashburn paced the NL with a .320 average. The NL, aided by franchise shifts, drew 10,164,596 fans, a gain of more than 1.3 million. The runaway victory of the Yankees held AL attendance to 7,296,034, a drop of a million.

BOWL GAMES: Air Force, although only in its second season of football, earned a trip to the Cotton Bowl and held a highly-touted Texas Christian team to a 0-0 tie. TCU's Marvin Lasater proved to be the hardest runner of the day. In typical run *(below)* Lasater reeled off seven yards in the fourth period. Tom Stevens *(l.)* of Syracuse found the Oklahoma Sooners line too tough, was stopped for no gain in first period of Orange Bowl game. The Sooners had too much over-all power for the Easterners and recorded a 21-6 victory. In the Rose Bowl, Iowa, the Big Ten title-holder, did the expected and walloped California, 38-12, in the biggest rout of the day. In the Gator Bowl, Mississippi edged past Florida, 7-3. The Sugar Bowl produced a mild upset when Louisiana State, voted the nation's top team, had to hold off a strong Clemson aggregation before posting a 7-0 win. LSU's Bayou Bengals were the only team playing a major schedule to finish unbeaten and untied. Their coach, Paul Dietzel, was named Coach of the Year. Ranked behind LSU were Iowa, Army, Auburn, Oklahoma, Air Force, Wisconsin, Ohio State, Syracuse and TCU. Other top teams were Notre Dame, South Carolina, Florida, Rutgers and Clemson. Top player was Army's Pete Dawkins *(see next page)*. Ranking closed to the fabled Cadet were Billy Cannon (LSU); Billy Austin (Rutgers); Randy Duncan (Iowa) and Joe Kapp (California).

JOE KUHARICH *(above)* took over the football hot seat when he replaced Terry Brennan at Notre Dame. Kuharich, former coach of the Washington Redskins, was working on the first year of a five-year contract when he went to N.D.

ALAN AMECHE plowed through gaping hole in the New York Giants line *(above)* to give the Baltimore Colts a 23-17 overtime win and the pro grid championship at the Yankee Stadium as a throng of 64,185 looked on. It was football's first official overtime struggle. Ameche's driving score thrilled the Baltimore fans; when Colts came home *(below)* 30,000 of them roared "Welcome home, champs." Over-all pro football attendance and Jimmy Brown of the Cleveland Browns were the year's big stories. More than 3,006,124 fans paid in excess of $9 million to see National Football League contests. Brown, a pile-driving fullback, set a ground-gaining record by breaking through for 1527 yards. He also matched the mark for the most touchdowns, 18, set in 1945.

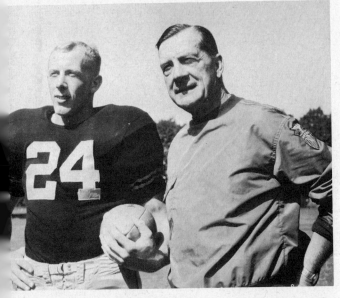

ARMY'S THIRD-RANKED FOOTBALL TEAM caught the fancy of the fans in a big way. Two reasons were Pete Dawkins *(l.)* and Coach Earl Blaik. Dawkins was the player of the year, winning the Heisman and Maxwell Trophies. The cadet, who ranked seventh in his class scholastically, became a Rhodes Scholar upon graduation. Coach Blaik, after his great season, during which he introduced the "Lonesome End" offense, left West Point. Dale Hall, a member of the famous Davis and Blanchard teams, succeeded Blaik. Navy's coach Eddie Erdelatz also stepped down, with Wayne Hardin taking over.

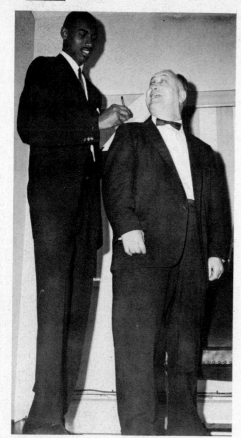

HARVARD'S VARSITY crew *(near lane, above)* noses out Syracuse to win the Eastern sprints. Both Harvard's lightweight and heavyweight crews upset English oarsmen at annual 120-year-old Royal Henley Regatta held on Thames River.

FUTURE of pro basketball seemed to be looking up in 1959, and one tall reason was Wilt (The Stilt) Chamberlain *(above)*, using back of Philadelphia Warriors' owner Eddie Gottlieb to sign pact. The Warriors signed the seven-foot, two-inch pivot man for reported $30,000, making him highest paid player in league. Tom Heinsohn *(15 below)* of the Boston Celtics leaps for rebound in championship series with Minneapolis Lakers. Celtics regained the title by sweeping Lakers in best-of-seven series.

CALIFORNIA BEARS and St. John's Redmen were the top basketball teams. The outstanding player for the second straight year was Cincinnati's high scoring rebounder, Oscar Robertson. California won the National Collegiate AA title by edging West Virginia 71-70. St. John's, powered by sophomore star Tony Jackson *(24 above)* defeated Bradley in a tightly fought game, 76-71, to win National Invitation Tournament. Jackson was voted Most Valuable Player in classic.

JON KONRADS, 16, holder of all free-style swimming records over 110 yards, kisses sister Ilsa after she set 880 mark.

PHENOMENAL AUSTRALIAN Herb Elliott *(below)* lowered the mile record to 3 minutes 54.5 seconds. John Thomas *(above)*, freshman at Boston U., set new high jump mark of 7 feet 1¼ inches. Don Bragg *(l.)* raised indoor pole vault record to 15 feet 9½ inches, and also won his event in U.S.-Russian meet held in July, in which U.S. men won 127-108, while U.S. women were defeated 67-40.

173

RACING'S TRIPLE CROWN was split three ways, but the front page news was near-fatal spill Eddie Arcaro took in the Belmont Stakes, won by Sword Dancer *(above, l.)* with Willie Shoemaker up. Arcaro, on Black Hills, was thrown to the turf after his horse's knees crossed. The horse was destroyed. Arcaro, shaken up, spent a few days in the hospital. Tom Lee on the inside won the Kentucky Derby with a burst of speed in the stretch *(l.)*. Willie Harmatz *(below)* kisses Royal Orbit in the winner's circle after coming first in the Preakness.

BUD WERNER of Steamboat Springs, Col., displays some of his ski form that has made him top U.S. threat in the 1960 Winter Olympics. Games will be held in Squaw Valley, Calif. Trials were in 1959.

FISHING, No. 1 participation sport, which grows more popular with each passing year, offered great moments. A Virginia fisherman, Charles Gifford, (above) enjoyed one while capturing 388-pound Blue Marlin. Auto racing stayed high on popularity list. Carroll Shelby, a Texan, (below) crosses finish line in Aston Martin racer after winning 24-hour endurance race at Le Mans, France. Only 13 out of 53 finished the race.

BOWLING, which is solidifying its position as the No. 2 participation sport, saw Don Carter (above) sweep most of the important titles, His wife, Laverne, holds trophy for the women's crown.

175

CAR OF THE FUTURE IS EXPERIMENTAL, TWO-ENGINE GM FIREBIRD III, FIRST EVER DESIGNED AROUND SINGLE STICK CONTROL.

GREATER ECONOMY AND SALES FOR 1959 CARS

Popular Rambler pulls American Motors out of red, first time in six years

THE AUTOMOBILE INDUSTRY bounced back from the depression and turned in a good performance during the 1959 model year. Sales were up nearly two million units over 1958.

General Motors led the field with a completely redesigned line. Buicks lost their familiar portholes, and sprouted a new set of fins, as did Chevrolet. Pontiac had a new body with longer axle for greater road stability.

American Motors' Rambler continued its meteoric sales climb. Earnings were sufficiently high that resumption of dividends was possible. Studebaker-Packard's Lark was introduced to join the Rambler in the small car market, and brought that company out of the red for the first time in several years.

The triumph of the Lark and Rambler sped plans for more small models. The "Big Three," Chrysler, Ford, and GM, tooled up for production so as to have small cars on the road by year's end.

Although small cars offer an economy of operation unknown to most U.S. drivers, sales indicate that the public still wants the standard size.

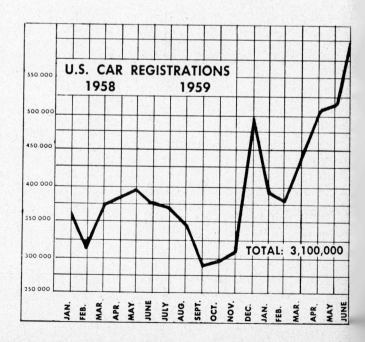

U.S. CAR REGISTRATIONS 1958 1959

TOTAL: 3,100,000

SLEEK RAMBLER was restyled in its first major change since 1956, but basic design was not altered. American Motor's President George Romney has stated on many occasions that he will not enter the horsepower race. AMC has stepped up its advertising and sales organizations. Romney expects to sell almost 500,000 units in 1960, and is aiming his sights at the coveted fourth spot in domestic automobile sales in the U.S.

CHRYSLER'S SWIVEL SEATS highlighted new features of 1959 Dodge. The swingout seats were designed to give maximum comfort to the ladies, who find it hard getting out of a car without worrying about wrinkled dresses. Other modern features included safety speedometer, push-button air conditioning, electronic mirrors, and automatic headlight-dimmers. New powerful 1959 Chrysler accelerated from 0-60 mph in 8.3 seconds.

STUDEBAKER'S LARK, the last gamble of a failing company, met with near-phenomenal success. Company President Churchill believes that they can make money even if sales drop to 100,000 units per year. This low break-even point was achieved by cutting such frills as heavy chrome, expensive dies, staff.

1959 CADILLAC COUPE features impressive expanse of glass in larger rear window and "jeweled" rear grille. Pointed rear fins set a new note in car design. Cadillac came out with new bumpers, hoods and fenders to give modern look to the traditional car of aristocracy. Cars featured air conditioning, heating units, electric door locks, "cruise control."

RENAULT DAUPHINE is sturdy enough to weather the storm of six curious youngsters, also puts in a good performance on the road. Renault's overseas sales have boosted the French firm's production to such an extent that it is now the world's sixth largest producer. Popularity of such little cars as the Dauphine boomed in 1959, taking 10% of total U.S. Market.

FOREIGN CARS CAPTURE
LARGER SHARE OF WORLD MARKET

Older companies such as Volkswagen, Renault and newcomers from Holland and Japan threaten U.S. position

PHENOMENAL SALES CLIMB of foreign cars in the U.S. continued in 1959, capturing 10% of the total domestic market. During the past year, production of non-American cars abroad surpassed that of the U.S. "Big Three" manufacturers. Their rate of increase could make this a permanent situation.

This change in the world production has seriously affected overseas markets for U.S. cars. Ten years ago, manufacturers here exported more autos to Europe than were imported to the U.S. Now the flow has been reversed. Italian cars outsell ours in Germany, and German models are more popular in Italy than U.S. cars.

The boom has encouraged the growth of old com-

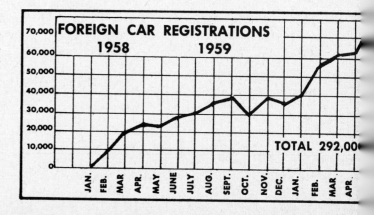

FOREIGN CAR REGISTRATIONS
1958   1959

TOTAL 292,00[0]

COVERED WITH AUTOGRAPHS of English assembly line workers, the 100,000th English Ford imported for sales in the U.S. is unloaded from deck of the Queen Elizabeth. Car was brought here to commemorate Ford's 10th year in imported car line.

MERCEDES-BENZ series-built sports car model 300 SL was designed for speed on the road and for easy handling. Cars like this provide rough competition for U.S. manufacturers.

DO-IT-YOURSELF car, said to be world's first, is shown partly assembled, *(front)* with English manufacturer, York Nobel, and completed *(back)*. Car was shown at the International Auto Show at New York's Coliseum in April, sells for $1000.

panies, and the birth of new ones. Japan's young industry produced only 42,000 units in 1958, but this year production tripled. Nissan and Toyota, leading producers, claim Hawaiian and West Coast sales made this possible.

Austin-Healey's Sprite, a British sports model selling for under $1800, has a waiting list in the U.S. Vauxhall sells as many cars here as in Britain.

The Volkswagen, whose price and style changed little since its introduction, remained the most popular import.

The more expensive models, such as Britain's Rolls-Royce, France's Facel-Vega, Germany's BMW and the Dart sports car, produced by the Daimler organization, appeared in more and more American garages.

HIGH ABOVE the streets of Tokyo, this new Japanese Toyopet Sedan is mounted on 10-story-high revolving tower in unusual advertising stunt. Japanese manufacturer made a hit on the West Coast with the Daihatsu trimobile truck, which met with enthusiastic reception by merchants and college students.

BILL: A lot they care.
EMILY: Also ... why, Bill Hawkey, whatever do you mean?

BILL: Well then how come when you go to stores, they're still selling other breads -- I mean right out in plain sight and all.

EMILY: Well, of course! That's the American way!

TV CARTOONS gained in popularity as advertisers learned how to use the light touch to sell. School teacher Emily Tipp *(above)* was animated by J. Walter Thompson as off-beat sales agent for Tip-Top bread. Script calls for Emily to stick to story of quality in spite of interruptions. Voices of Carl Reiner and Margaret Hamilton add to pixy quality of film.

ERA OF BIGNESS OPENS FOR ADVERTISERS

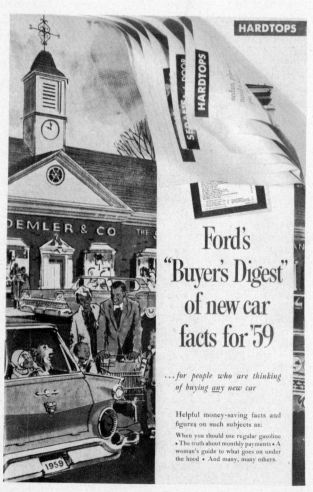

HARDTOPS

Ford's "Buyer's Digest" of new car facts for '59

...*for people who are thinking of buying any new car*

Helpful money-saving facts and figures on such subjects as:

When you should use regular gasoline • The truth about monthly payments • A woman's guide to what goes on under the hood • And many, many others.

$780,000 AD covered 36 pages of once ad-free Reader's Digest, set new record for size in consumer magazine advertising. Ad was designed as guide for mobile living, looked like editorial.

ADVERTISING, which suffered from lack of investment in the second half of 1958 as national advertisers became alarmed over the extent of the recession, recovered substantially in 1959. As consumer spending strengthened, it resumed the favorable pattern of growth interrupted in 1958, and started reshaping itself into a big, big business.

Volume reached $11 billion, after staying close to the $10 billion level for the previous two years. As the year opened, 31% of the money was spent in newspapers, 13% in television, 8% in magazines, 6% in radio, 5% in trade papers, 2% for outdoor posters and the rest in other media such as direct mail, premiums, and store displays. TV was the big gainer, as radio fell off the most.

The very largest corporations and their advertising agencies tended to dominate advertising more than ever. The largest advertisers lumped their investments in heavily promoted TV shows, special all-advertising supplements in newspapers, multi-page and oversize ads in magazines and giant three-dimensional painted bulletins at highway intersections.

Advertisers strained to outdo each other with give-away promotions. Although big money quiz shows were publicized out of business by charges of rigging and kick-backs to quiz masters, a new kind of give-away—The Sweepstakes—came into prominence. To enter a Sweep-stake, all the consumer had to do was send name and address to the advertiser. No jingles to write; no purchase required. Because no "consideration" was involved, these giant give-aways were not hampered by lottery laws. In the race to give away over $100,000 each were General Mills, Post Cereals Division of General Foods, DuPont, and others.

Nickle-and-dime give-aways were also highly publicized. There were more two-for-one sales heavily adver-

WHISKEY FOR A LADY, previously taboo in ads, became acceptable as Distilled Spirits Institute lifted 25-year ban on females. Saturday Evening Post took first liquor ads in 62 yrs.

SIMPLE SYMBOLS were used widely to tell complicated stories quickly. When El Al Airlines' ad agency learned that new jets cut time to London 20%, it cut 20% off ocean photo.

tised, coupons good for cents-off in grocery stores, trading stamps. A new magazine designed specifically to carry coupons appeared. Advertisers added coupon flaps to full-page ads. There was such a flood of coupons in some issues that the value of coupons inside exceeded their newsstand price.

The largest national advertiser was General Motors, spending 145 million dollars—three quarters of it split into magazines, newspapers, and TV. Proctor and Gamble spent 110 million; Ford 104; General Foods 87; Lever Brothers 80; General Electric 73 million dollars. The largest retail advertiser in the United States and undoubtedly in the entire world was Sears, Roebuck, which spent almost 70 million dollars on advertising—three-quarters of it in newspaper ads for its retail outlets.

The largest advertising agencies grew larger in a year marked by 150 major agency mergers. Most of mergers were among middle-sized agencies; but the importance of the top few key agencies also increased.

The largest agency, J. Walter Thompson, handled 303 million dollars in billings in 1958; McCann-Erickson over 265 million; Young & Rubicam 225; BBDO 209; Ted Bates 107; Benton & Bowles 103; N. W. Ayer 102; Leo Burnett, 102 million dollars.

SKIN FOR "LES" GIRLS drew raised eyebrows and extra attention for Cole of California. Picture is composite of girls posed separately on Long Island to avoid embarrassment.

181

THE ACADEMY of Television Arts and Sciences, which presents the annual Emmy Awards, came in for severe criticism during the year over the complicated structure it set up for handing out 42 statuettes. Some critics felt the system had been tailored to mediocre standards instead of recognition of achievement. Above are four of this year's selections: Bob Hope, a special award; Jack Benny, Best Comedy Series; Barbara Hale, Best Supporting Actress; Raymond Burr, Best Performance in a Dramatic Series. Below, Fred Astaire (r.), with Robert Young, took 9 Emmies for his hour-long TV debut.

"SATURATED" TV
GROSSES $1 BILLION

Quiz shows decline as western films ride high

DURING the early part of 1959, TV set circulation reached the predicted saturation point. Nearly 90 per cent of the homes in the country were reported to have TV.

Advertising revenues continued to grow at a phenomenal rate. The Federal Communications Commission, in its latest report on broadcast revenues, estimated that in 1958 the three TV webs and 514 stations realized $1.03 billion, a rise of 9.2 per cent over the total recorded for the calendar year of 1957.

Western shows continued to dominate programming. Quiz shows came under heavy fire of charges hinting

fraud, killing off their nighttime use but apparently not affecting their daytime popularity. A New York Grand Jury conducted an investigation of claims that the big money quiz shows had furnished answers to particular contestants who had strong audience appeal. The investigation resulted in a presentment instead of an indictment. This touched off a new controversy when Court of General Sessions Judge Mitchell D. Schweitzer kept the presentment secret at the request of the program producers.

The Federal Communications Commission ruled that, under Section 315 of the Communications Act, stations

MENOTTI'S OPERA, "Maria Golovin," was part of NBC series in which the web invests approximately $750,000 each year. Operas draw 8 million viewers but are too expensive to be profitable.

QUIZ SHOWS which enjoyed phenomenal success hit a quick demise after charges of questionable practices. Jack Barry *(below)*, emcee, co-producer of "Twenty One," broods after the last show.

PER YEAR

NEWS PROGRAMS, featuring personable commentators interpreting national and world events, continued to gain stature as TV fare. Chet Huntley *(below l.)* and David Brinkley, a new team introduced by NBC-TV, received wide critical acclaim and several awards for their news coverage and analysis. Huntley reports from New York, Brinkley from Washington. Huntley also starred in hour-long Sunday show.

and networks which aired film clips of a public official in a news show must grant equal time to any political opponent. The ruling was made on request of Lar Daly, perennial unsuccessful candidate for mayor of Chicago under the label of an obscure political party.

President Eisenhower termed the decision "ridiculous" and the Attorney General requested the FCC to reconsider the decision. The FCC did so but renewed the original finding. Both Senate and House of Representatives committees started hearings on all Section 315 requirements, and need for new revisions.

DAVID BRINKLEY

BIG DEAL of the year is signed by Perry Como with Kraft Foods Company. The $25 million pact calls for two years services as performer-producer, 10 years as consultant. Como should net $2 million. At signing are *(l. to r.)* R. E. Kintner, NBC president, J. C. Loftis, Kraft president, R. Sarnoff, chairman of NBC.

FIRST FILM for TV sent by telephone cable across the Atlantic was of Queen Elizabeth's departure for Canada. Only 100 minutes after Queen Mother, Princess Margaret waved goodbye, Americans saw the event. Photo *(r.)* taken from television screen during the telecast in the U.S., shows their airport farewells.

TV AUDIENCES were startled by announcement that Edward R. Murrow, CBS star commentator, would take year's leave of absence. Rumors of tiff with top CBS management were rampant. "Inside information" had it that Murrow had grown bigger than the web and strained relations had resulted.

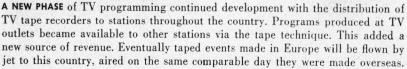

A NEW PHASE of TV programming continued development with the distribution of TV tape recorders to stations throughout the country. Programs produced at TV outlets became available to other stations via the tape technique. This added a new source of revenue. Eventually taped events made in Europe will be flown by jet to this country, aired on the same comparable day they were made overseas.

NBC-TV'S "TODAY," show starring Dave Garroway touched off major labor controversy when a technician's union called a strike to protest airing of tape programs made in Europe with Brigitte Bardot. Strike resulted in complete defeat of union by web. During the strike NBC administrative personnel handled all the technical chores to keep network programming schedule on the air.

ARTHUR GODFREY, star of many of his own shows on radio and TV, became the victim of lung cancer. Successful operation for removal of tumor required long convalescence. His value to CBS is most clearly evident in report he brought web $12 million in billings each year. The freckled, red-headed performer was expected to resume activities during the 1959-60 season.

URBAN RENEWAL SPARKS BOOM

Frank Lloyd Wright, dean of U.S. architects, dies at 89

FRANK LLOYD WRIGHT, dean of U.S. architects, died on April 9 at the age of 89. Colorful, controversial and much-quoted, Wright had been, in the opinion of many, the world's greatest living architect.

His philosophy of building was expressed in low, terrain-conforming homes, which came to be known as "prairie architecture," and in functional office buildings of modest height, using such materials as concrete, glass brick and tubing.

He hated skyscrapers, although he had received his early training, in Chicago before 1900, from Louis Sullivan, "father of the skyscraper."

Partly because of his scathing condemnation of the "topless towers" so dear to the hearts of most' U.S. architects, Wright was much admired in Europe but largely a prophet without honor in his own country for many years.

During the 40s and 50s, however, his reputation was firmly established on both sides of the Atlantic.

One of his most famous buildings was his own home, Taliesin ("shining brow" in his ancestral Welsh), in Spring Green, Wisconsin.

Other Wright showplaces throughout the nation were the Midway Gardens in Chicago, the Larkin Co. administration building in Buffalo, N.Y., the S. C. Johnson building in Racine, Wisc., and Falling Water, the Bear Run, Pa., home of Edgar J. Kaufmann.

His only New York commission was the Guggenheim Museum of Non-Objective Painting, which was nearing completion when he died.

The "little temple in a park," as the architect called his cylindrical design, aroused a typical Wright furor. His admirers hailed it; his critics called it a "washing machine," a "hot cross bun," a "marshmallow," and other terms of ridicule.

The Wright legacy was seen in many of the new office buildings, shining with glass and surrounded by terraces and fountains, that rose in every major U.S. city during the

FRANK LLOYD WRIGHT was born June 8, 1869, at Richland Center, Wisc., the son of a minister and a school teacher. He broke with tradition at the outset of his professional career by going to Chicago rather than to Paris to study and was an architectural radical all his life. He twice incorporated himself, selling shares in his earning potential to friends, when financial going was rough. Active as ever in his 80s, he denounced compulsory retirement at 65 as a "murderous custom."

year as the building boom continued.

Most cities were embarking on long-range, multi-million dollar programs to halt creeping obsolescence in their business districts.

The new "downtowns" envisioned by urban planners featured ample space for traffic circulation and parking (a few suggested solution of the traffic strangulation problem by the

more drastic method of barring cars from downtown areas) and walk-to-work housing integrated with new office buildings.

Need for new housing—urban and suburban, public and private and at all income levels—was equally pressing. Future of the construction industry was a vital element in the expanding economy of the nation.

WRIGHT DESIGN for Beth Sholom Synagogue in Philadelphia was one of his last. Among many honors architect received in his later years were Gold Medal Award of the National Institute of Arts and Letters, Gold Medal of the American Institute of Architects, Britain's Royal Gold Medal for Architecture, Italy's Star of Solidarity and Gold Medal of Florence.

CONSTRUCTION BOOM was a noisy nuisance for New Yorkers, but it also provided a new kind of lunch hour entertainment. Fences around most of the new buildings had peepholes

LARGEST ROMAN CATHOLIC CHURCH in the U.S., the National Shrine of the Immaculate Conception, moved closer to completion in Washington, D.C. Plans for the massive church, 459 feet long and 237 feet high, had been drawn up in 1919. It was built entirely without structural steel, using masonry, brick, tile and stone. Estimated cost was $30 million.

for "sidewalk superintendents." One company, Western Electric, even installed telephones *(below)* which passers-by could pick up for running account of construction progress.

WORLD'S LARGEST geodesic dome built at Baton Rouge, La., houses the tank car repair and maintenance facilities of Union Tank Car Co. of Chicago. Big enough to house a major league baseball diamond or football field, the umbrella-like structure measures 384 feet in diameter, rises to height of 120 feet. It is made of 321 six-sided steel panels welded in by rods and pipes.

NATION'S CAPITAL received a new monument when the Robert A. Taft Memorial Bell Tower was dedicated early in 1959. The slender white shaft stands on Capitol Hill, to left of Capitol Building, is floodlighted at night (r.). It honors Sen. Robert A. Taft of Ohio, the widely respected "Mr. Republican," who died in 1953.

NATION'S FIRST fully mechanized post office and mail processing plant, ultra-modern inside and out, went into construction in Providence, R.I. "Post Office of Tomorrow" (estimated cost $20 million) was scheduled for 1960 completion.

BRAZIL'S NEW CAPITAL, Brasilia, was being built from the ground up on huge nation's central plateau. Chapel (below) for presidential residence, Sunrise Palace, was among buildings finished in 1959. Oscar Niemayer was chief architect.

HUNGARIAN-BORN Dr. E. P. Wigner *(l.)*, Princeton University, receives the Atomic Energy Commission's Enrico Fermi Award from AEC Chairman John McCone. Established in 1946, the commission honored Dr. Wigner for work in development of nuclear reactors related to atom research.

SEVENTY-THREE YEAR OLD Prof. George de Hevesy works at his laboratory in Stockholm, Sweden, after being named second winner of $75,000 "Atoms For Peace Award." A native Hungarian and one-time winner of the Nobel Prize in Chemistry, the scientist was chosen from 111 candidates from 19 countries for his pioneering research in the use of radioactive isotopes. Professor de Hevesy found isotopes could be used as indicators of biochemical processes in living organisms.

AWARDS

WINNERS of National Institute of Social Sciences Gold Medals display their prizes at Waldorf Astoria. They are, left to right, James R. Killian, Singer Marian Anderson, Herbert Hoover, Institute President Frank Pace Jr., and Robert Anderson.

THE AMERICAN ACADEMY of Arts and Letters presented its Award of Merit Medal for the Novel to Britisher Aldous Huxley at its annual ceremony on May 20. Many of the best-known U.S. artists, writers and composers attended event.

LINEUP of Nobel Prize winners is conspicuous because of absence of Soviet poet Boris Pasternak, who won Literature Prize, refused due to communist pressure. Winners are *(l. to r.)* for Medicine, Dr. George Wells Beadle, 55, of the U.S. and Professor Edward Lawrie Tatum, 48, U.S.; for Physics, Dr. Igor E. Tamm of Moscow; for Chemistry, Dr. Frederick Sanger, 40, of England; for Physics, Dr. Pavel A. Cherenkov and Dr. Ilya M. Frank, both of Moscow; for Medicine, Dr. Joshua Lederberg, 33, U.S.

REVIVAL OF LYNCH LAW SHOCKS THE NATION

A SHOCKED NATION learned in 1959 that the shameful era of the lynch mob had not yet come to an end. The tragic proof was offered by the body of Mack Charles Parker, pulled from the Pearl River near the Mississippi-Louisiana border *(above)*. Parker, a 23-year-old Negro truck driver, was being held in the Poplarville, Miss. jail on a charge of raping a pregnant white woman. Shortly before midnight on April 25, a band of masked and gloved raiders broke into his cell, dragged their victim feet-first down the concrete stairs and disappeared into the night. Parker's body was found nine days later. Mississippi Governor James P. Coleman promptly called in F.B.I. help. Concluding no federal law had been violated, the F.B.I. turned over the results of its investigation to local authorities. The next step lay in the hands of a Mississippi grand jury.

TAKING REFUGE in the Fifth amendment, Vito Genovese *(r.)*, described by Senator John McClellan as one of "the top gangsters in the country," refused even to tell his occupation in an appearance before the Senate Rackets Committee. Some of organized crime's leaders ran into trouble in 1959. In February, crime lord Frank Costello was divested of his citizenship in a court decision that opened the way for deportation action. In May, 21 bigtime gangster guests at the infamous 1957 Apalachin crime convention were rounded up by federal agents and booked on the unusual charge of conspiracy to obstruct justice, on the basis of their concerted refusal to talk about the goings-on at the Apalachin meeting. Government officials faced a tough court fight in their effort to get a decision that might put the 21 mobster leaders out of circulation for a period of at least five years.

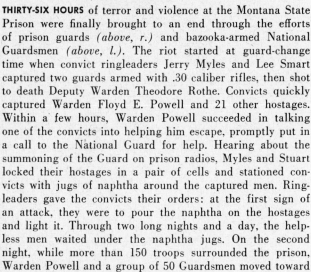

THIRTY-SIX HOURS of terror and violence at the Montana State Prison were finally brought to an end through the efforts of prison guards *(above, r.)* and bazooka-armed National Guardsmen *(above, l.)*. The riot started at guard-change time when convict ringleaders Jerry Myles and Lee Smart captured two guards armed with .30 caliber rifles, then shot to death Deputy Warden Theodore Rothe. Convicts quickly captured Warden Floyd E. Powell and 21 other hostages. Within a few hours, Warden Powell succeeded in talking one of the convicts into helping him escape, promptly put in a call to the National Guard for help. Hearing about the summoning of the Guard on prison radios, Myles and Stuart locked their hostages in a pair of cells and stationed convicts with jugs of naphtha around the captured men. Ringleaders gave the convicts their orders: at the first sign of an attack, they were to pour the naphtha on the hostages and light it. Through two long nights and a day, the helpless men waited under the naphtha jugs. On the second night, while more than 150 troops surrounded the prison, Warden Powell and a group of 50 Guardsmen moved toward the embattled cell block. A bazooka blast signaled the start of the attack. Within moments Guardsmen had reached the hostages. They were uninjured; startled convicts had found time to pour only one naphtha jug. But lying dead in the prison's northwest tower were mutinous ring leaders Myles and Smart, apparently victims of murder (Myles) and suicide (Smart). Two Guardsmen were slightly wounded.

A month before the Deer Lodge rebellion made headlines in April, violence had erupted at the Walpole State Prison, about 20 miles southwest of Boston, Mass. There, on the morning of March 7, six convicts attempted to escape over the wall, only to be thwarted by a guard who toppled the ladder they had raised. The convicts succeeded in seizing seven hostages, including Warden John A. Gavin, Prison Chaplain the Rev. Edward F. Hartigan, and two deputy wardens. The mutineers drenched their hostages with gasoline and threatened to turn them into human torches. But less than three hours after the uprising started, about 50 state police troopers, armed with machine guns, stormed through windows and doors to bring an end to the rebellion.

191

SECOND TRAGEDY entered the life of former Brooklyn Dodger catcher Roy Campanella, paralyzed in a 1958 automobile accident, when his son was seized by police in a street fight of juvenile gangs, later charged with burglary as well. Accompanying David Campanella *(above)* in his appearance at Children's Court was his mother, Mrs. Ruthe Campanella. The boy was eventually put on probation for an indeterminate period. Police expressed surprise at the discovery that young Campanella was involved with a gang of juvenile toughs. Ironically, his father, who rose from Philadelphia slums to become one of major-league baseball's outstanding players, has been actively engaged for several years in working among youngsters to help curb juvenile delinquency.

DIRE WARNINGS of racial bigots and diehard segregationists, harping on the theme of possible Negro assaults on white women, were given a reverse twist by events in Tallahassee, Florida. There, four white youths, William Collinsworth, Patrick Scarbourough, Ollie Stoutamire and David Beagles were seized by police on May 2, placed under arrest on charges of having raped a Negro co-ed at Tallahassee's all-Negro Florida A. & M. University. Two days later, fellow students of the rape victim boycotted classes to attend an all-day "passive resistance" rally. Four days later, on May 6 the four youths were indicted on a charge of rape; on June 22 Judge W. May Walker, acting on a plea of mercy from all-white jury, sentenced the four to life imprisonment. In similar cases heard in South Carolina a few days later, 70-year-old Judge J. Henry Johnson of the General Sessions Court passed the death sentence within the space of two hours on Israel Sharpe, a Negro, for the rape of a white woman, and Pvt. Fred Davis of the U.S. Marine Corps, a white man, for the rape of a Negress. This was the first time that a white man was slated to die for the rape of a Negress.

FRIGHTENING GLIMPSE into the dark world of a troubled child's mind was afforded by the case of 8-year-old Melvin Dean Nimer *(above with his uncle)*. The boy's parents, Dr. and Mrs. Melvin Nimer, were stabbed to death in their Staten Island (N. Y.) home. Melvin told police they were slain by a masked intruder, then changed his story, confessed he had stabbed them. After that came a series of conflicting stories and the boy, held as a material witness, was sent to Bellevue Hospital for psychiatric observation. Reporting that he had "an emotional disturbance that requires close psychiatric supervision," officials finally released the boy to the custody of relatives. No one seemed quite sure which—if any—of Melvin's many conflicting stories was the truth.

CRIME of passion brought a sentence of 2 to 21 years in the Indiana Women's Prison for Connie Nicholas (*r.* with defense attorney Frank Symmes as she hears sentence pronounced). The jury had found her guilty of voluntary manslaughter in the slaying of the man she claimed she loved.

DISTRAUGHT father Frank Chionchio (*below*) pleads for the return of his day-old daughter, kidnapped from a Brooklyn hospital less than three hours after birth. Child was found unharmed ten days later. Mrs. Jean Iavarone, widowed mother of eight children, was held on kidnapping charges.

MOTHER-IN-LAW trouble, stock subject for humorists, proved a source of tragedy rather than comedy in California where Mrs. Elizabeth Duncan (*below*) was condemned to death March 21 for hiring two men to murder her daughter-in-law, Olga. Trial made public a story of Momism in its most virulent form. Failing to break up her son's marriage with a fraudulent annulment, mother Duncan resorted to surgery of death.

SCANDAL of housing conditions in New York City slum areas led to arrest of Banton L. Wyckoff (*below*) in Teaneck, N.J. Operator of five tenements in Manhattan, Wyckoff was named in five criminal informations returned by a New York County grand jury in February. District Attorney Hogan reported more than 425 violations had been listed against "slumlord" Wyckoff's buildings.

193

OCCUPATIONAL HAZARDS threaten the lives of workers in many trades and professions. Advances in science and technology have produced safety devices that make many a man's work safer, as well as easier, but the threat of disaster still remains the constant companion of many workers. The ancient nightmare of the miner once again became a reality in Summersville, West Virginia, where 17 men were trapped underground in a coal-mine explosion. Here, the body of one of the victims is brought to the surface by grim-faced rescue workers.

NATURE AND MAN IN TRAGIC COLLABORATION

The ancient enemies of man—wind and weather, fire and water—continue, as always, to take their toll in life and property. To them have been added the special hazards of a modern, highly complex, technologically advanced civilization. In 1959 men met disaster in huge jet-powered aircraft, in luxurious ocean liners, in high-speed railroad trains. And, so familiar had become the ever-increasing slaughter on the nation's highways that the grim statistics of automobile deaths no longer seemed news in the U.S.

FIRE sweeps through a Chicago parochial school as horrified parents, whose children may have been among the dead, watch. The worst school fire in Chicago's history claimed 87 children and 3 nuns as victims, many of whom leaped from windows in panic. Flames spread so rapidly that scores of children were found dead at their desks, although more than 1000 of the 8-14-year old children were rescued. Nation-wide horror over tragic blaze prompted many U.S. cities to undertake immediate investigation of fire hazards in their schools.

TRAIN DISASTER carried more than 20 passengers to their deaths in Newark Bay when a commuter train plunged through an open drawbridge. Two locomotives and two passenger cars were submerged immediately, while a third coach was left hanging between trestle and water. Officials from federal and state agencies joined railroad personnel in searching for cause of tragedy. Investigators *(r.)* inspect the derailing device on the death bridge, where it was determined that the train had been derailed but not halted by the automatic safeguard, which went into operation only after the train had passed three warning signals.

THREE MINUTES after a tornado struck St. Louis in February, 19 persons were dead, more than 300 were injured, and shattered homes *(above)* bore silent witness to the force of the violent wind. The storm struck before any warnings could be issued, and left a path of devastation across a quiet residential area and small business section of the city.

DAMAGE to buildings in Oswego, N.Y. *(above)* reached well over $1 million as buildings sagged and collapsed under the weight of successive snowfalls that reached a total accumulation of more than 80 inches. Severe winter weather plagued other areas of country in January, when a two-day storm left 71 dead in a fifteen-state area of the Midwest. The Red Cross estimated that 9500 families suffered storm losses in Ohio, Pennsylvania, Indiana, New York. Especially hard hit was Columbus, Ohio, where 2500 were made homeless.

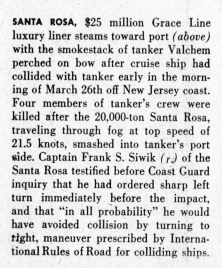

SANTA ROSA, $25 million Grace Line luxury liner steams toward port *(above)* with the smokestack of tanker Valchem perched on bow after cruise ship had collided with tanker early in the morning of March 26th off New Jersey coast. Four members of tanker's crew were killed after the 20,000-ton Santa Rosa, traveling through fog at top speed of 21.5 knots, smashed into tanker's port side. Captain Frank S. Siwik *(r.)* of the Santa Rosa testified before Coast Guard inquiry that he had ordered sharp left turn immediately before the impact, and that "in all probability" he would have avoided collision by turning to right, maneuver prescribed by International Rules of Road for colliding ships.

WRECKAGE of an Electra turbo-prop airliner *(above)* is removed from the East River. Sixty-five persons died in crash.

DEATH claimed this little Negro tot despite valiant efforts of fireman to breathe life into him. Baby died in fire.

FIREMEN pour water on ruins *(below)* that remained after explosion and fire raced through "Fountain of the World" religious colony in California. Nine persons, including leader of sect, Krishna Venta, were reported killed. It was later announced that blast was caused by bomb. California was the scene of another disaster that produced an act of heroism when a college girl risked her life in an attempt to save a boy attacked by a 500 lb. killer shark near San Francisco. The girl, Shirley O'Neill, was in line for Carnegie Medal of Honor.

The Passing Scene

People and events that made big
and small headlines during the year

FABULOUS GIFT from New York gem dealer Harry Winston was the legendary Hope Diamond, which Winston donated to the Smithsonian Institution in Washington, D. C. Long famed for the curse of bad luck it is supposed to bring to its owners, the 44½ carat stone is one of world's best-known diamonds, but not the largest.

FABULOUS JOURNEY was made by 37-year-old Christopher Grabowski, shown as he arrived in New York City after completing a solo crossing of Atlantic in a 25-ft. sailing boat. Grabowski, a Polish Air Force veteran, sailed from Tangier April 12 and arrived in U.S. 85 days and 6000 miles later, with provisions left.

◄ **STORY-BOOK ROMANCE** in real life kept the eyes of the world focused on the tiny village of Sogne, Norway in the summer of 1959. There Steven Rockefeller, son of New York's Gov. Nelson Rockefeller and scion of one of the world's great fortunes, was joined in marriage to Anne Marie Rasmussen, daughter of a retired Norwegian grocer. Cinderella had met her Prince Charming in the U.S., where she had spent a year as a housemaid in the Rockefeller home. The announcement of the couple's engagement and wedding plans was the signal for the invasion of quiet Sogne by a host of reporters, photographers, Rockefellers and the merely curious; and what was planned to be a simple ceremony in a small rural church turned into the most publicized nuptials since Grace Kelly wed her Prince. The newlyweds chose the U.S. for their honeymoon.

FRIGHTENED spectators and circus employes scramble for safety as Ponto, an 800-lb. lion, charges across the arena in Madison Square Garden after breaking out of his cage during a circus performance in March. A few minutes after this picture was taken, Ponto's bid for freedom ended when he was trapped in the lobby by an aerialist's net.

PLASTIC BAGS joined such familiar items as matches and candy-coated medicines on the list of household hazards for children. From all across the U.S. came reports of the deaths of small children who suffocated after becoming entangled in the slippery, static-charged folds of plastic. Two-year-old model shows how easily it could happen.

STOCKHOLDERS OF AMERICAN TELEPHONE AND TELEGRAPH CO. SIT FOR PORTRAIT OF THE U.S. CAPITALIST, 1959 VERSION

Beauty Parade

MISS AMERICA of 1959, 21-year-old Mary Ann Mobley of Brandon, Miss., won her title late in 1958 at the nationwide competition of U.S. beauties held every year at Atlantic City, New Jersey.

MRS. AMERICA, who was chosen in a competition at Fort Lauderdale, Fla. on June 20, is Mrs. Margaret Priebe of Des Moines, Iowa. Mrs. Priebe, who managed to defeat 51 other contestants for the title, is the mother of four.

MISS UNIVERSE begins her reign from a throne at Long Beach, Calif. Tokyo fashion model Akiko Kojima was the first Asian ever to win the title in the international beauty pageant, now in its eighth year. Embarrassed Akiko later denied reports that her shapely curves resulted from surgery instead of nature.

MISS FESTIVAL of 1959, named at the annual Cannes Film Festival in France, was 20-year-old Cecilia Cooper. A New York model, she was first Negro to win the title.

ADVENTUROUS CREW of a balloon optimistically named *Small World (r.)* set off from Tenerife, in the Canary Islands, on a voyage to America. After covering 1200 miles by air in 3 days, they spent 21 days at sea before the battered gondola of their balloon *(below)* was found near Barbados. Picked up by fishermen, crew members finally arrived in New York City *(above)* by plane.

GROUNDED GENERAL, Air Force Vice Chief of Staff Curtis LeMay, forsakes his jet planes, but not his customary cigar, to try out his skill at piloting a "Go-Cart" — gasoline-powered, 65 m.p.h. top speed.

PROUD SHIP, the aircraft carrier *USS Wasp*, cruises off the Battery, New York City, in a June celebration of the 350th anniversary of the discovery of the Hudson river. A few weeks later, explosion brought death to several of the crew members while the *Wasp* operated off Quonset Point, R. I.

ONCE-PROUD SHIP, the 45,000-ton French liner *Île de France*, shown *(l.)* in happier days, met a strange fate. Built in 1927, she was no longer profitable in competition with swifter vessels on the Atlantic run. Her owners sold her to a Japanese scrap merchant, but she received a brief reprieve when movie producer Andrew Stone acquired her as the chief prop for a film titled "The Last Voyage." Then, in June, following his script, realist Stone rolled his cameras as flames and flying debris filled the air and the *Ile de France* was deliberately blown up. Her frequent missions of mercy had won the ship the title of "St. Bernard of the Atlantic." She had made the headlines as recently as 1956, when she rushed to pick up passengers from the stricken *Andrea Doria*, which sank after a collision off Nantucket in 1956. The *Ile* rescued 753 survivors.

ENERGETIC OCTOGENARIANS, poet Carl Sandburg *(above, l.)* and photographer Edward Steichen arrive in Sweden for a visit, their energy and creative activity apparently undiminished by the fact that both are 81 years old. The two famous men are brothers-in-law.

YOUTH AND AGE met at an airport in French Equatorial Africa in July, when 13-year-old Bobby Hill *(below, r.)* arrived with $400,000 worth of medical supplies for Dr. Albert Schweitzer *(c.)*. Supplies were donated by Italian individuals and corporations in a drive sparked by a letter Bobby, son of a G.I. in Italy, had written to a NATO general.

FAMOUS DIPLOMAT, Dr. Ralph Bunche, winner of a Nobel Peace Prize, disclosed in July that the West Side Tennis Club in Forest Hills, scene of the biggest U.S. tournaments, had refused membership to his son because Negroes and Jews were not admitted. Uproar ended with the resignation of club's president.

In Memoriam

SAMUEL HOPKINS ADAMS, 87, novelist *(It Happened One Night, The Harvey Girls);* in So. Carolina, Nov. 15, 1958.

ZOE AKINS, 72, Pulitzer Prize-winning playwright *(The Old Maid,* 1935); in Los Angeles, Calif., Oct. 29, 1958.

MAXWELL ANDERSON, 70, 1933 Pulitzer Prize-winner for plays in blank verse *(Winterset, High Tor; Lost in the Stars* in collaboration with Kurt Weill); in Stamford, Conn., Feb. 28.

VINCENT ASTOR, 67, philanthropist, board chairman of *Newsweek;* in New York City, Feb. 3.

ETHEL BARRYMORE, 79, actress, sister of the late Lionel and John Barrymore; in Beverly Hills, Calif., June 18.

MEYER BERGER, 60, *N.Y. Times* reporter and columnist, 1950 Pulitzer Prize winner; in New York City, Feb. 8.

ERNEST BLOCH, 78, composer of works based on Jewish themes; in Portland, Ore., July 15.

RAYMOND CHANDLER, 70, detective story writer *(The Big Sleep, Double Indemnity);* in La Jolla, Calif., March 26.

HARRY D. COLLIER, 83, president of Standard Oil of California and former board chairman of Arabian Oil of California; in San Francisco, Calif., Jan. 30.

BILL CORUM, 63, *N.Y. Journal American* sports writer, president of Churchill Downs; in New York City, Dec. 16, 1958.

LOU COSTELLO, 53, comedian, one-time partner of Bud Abbott; in Beverly Hills, Calif., March 3.

JAMES MICHAEL CURLEY, 83, four times mayor of Boston, governor of Massachusetts, and U.S. Representative; in Boston, Nov. 12, 1958.

CECIL B. deMILLE, 77, pioneer producer of movie extravaganzas (1953 Academy Award for *The Greatest Show on Earth, The Ten Commandments);* in Hollywood, Calif., Jan. 21.

CLARENCE DERWENT, 75, actor, president of American National Theatre and Academy; in New York City, Aug. 6.

MAJ. GEN. WILLIAM JOSEPH (WILD BILL) DONOVAN, 76, World War I hero, World War II chief of Office of Strategic Services; in Washington, D.C., Feb. 8.

JOHN FOSTER DULLES, 71, U.S. Secretary of State, in Washington, D.C., May 24 *(see pages 16-17).*

SIR JACOB EPSTEIN, 78, controversial sculptor of works on Biblical themes; in London, England, Aug. 19.

DOROTHY CANFIELD FISHER, 79, novelist, *(The Deepening Stream),* literary critic; in Arlington, Vt., Nov. 9, 1958.

EDGAR ALBERT GUEST, 77, verse writer known as the "Poet of the People;" in Detroit, Mich., Aug. 5.

FLEET ADM. WILLIAM FREDERICK ("BULL") HALSEY, JR., 76, commander of U.S. Third Fleet in Pacific during World War II; at Fisher's Island, N.Y., Aug. 16.

DUNCAN HINES, 78, restaurant and hotel authority *(Adventures in Good Eating, Lodgings for a Night);* in Bowling Green, Ky., March 15.

WILLIE HOPPE, 71, winner of 51 world billiard championships, 1906-1952; in Miami, Fla., Feb. 1.

CHARLES FRANKLIN KETTERING, 82, engineer and inventor, co-founder of Sloan-Kettering Institute for Cancer Research; in Dayton, Ohio, Nov. 25, 1958.

WANDA LANDOWSKA, 80, harpsichordist, widely acclaimed interpreter of Bach; in Lakeville, Conn., Aug. 16.

DR. ERNEST O. LAWRENCE, 57, 1939 Nobel Prize winning physicist for invention of the cyclotron; in Palo Alto, Calif., Aug. 27, 1958.

DANIEL FRANCOIS MALAN, 84, former South African prime minister, founder of apartheid white supremacy laws; in Capetown, Feb. 7.

ALFRED J. McCOSKER, 72, ex-chairman and president of radio station WOR, co-founder of Mutual Broadcasting System; in Miami, Fla., July 1.

EUGENE MEYER, 83, chairman of the *Washington Post and Times Herald,* financier and banker; in Washington, D.C., July 17.

EDWARD CARDINAL MOONEY, 76, Roman Catholic archbishop of Detroit; in Rome, Italy, Oct. 25, 1958.

MARY FRANCES HOYT MOSES, 100, first woman appointee to U.S. Civil Service, 1883; in New York City, Oct. 19, 1958.

MEL OTT, 49, N.Y. Giants outfielder, set National League record of 511 home runs; in New Orleans, Nov. 15, 1958.

POPE PIUS XII, 82, in Castel Gandolfo, Italy, Oct. 9, 1958 *(see pages 122-123).*

TYRONE POWER, 44, actor *(Blood and Sand, Witness for the Prosecution);* in Madrid, Spain, Nov. 15, 1958.

DONALD QUARLES, 64, Defense Secretary; in Washington, D.C., May 8 *(see page 22).*

DANIEL REED, 83, senior Republican in Congress from N.Y., chairman of Ways and Means Committeee; in Washington, D.C., Feb. 19.

ROBERT W. SERVICE, 84, poet *(The Shooting of Dan Mc-Grew);* in Lancieux, France, Sept. 11, 1958.

DOROTHY SHAVER, 61, president of Lord and Taylor department store; in Hudson, N.Y., June 28.

TRIS SPEAKER, 70, baseball "immortal;" in Whitney, Texas, Dec. 16, 1958.

ALFRED N. STEELE, 57, board chairman of Pepsi Cola Co., husband of actress Joan Crawford; in New York City, April 19.

DR. ABRAHAM STONE, 68, pioneer in birth control, medical director of Margaret Sanger Research Bureau; in New York City, July 3.

CHARLES VIDOR, 59, motion picture director *(Ladies in Retirement, The Swan);* in Vienna, Austria, June 4.

MAURICE de VLAMINCK, 82, French "fauve" landscape and still-life painter; near Paris, France, Oct. 11, 1958.

SIR HUBERT WILKINS, 70, Australian polar explorer who took first submarine under Arctic ice, 1931; in Framingham, Mass., Dec. 1, 1958.

FRANK LLOYD WRIGHT, 89, architect, in Phoenix, Ariz., April 9 *(see pages 186-187).*

"Before we get started, am I correct in saying that you work for me?" NEWS FRONT

"Well, if you won't give me a raise, I'll be forced to go over your head and pray for one."

"Could you spare the price of coffee and doughnuts, Mister? I lost my Diners' Club card."

CARTOONS

"You're overselling, Martin."

BERNHARDT

"In a way, it's a good thing that crime *doesn't* pay.
If it did, the competition would be terrific."

"Isn't science wonderful! To think we're sitting here tonight in our own living room watching a movie they made 20 years ago!"

"Why can't you be like other men and just devour me with your eyes?"

"You'll recall, Henderson, that when I hired you back in 1923 I warned you that the job might be temporary . . . Well . . ."

"I'm sorry, comrade—but in the confusion of living as one of them and pretending to be spying on us, when actually I'm one of us pretending to be one of them spying on us, I sent my secret report to *their* government."

"Harvey was replaced by a machine that cost only thirty-two dollars and sixteen cents."

"I will now distribute these weapons—your uncle's will leaves his money to his sole survivor."

scheffy

he New York office wants to know what kind of idiot is running this department. What'll I tell them?"

"You're on your own now, dear."

". . . a special news bulletin! Our leading scientists say the earth may explode before midnight. Here are the details . . . after this word from our sponsor."

Special Features

Picture news articles
on significant events
in the year's headlines

100 YEARS OF OIL

PETROLEUM PAGEANT

ON AUGUST 27, 1859, in Titusville, Pa., Edwin L. Drake completed drilling the first U.S. petroleum well, and proved that "Seneca Oil," long esteemed as a liniment and general panacea, could be produced in commercially profitable quantities.

In 1958 the U.S. produced 2.46 billion barrels of petroleum crude, and other nations 4.1 billion, for a global total of 6.56 billion.

The dates span a century which transformed the world.

Petroleum made possible the internal combustion engine, in which the fuel itself expands to create power, cutting to one stage what takes the steam engine two.

It thus made possible the automobile, which revolutionized domestic transportation in every country on earth, and the airplane, which has married the continents and almost abolished physical distance.

And every wheel that turns, in every industry everywhere, is lubricated by a petroleum product.

Oil, in practical terms, is by far the world's most precious single commodity. The search for it, begun 100 years ago in the leafy Pennsylvania hills, today is pressed incessantly in every jungle and forgotten desert across the globe. (Oil alone gave importance to the Middle East, forgotten for two millenia, now a focal point in the struggle between freedom and Communism.)

The oil industry, even in the U.S. where it was born, is thus inescapably international.

Yet it is most appropriate that oil's Centennial be celebrated this year by the U.S. industry, for the "Age of Oil" remains primarily American, just as its predecessor in changing the world, the "Age of Steam" was in essential character British.

In the following pages the editors review the significant highlights of oil's first century.

*Original Drake well (above) at Titusville, Pa., is back-
drop for tophatted Edwin L. Drake (r.) industry pioneer
who failed to make fortune, lived in final years on small
pension from state. In contrast is modern Shell Oil Co.
marine drilling rig (l.) in Gulf of Mexico of Louisiana.
Petroleum search has spread from land to bottom of sea.*

COURTESY OF THE ROAD was important in the dusty 1900s. Oil made the automobile possible, and automobile's insatiable thirst for gasoline in turn created the modern oil industry.

Within 24 hours after Drake had "struck oil," the oil fever had set in. (It has never abated.) Land in the area skyrocketed in value, as it has everywhere since where oil has been discovered.

The early 1860s were studded with petroleum firsts.

On Jan. 22, 1860, Luther Atwood obtained the first patent for "cracking" crude. His process made possible mass production of light illuminating oils, the first large commercial petroleum use. It led, eventually, to the vast petrochemical industry, which alone represents an investment of close to $8 billion, and produces everything from soaps to synthetic rubber.

On Nov. 6, 1860, the new industry's first refinery, which cost $15,000, went into production. (On May 23, 1957, the Tidewater Oil Co.'s new Delaware refinery, the largest ever built as a unit, was officially dedicated. It cost $200 million.)

On May 12, 1861, Pennsylvania's first "deep" well started flowing at a depth of 450 feet. (The deepest modern well, in Louisiana, currently is producing oil at a depth of 21,500 feet, or four miles.)

On Jan. 7, 1865, a well was brought in on Pithole Creek after it had been located by hazel twig "dowsing." (Today's oil industry uses every available scientific method to find new fields. Principal tools are the seismograph, which measures vibrations reflected by a subterranean explosion, the gravimeter, which measures minute differences in gravity's pull, and the magnetometer, which records variations in the earth's magnetic field.)

The new well led to the overnight rise of Pithole City, which by September had 15,000 people, 50 hotels—and hundreds of saloons. But by January, 1866, after the new local wells had run dry, it was an empty ghost town.

1865 also saw completion of the first successful pipeline, which ran five miles to Pithole from the Miller Farm producing area. (The U.S. today has close to 200,000 miles of pipelines, not much below the railroad mileage.)

The same year produced the first oil millionaire, James Farr, who sold his interest in a 200-acre farm for the equivalent of $5 million in gold and an estimated $1 million annually in royalties.

On Sept. 12, 1866, the first well in Texas was brought in. (On Jan. 10, 1901, the great Spindletop gusher, which ushered in the era of Texas predominance and scientific oil production, roared in with an initial flow of 100,000 barrels per day.)

And, in the 1860s, John D. Rockefeller entered the oil business.

He needed adequate supplies to insure continuous operation of his refinery, and ample markets in which to sell its products. The new Standard Oil Co. expanded horizontally and vertically. In 1882, when he and his partners formed a trust agreement, they controlled 40 companies in every phase of the oil industry.

The Standard companies pioneered in improving production, in developing new products, in distribution and marketing, in lowering prices. They brought a measure of order into what had been economic chaos.

But the price, for many rivals, was high. Some survived as independents, and still are thriving. Some merged, willingly or not, with Standard. Others were forced out of business.

Meanwhile production was spreading across the nation. After Pennsylvania came West Virginia, New York, Ohio, Kentucky, Texas, Indiana, Illinois, in 1875 California, in 1892 Kansas. Then came Oklahoma, Louisiana, Arkansas, New Mexico, Mississippi, Nebraska, Wyoming, Alabama, Alaska, the Dakotas, 30 states in all.

For many decades, kerosene and similar illuminating gases were the major commercial petroleum products. Gasoline, which formed as much as one-fourth of crude, was almost worthless. Often it was just thrown away.

Then came the automobile.

In 1892 Charles E. Duryea built the first U.S. car. Auto sales were under 5000 in 1900, 181,000 in 1910, 895,000 in 1915, 1.9 million in 1920, 6.6 million in 1950.

Today, there are more than 67 million cars, trucks and buses registered in the U.S.

The automobile was prince, gasoline Cinderella.

The problem was not how to get rid of gasoline, but how to produce more, and more, and more.

In 1913 science came to the rescue. William M. Burton patented the thermal cracking process, which broke up the heavier elements of the crude into lighter, smaller gasoline molecules.

The gasoline thus obtained was not only greater in quantity than that produced by the old fractional distillation method, which sorted out the crude's components without changing them, but far superior in quality. A further improvement was catalytic cracking, which dispensed with thermal's high pressures, and produced even more gasoline.

Another major scientific advance was polymerization, which, the exact opposite of cracking, builds big molecules, practically to order, out of small ones. The two together have made possible such petrochemical marvels as orlon, dacron, fiberglass, the synthetic rubbers (now two-thirds of all new rubber used in industry), plastics, inks, waxes, medicines, and thousands more, including lipstick and rouge.

The basis of the present pattern of industry organization had, meanwhile, been established. The dominating Rockefeller interests earlier had been reorganized into a number of companies headed by the Standard Oil Co. (N.J.). The government in 1906 brought suit against the latter under the Sherman Act, forcing it, after years in the courts, to divest itself of control of 33 operating companies. These became vigorous competitors, some retaining the Standard name, some discarding it.

In 1935 Congress approved the Interstate Oil Compact

LUCAS GUSHER at Spindletop, greatest to date, ushered in 1901, era of Texas oil predominance, with flow of 100,000 barrels per day. First Wright airplane flight (l.) Dec. 17, 1903, was an even more significant augury of future of oil industry and the entire world.

KIEFER, OKLA., (below) typified boom towns which grew overnight when oil fever set in. First one, Pithole City, Pa., mushroomed and died within a single year—1865.

Commission to "conserve oil and gas by the prevention of physical waste."

On Aug. 15, 1945, the day Japan surrendered, Louisiana granted the first off-shore lease. More than $1.5 billion dollars now are invested in more than 5 million acres of ocean bottom.

U.S. oil today is 42,000 companies directly employing 1.7 million persons, and indirectly making work for millions more.

It is, above all, daily production of 7.5 million barrels of the industrial lifeblood of the U.S.

WORLD OIL PRODUCTION 1957 and 1956

MILLIONS OF METRIC TONS—7.5 BARRELS TO TON

WESTERN HEMISPHERE			EASTERN HEMISPHERE			
	1957	1956			1957	1956
U.S.A.			MIDDLE EAST			
Crude Oil	346·4	347·1	Bahrein		1·6	1·5
Natural Gasoline	34·0	33·4	Iran		34·9	26·2
			Iraq			
Total	380·4	380·5	Kirkuk/Mosul	12·2		
			Basrah	9·1		
CARIBBEAN			Khanaquin	0·2		
Venezuela	141·5	125·6			21·5	30·8
Colombia	6·4	6·2	Kuwait		56·4	54·1
Trinidad	4·9	4·1	Neutral Zone		3·4	1·7
			Qatar		6·5	5·8
Total	152·8	135·9	Saudi Arabia		48·1	47·9
CANADA	24·1	22·8	Total		172·4	168·0
MEXICO	12·4	12·9	WESTERN EUROPE		12·2	10·4
ARGENTINA	4·8	4·3	EAST INDIES		20·7	18·6
PERU	2·5	2·4	U.S.S.R.	98·0		
OTHERS	2·8	1·9	EASTERN EUROPE, ETC.	12·8		
					110·8	97·0
			OTHERS		3·4	3·0
TOTAL WESTERN HEMISPHERE	579·8	560·7	TOTAL EASTERN HEMISPHERE		319·5	297·0
TOTAL WORLD 1957 — 899·3						
TOTAL WORLD 1956 — 857·7						

MAJOR AREAS AS A PERCENTAGE OF WORLD TOTAL PRODUCTION IN 1957

WESTERN HEMISPHERE	PERCENTAGE
U.S.A.	42%
Caribbean	17%
Canada	3%
Other West	3%
TOTAL WESTERN HEMISPHERE	65%

EASTERN HEMISPHERE	PERCENTAGE
Middle East	19%
East Indies	2%
Other East	2%
U.S.S.R., etc.	12%
TOTAL EASTERN HEMISPHERE	35%

WORLD OIL CONSUMPTION 1957 and 1956

(Crude Oil Equivalent)

MILLIONS OF METRIC TONS—7.5 BARRELS TO TON			1957 SHARE OF TOTAL
	1957	1956	
U.S.A.	425	425	48%
Canada	39	36	4%
Mexico	13	12	2%
Caribbean	18	17	2%
Other West	45	41	5%
TOTAL WESTERN HEMISPHERE	540	531	61%
Western Europe	136	136	15%
Africa	28	27	3%
Middle East	19	17	2%
East Indies	6	5	1%
Australasia	11	10	1%
Other East	38*	33	5%
Eastern Hemisphere, excl. U.S.S.R., etc.	238	228	27%
U.S.S.R., etc.	105	92	12%
TOTAL EASTERN HEMISPHERE	343	320	39%
WORLD, EXCL. U.S.S.R., ETC.	778	759	88%
WORLD	883	851	100%

* Includes unascertainable stock change.

U.S. FLAG tankers formed only 16% of world tanker tonnage in 1957, but U.S. oil industry used 25% of total. New U.S. tankers are 30,000-ton.

RAIL transport still is important to industry, although percentage carried has not kept pace with output rise. Tank cars number 140,000.

BRITISH PETROLEUM CO. scientist uses gravimeter in search for oil in Libya, North Africa.

While U.S. is largest single producer, rest of world in 1958 produced some 4.1 billion barrels.

217

4-POINT PLANS FIGHT DOWNTOWN DECAY

Many of the nation's downtowns are dying. If they do, urban experts agree, the entire urban areas of which they form the centers will be blighted, too. The problem is pressing, not only for such vast complexes as New York and Los Angeles but for most of the medium-sized cities. Is there any cure?

"IF DETROIT were obliterated, surrounding towns would be hard put to exist. They would never be healthy until Detroit was rebuilt and repopulated."

These words of Walter S. Schmidt, white-haired dean of U.S. urban planners, sum up what every metropolitan area in the nation is learning.

That is that the economic health and growth of the entire urban complex, including the remotest suburbs and "exurbs," depend on the survival and prosperity of its hard core, its historic "downtown" section.

Dry rot downtown, manifested in building obsolescence, traffic strangulation and declining revenues, sooner or later must spread to the farthest periphery.

To combat it, and rehabilitate the vital core districts, the country's major metropolitan areas have embarked on programs costing, altogether, many billions of dollars.

PITTSBURGH'S "GOLDEN TRIANGLE" where Ohio is born from confluence of Allegheny, Monongahela rivers, today *(l.)* looks like this after expenditure of $3 billion on rebuilding of area. In 1939, district, site of ancient Fort Pitt, established by British in 1758 after expulsion of French, was blighted dead end *(c.)*. Artist's conception *(r.)* shows triangle with new arterial bridges scheduled for completion in 1961. Area's rehabilitation actually increased traffic congestion.

219

Los Angeles, Detroit, Baltimore programs among largest

While plans vary from city to city, and from a few thousand dollars allocated for a parking study to Pittsburgh's multi-billion-dollar rehabilitation of its "Golden Triangle," almost all have four essentials.

They are 1) ample provision for free traffic circulation and access to the area, 2) ample provision for parking, whether in open spaces, garages or underground, 3) coordinated use of the entire area and 4) return of part of the area to desirable housing use.

Representative of large-scale plans is Los Angeles' $339 million Bunker Hill Project, designed to revitalize 135 acres in the heart of the city between the civic center and the retail district.

It will be financed by $74 million from the Federal Government (a $59 million loan and a $15 million grant), $15 million raised by the city through tax allocation bonds and $250 million from private investors.

What Bunker Hill will be worth to Los Angeles can be judged from the expected return in one field alone, taxes.

In the fiscal year 1957-58 the entire tax revenue from the area was only $94,210 while the cost of city services supplied it was $298,624, a net loss of $204,414.

When the project is completed, the Los Angeles Com-

URBAN LAND INSTITUTE panel tours downtown tunnel of St. Louis' Terminal Railroad to check possible use for commuter trains. New rapid transit facilities are said to be possible solution for problems caused by downtown auto congestion.

munity Redevelopment Agency predicts, the annual tax return will be $4.4 million, 46 times the present yield.

Bunker Hill will meet all four of the requisites by offering unhindered access to and from the nearby freeway outlets; parking space for 4000 and, eventually, 20,000 additional cars; light, airy, planned space for retail trade and offices; and a residential development which will give Angelenos the opportunity, previously almost mythical, to walk to work.

Backstopping downtown rehabilitation throughout the country is the Urban Land Institute, of Washington, D.C., a non-profit body whose experts are on call to help every metropolitan area set up a workable program.

An Institute survey and program for revitalizing downtown Detroit, while still largely in the planning stage, already is making itself felt in real estate values—and tax assessments. Harry V. Wade, until recently editor of the *Detroit News*, reported:

"Downtown building owners already are moaning over boosts' in assessments of their property.

"We feel for them, but after all, that is what we set out to do.

The plan includes $16.1 million for increased parking facilities and, of this, $4 million for an underground garage which can house 1050 cars already has been approved.

What deterioration costs in concrete cases is revealed by an Institute survey of downtown Peoria, Ill. It showed that lack of space for retail stores, including lack of adequate parking facilities, was costing merchants $25 million a year in lost business, residents 1500 jobs and the city $200,000 annually in taxes.

Elimination of auto-caused congestion, by increasing parking space, by rerouting traffic or, most drastically of all, by barring cars from the core areas, is at the heart of most plans.

LOS ANGELES' Bunker Hill Project will occupy decaying area outlined in photo. The existing huddle of obsolescent buildings will be replaced by uncluttered area of new office buildings and many light, airy modern apartment houses.

DETROIT'S new Convention Hall (above) will, when completed, form focus of rehabilitation of city's historic lakefront area. Spearhead of the program, which includes $16 million for new parking, is the Detroit Tomorrow Committee.

MAKING DOWNTOWNS attractive to their largest group of users, office girls, is part of problem. Houston planners (below) offer free assistance in making out income tax returns. Other inducements include lunch hour fashion shows.

Seattle intends to add room for 2640 more cars (plus walk-to-work housing) and Abilene, Texas, room for 1750. Trenton, N. J., and the Kansas City area plan through traffic loops around the revitalized downtown districts. Grand Rapids, Mich., plans new through expressways to ease traffic pressure, and Pittsburgh two new bridges to increase access to and exit from its "Golden Triangle." Houston will reorganize all traffic.

Fort Worth, Texas, congested by the daily downtown visits of 75,000 cars—a number expected to double within a decade unless something is done about it—is considering banning all autos, and building pedestrian malls to replace existing streets.

New parking facilities are a vital part of Baltimore's $127 million Charles Center project, under which all but five buildings in 22 downtown acres are being razed. They will be replaced by, in addition to huge parking spaces, a transport terminal, a hotel, eight office buildings and three public parks. The project, when completed, will add $2 million to Baltimore's tax income.

Suitable industrial facilities, the Urban Land Institute insists, must be included in most plans if they are to attain their objective, since railroad terminals usually are in downtown areas.

Best way to do this, the Institute believes, is integration of industrial parks.

And plans must be integrated and comprehensive, experts agree. In discussing the future of downtown Dallas, which faces problems similar to most other centers, W. W. Overton, Jr., chairman of the Texas Bank and Trust Co., stated:

"No longer can cities afford to correct mistakes made by individuals because of lack of planning."

Abilene's city manager, Henry D. Nabers summed up the over-all situation this way: "A city as a whole can be no better than its downtown area."

BANNING OF CARS is one drastic solution to automobile congestion. Artist's conception shows Fort Worth street transformed into shopping mall. Pedestrian bridge overhead connects hotel on right with multi-story parking garage.

DEFENSE

THREE times in a six-month period the U.S. Armed Forces have shown that they can "get there fustest."

In May, 1958, within 14 hours of Pres. Eisenhower's decision to extend armed protection, if needed, to Vice President Nixon during the final stage of his South American tour, the Air Force had acted. It had flown 498 paratroopers with full equipment to Caribbean bases close to mob-threatened Caracas, Venezuela.

In July, on the very day the U.S. announced it was sending troops to Lebanon at the request of then President Camille Chamoun, a Composite Air Strike Force flew to Adana, Turkey, to back up Marines landing south of Beirut.

In August, when the Chinese Communist bombardment of Quemoy and its tiny neighbors seemed to presage an attempt to invade Formosa, another Composite Air Strike Force was flown across the Pacific to the Nationalist stronghold.

But inability to complete Confederate Gen. Nathan Bedford Forrest's strategic formula, to get there by air not only "fustest" but "with the mostest" is perhaps the gravest of current U.S. military weaknesses.

The force flown to the Caribbean by the 314th and 63rd Troop Carrier Wings at the time of the Nixon incident was intended—and strong enough—merely for police action.

The Composite Air Strike Force which flew to Adana was drawn from troops in Germany, not from Tactical Air Command units in the U.S. which had received special "brush-fire" training for just such eventualities.

U.S. today could fly only one division to danger area

HOW MUCH AIRLIFT?

The reason, it was reported at the time, was that enough airlift was not available in the U.S. —and thus the risk of temporarily weakening West Europe NATO forces had to be taken.

The Formosa flight was but the spearhead of a still continuing Formosa buildup and, like the Adana venture, was primarily important to show U.S. will and military capability.

Gen. O. P. Weyland, chief of the Tactical Air Command, recently stated that "we are unable to transport and air support a force of much more than division size on a single lift."

The *Army Information Digest* said:

"The U.S. *should* be able to airlift a decisive limited war force to any place in the world in four or five days . . .

"But there is an alarming lack of modernization in our troop-and-supply-carrying air fleet."

COMBAT INFANTRY deploy at top speed from Army helicopter. Troops are action-ready, but could enough be flown in time to danger point?

OBSOLETE PLANES CHIEF WEAKNESS

The first full bitter cost of airlift inadequacy was paid by Great Britain and France, not the U.S.

Had the island-hopping Mediterranean airlift which brought their forces to Suez in the fall of 1956 been completed even one day faster, most experts believe, the entire Canal area would have been occupied and Egypt's President Nasser toppled before the UN, prodded by the Soviet Union and the U.S., could have intervened.

But, for lack of transport planes, the Allied troops were late, the two nations were forced to beat an ignominious retreat—and Soviet prestige in the Middle East soared at the expense of the West.

Suez emphasized what was first demonstrated in Korea, when the airlines and commercial charter companies were pressed into service with the Military Air Transport Service to do the airlift job with planes which, mostly, were neither designed nor suited for it. As Donald Douglas, Jr., president of the Douglas Aircraft Co., recently pointed out, Korea was a lesson in the lack of proper airlift preparedness.

An airborne division contains 11,486 men; to move it, with supplies and equipment, means airlifting 7000 tons. (A standard infantry division has 13,748 men, with more—and heavier—equipment.) By the 10-tons-per-plane estimate used as a working rule of thumb, 700 planes would be needed to airlift an airborne division.

To meet an airlift emergency, the Armed Forces can call immediately upon some 1725 planes, more than two-and-one-half times, on paper, the number needed for a division lift.

But many of these, including the 368 airliners of the Civil Reserve Air Fleet, are primarily passenger planes, although the greater need is for cargo capacity. Besides, abruptly pulling airliners out of civilian service would cripple vital domestic schedules.

The 600 planes of the Air Force Reserve, manned by "weekend warrior" crews, are slow C-119 transports with only three tons capacity.

Out of the 1725 available planes, less than 200 are jet-prop powered, the rest have piston engines.

Ideal for transporting the streamlined "pentomic" division are the Lockheed Hercules C-130 and the Douglas Cargomaster C-133, both turbine-powered (jet-prop) aircraft.

The C-130 can carry 92% of the different items needed by an airborne division—and carry them 4000 miles without refueling.

The Tactical Air Command estimates it can load 12-and-one-half tons into each C-130 for deployment to Europe or Africa, and seven-and-one-half for a Far East flight. (More space is needed for fuel.)

But the Air Force has only about 160 C-130s (96 in TAC), and to support for a month a Composite Air Strike Force Wing would require continuous use of 49. Sustaining a division would require some 150.

The Douglas Cargomaster C-133 has a capacity of almost 50 tons, but the Air Force has only a handful.

Why is U.S. airlift capacity low?

Primarily, because defense emphasis has been placed on nuclear deterrent rather than tactical potential, on a "bigger bang for a buck."

Airlift, in comparison with such more "glamorous" and publicized military activities as the Strategic Air Command and missile development, has received very low budget priority.

But there is another problem; just how much airlift is enough? How many "brushfire" crises will erupt on the Free World periphery, and how far will they be from the continental U.S.? Will two or more occur at the same time?

Should the U.S. develop, now, airlift capacity for a full-scale, multifront global war?

There is, industry and the military agree, no perfect solution.

PISTON-POWERED Douglas Globemaster, with 36-ton carrying capacity, remains U.S. airlift backbone. Some 300 are still in service, but plane is too slow by jet standards.

FUJIYAMA forms backdrop for globe-ranging Lockheed turboprop Hercules, most modern transport now in mass use by United States forces.

DOUGLAS TURBOPROP CARGOMASTER has same 4000-mile range as Hercules, almost 50-ton carrying capacity. But Air Force has only a few on hand or on order. Major airlift need is more turboprops, which fly faster, land in less space, than piston planes.

U.S. MILITARY AIRLIFT PLANES

COMPANY	TYPE	Pounds	CAPACITY Cu. Ft.	Troops	CRUISING SPEED	RANGE (non-refuel)
Lockheed	Hercules Turboprop C-130	36,900- 40,000	4,300	92	370 mph	4000 m. (max. range) 1750 m. (max. payload)
Lockheed	Constellation C-121 or R7V	40,000	5,500	58-94	334 mph	4447 m. (max. range) 2837 m. (max. payload)
Douglas	Cargomaster Turboprop C-133	41,700- 95,000	13,500	....	315 mph	4000 m. (max. range) 1750 m. (max. payload)
Douglas	Globemaster C-124	74,000	....	200	250 mph	4000 m.
Douglas	Liftmaster C-118 or DC-6	....	....	54-89	315 mph	5000 m.
Douglas	C-54, R5D5 or DC-4	6,300- 13,000	....	50	177 mph	2415 m. (max. range) 1150 m. (max. payload)
Douglas	C-47, R4D7 or DC-3	7,500	....	21-30	167 mph	2200 m. (max. range) 1440 m. (max. payload)
Stroukoff Aircraft Co.	Assault Transport YC-134	30,000	....	....	250 mph	4750 m. (max. range) 600 m. (max. payload)
Boeing	KC-135	....	6,660	....	over 600 mph	4000 m.
Boeing	Stratocruiser C-97	....	....	130	over 300 mph	4300 m.
Convair Div. General Dynamics	C-131	....	....	48	200 mph	2150 m.
Fairchild	Provider C-123B	16,000- 18,000	....	60	186 mph	3450 m. (max. range) 1150 m. (max. payload)
Fairchild	C-119	6,850	3,150	62	175 mph	3480 m.

SOVIET MILITARY AIRLIFT PLANES (all Jet, Jet Prop)

Government	TU-104A TJ	....	....	70	445 knots	2200 m.
Government	TU-110 TJ	....	....	100	445 knots	2500 m.
Government	Ukrainia TP	50,000	....	....	350 knots	2850 m.
Government	TU-114 TP	110,000	....	170	400 knots	4500 m.
Government	AN-4 TP	30,000	....	....	300 knots	2250 m.
Government	IL-18 TP	30,000	....	....	350 knots	1750 m.

But the most practicable approach the experts also agree lies in combining modernization with flexibility and capacity for rapid expansion.

Douglas engineers assert that a fleet of 107 turboprops (such as the C-133) could, with more efficiency and economy, replace the entire present MATS fleet.

Dr. Allen R. Ferguson, research director of Northwestern University Transportation Center, proposes that the Air Force lease, not buy, its turbine-powered transports.

He claims that this would greatly increase flexibility, and that "it should be possible to compute a rental less than the cost of operating the existing (MATS) piston fleet and still be enough to provide an adequate return for the lessors."

For actual combat conditions, the Stroukoff Aircraft Co. is developing an attack transport, the YC-134, which can land "almost anywhere." But it is still experimental.

Not only is flying troops abroad to trouble spots, as needed, cheaper than permanent garrisons, but world developments are making it more desirable. A leading authority writes:

"It is only a matter of time before we will find it better diplomacy to bring our troops home from West Germany, Italy and South Korea than to leave them there. The ideal arrangement would be to have only token forces abroad and the bulk ready to fly in at short notice."

But as Maj. Gen. Robert F. Sink, commander of the 18th Corps (Airborne), stated recently:

"If we don't have the means of getting transportation . . . why, Hell, we stay at home."

IDEAL FOR USE in combat airlift would be STOL (Short Takeoff and Landing) planes shown as conceived by an Air Force artist. But they are still on the drawing board. Essential practical step is full conversion to turboprops.

SIGNIFICANT AIRLIFTS

1948-9	Berlin Airlift
1950-2	Korean War support
1953	Arabs to Mecca
1954	Medicine to India
1954	Indo-China war
1955-6	DEW Line Construction
1956	British and French airlifted troops to attack Suez
1956	U.N. troops airlifted to maintain peace
1956	Hungarian refugees
1957-8	South Pole and Antarctic I.G.Y.
1958	Caribbean airlift for Nixon safety
1958	Lebanon landings
1958	Formosa

AVAILABLE U. S. AIRLIFT
(unofficial estimates)

COMMAND	TOTAL PLANES AVAILABLE
Tactical Air Command (TAC)	240 (96 C-130s, 96 C-123s, 48 C-119s)
Military Air Transport Service (MATS)	417 (various types)
Strategic Air Command (SAC)	100 (C-130s, KC-135s, others)
Air Force Reserve	600 (all C-119s)
Civil Reserve Air Fleet (Civil Airliners)	368 (all four-engine airlines)
TOTAL	1725

ARMY'S GLOBAL DEPLOYMENT INCLUDES MILITARY ASSISTANCE ADVISORY GROUPS AND MISSIONS IN SOME 75 COUNTRIES

FREEDOM'S FRONT

Combat-ready U.S. Army majo

how to expand in all-out emergency sti

W E STILL need an army.
Mass air (or missile) delivery of conventional destructive power is not, despite the arguments of air theorists from Billy Mitchell and the Italian Giulio Douhet to the present, sufficient to bring about a favorable decision, even the negative one of successful defense.

To cite but two examples, German

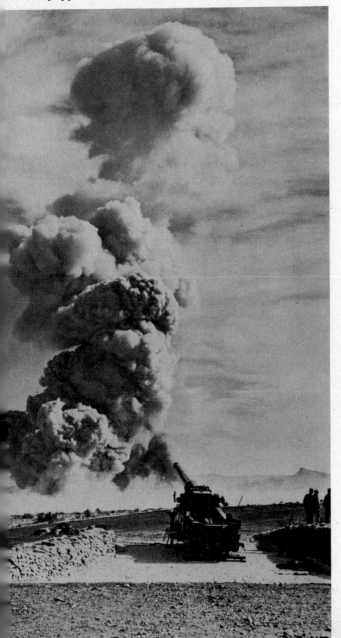

ARMY TANKS *(above)*, rushed by air to Lebanon, mass on Beirut Airfield in demonstration of U.S. ability, readiness to come to instant support of ally. Mushroom cloud *(below)* from first atomic shell fired by cannon ushered in new artillery era. All of the major Army combat forces now are equipped to make use of tactical nuclear weapons.

THE ARMY'S MISSILE FAMILY

Intermediate Range Ballistic Missiles

JUPITER, liquid propellant, now in production. Jupiter furnished the basic thrust for the EXPLORER satellites, three of which were placed in orbit, and the PIONEER III Space Probe, which penetrated space 65,000 miles.

Surface-to-Air

NIKE AJAX, liquid propellant, solid fuel booster rockets. At present main air defense of continental U.S. Characteristics classified, but performance has exceeded expectations. Areas protected by Ajax include:

> Cleveland; Fairfield, Calif.; Hanford, Wash.; Hartford-Bridgeport, Conn.; Limestone, Me.; Milwaukee; Buffalo, N. Y.; Norfolk, Va.; Providence; Rapid City, S. D.; San Francisco; Seattle; Spokane.

NIKE HERCULES, similar to AJAX, which it is augmenting, but with greater speed and range. Can carry atomic warhead. Areas protected include:

> Boston; Chicago; Detroit; Los Angeles; New York; Philadelphia; Pittsburgh; Washington-Baltimore.
> HERCULES sites are on the construction schedule for: Cincinnati; Dallas; Fort Worth; Kansas City; St. Louis; Minneapolis-St. Paul.

NIKE installations eventually will be controlled throughout the U.S. by the MISSILE MASTER coordinating electronic control system. The first installation is in operation in the Washington-Baltimore area. The second is scheduled to become operational in New York.

NIKE ZEUS, anti-missile missile and third "generation" of NIKE "family." Being developed under high priority.

PLATO, anti-missile missile in early development.

VIGILANTE, classified, in early development.

HAWK, solid propellant. "Bullet with a brain" for use against low-flying aircraft. Under test.

Surface-to-Surface

REDSTONE, liquid propellant, 200-mile range. Became operational in 1958. Atomic or high explosive warhead.

PERSHING, solid propellant. Smaller size and weight give it greater mobility than REDSTONE, which it will replace.

CORPORAL, liquid propellant. 75-mile range. Operational. Atomic or HE warhead.

SERGEANT, solid propellant. Will replace CORPORAL. Can be transported by air.

LACROSSE, solid propellant. Truck-mounted close and general support weapon.

HONEST JOHN, solid propellant. Free flight, mounted on truck transporter-launcher. Atomic or HE warhead, range equivalent to that of long-range artillery. Operational.

LITTLE JOHN, solid propellant. Free flight, HONEST JOHN's "little brother." Range equivalent to that of medium-range artillery. Can be transported by air. In production.

DART, solid propellant. Anti-tank missile designed to penetrate heaviest armor.

ARMY

Training level in both groups is high, with National Guard training attendance in 1958 95% for officers and 88% for enlisted men, and reserve unit attendance 87% for officers and 76% for enlisted men.

But the National Guard and the Organized Reserve are not, by themselves, the answer to the problem of obtaining sufficient manpower.

They form, in numbers, a strictly limited resource.

And, as the last relics of state and local military autonomy, Guard units are inextricably enmeshed in politics. By their very nature they must resist —if in the long run unsuccessfully— Army efforts to increase its control of them in the interests of greater military efficiency.

(The Guard's size, particularly the number and distribution of units, is a burning issue in the present Congress, as in most earlier.)

As has become more and more apparent since the Napoleonic Wars introduced mass armies, only some form of conscription can supply the men needed.

But, in the present U.S., military service by all fit young men is militarily unnecessary, socially undesirable and politically impossible.

How, then, fairly and equitably, can some be called up while the majority escape the burden?

The Army's best brains are attempting to work out the answer.

Meanwhile, at the Defense Department's request, Congress has extended the present Selective Service System for four more years.

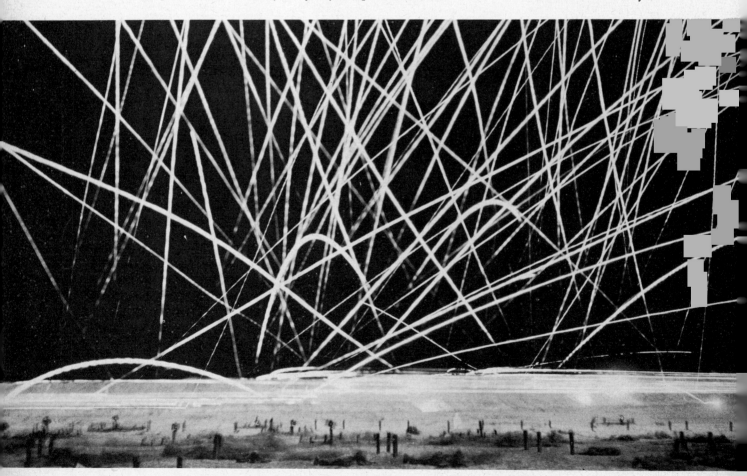

UNFLAGGING training, such as rifle practice *(above)*, produces crack paratrooper *(r.)* striding confidently from drop zone in Salerno, Italy, with full equipment after successful drop. Modern U.S. soldier must be ready to use any weapon, fight any kind of war.

VIVID PATTERN is etched in night sky by tracer bullets *(l.)* at Signal Corps training center in Georgia. 1st Lieut. Newman A. Howard *(above)* commands Non-commissioned Officers Leaders School at Ft. Belvoir, Va., Engineer Center. Trained NCOs, in modern era, are essential "backbone of the Army."

PAST-60 VOTE COULD SWING 1960 ELECTION

Senior citizens form over one-fifth of voters

*1960 over-60 group will total 23 million,
13% of population, 21% of potential voters.
1956 Eisenhower margin was only 15.4%.*

GRANDFATHER of aid to aged is Dr. Francis Townsend *(far l.)*, who at 92 still is vigorous fighter for pensions. Republican drive for "senior" votes is spearheaded by Mrs. Clare B. Williams. Democratic efforts are led by Sen. Pat McNamara *(at l. c.)* and Rep. Aime J. Forand of Pawtucket, R.I.

VOTERS OVER 60 will have the power to elect the next President of the U.S.

In 1960, according to the Census Bureau, persons 60 and over will number approximately 23 million.

That will be 13% of the entire estimated population of 178.5 million.

It will also be 21% of the estimated over-21 voting population of 108 million.

Most important of all, it will be 36% of the approximately 63 million who can be expected to cast ballots if the same proportion of voters turn out as in 1956. Then, the total Presidential vote was 61.1 million.

Of these, 35.6 million, 57.3%, voted for President Eisenhower, and 26 million, 41.9%, for Adlai Stev-

both parties court their support

enson. The difference was 9.5 million, 15.4% of the total.

In the 1958 election, with only seats in the House and Senate at stake, the total dropped to 45.8 million, and the percentages were almost exactly reversed. The Democrats obtained 25.7 million, 56.4%, and the Republicans 19.7 million, 43.2%.

Although reliable analyses of the senior vote do not exist, experts of both parties believe it went overwhelmingly for President Eisenhower in 1958, and switched to the Democrats—or stayed home—last year.

The Republican National Committee has given Mrs. Clare B. Williams of Florida, assistant chairman for women's affairs, the job of wooing older voters. One of her assignments is to set up a network of "Senior Republican Clubs," under a Senior State Chairman, in each state.

Republican courtship of the oldsters also will be helped by the Federal Council for the Aged set up by President Eisenhower, which is scheduled to report in the coming months, and by the National Advisory Council, which will help organize the White House Conference on Aging.

Control of both houses of Congress places the Democrats in a strategic position to attract senior voters.

Rep. Aime J. Forand (D-R.I.) has introduced a bill to extend health insurance coverage to all persons eligible for social security payments. (43%, according to the Department of Health, Education and Welfare, now have voluntary health insurance.)

It would pay all hospital, surgical and convalescent expenses, and would be financed by an addition of onefourth of 1% to social security taxes.

Supporters include the AFL-CIO and opponents the powerful American Medical Association.

Sen. Pat McNamara (D-Mich.) heads a special Senate subcommittee on Problems of the Aged and Aging, and soon will begin hearings.

Still another version of the Townsend Plan, which would pay "senior citizens" $200 monthly, is before Congress. Its champion, 92-year-old Dr. Francis Townsend, has been urging it since the early 1930s.

Politicians, at least, cannot be charged with neglecting the aged.

235

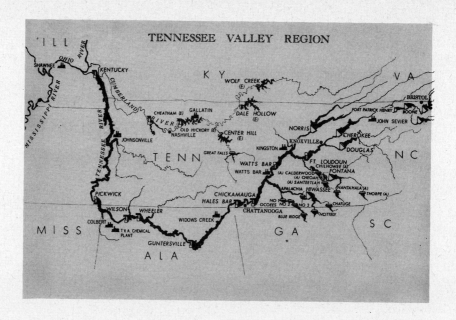

After 25 years gigantic project's power activities are still subject of controversy. But transformation of backward region, creating mammoth recreation area, flood control and farm services are assets to all U.S.

TVA

Should the 25-year-old, $2.1 billion Tennessee Valley Authority, already the nation's largest single electric power producer, be permitted to sell revenue bonds to expand production further?

Legislation giving it limited authority to do so was finally adopted by Congress after rejection in previous sessions.

President Eisenhower, who is known to sympathize with private utility and other critics who hold that TVA is unfair competition, signed the bill. But he did so only after receiving assurances from Congressional leaders that TVA's new powers would not diminish Executive authority over its operations.

TVA champions insist that power capacity, already over 10 million kws (more than all of France), must be increased at least 10% annually merely to keep pace with existing demand.

They claim that TVA's tax-free net income ($55 million in fiscal 1958 less $10 million paid the Treasury "on the assumption that funds necessary for increased generating

capacity would be available through revenue bond financing") is nowhere near sufficient.

Critics complain that its tax-free status enables it to charge only 1.2 cents per kwh for power, compared to the national average of 2.6 cents, thus subsidizing unfair competition with privately owned utilities.

TVA advocates assert this rate serves as a "yardstick" keeping down consumer costs throughout the country. They add that cheap TVA power—plus other Authority activities—has transformed a once impoverished and diseased backwater into an area internationally famous as a demonstration of the potential of the "American Way," and thus a major Cold War asset.

There are two aspects of TVA power undreamed of when the Authority came into official existence in 1933.

It was planned primarily as a great hydro-electric system (as late as 1950, 90% of its output came from power dams). But today more than 75% of its power comes from steam generators. It is the nation's largest coal buyer, with purchases averaging $80 million annually, and

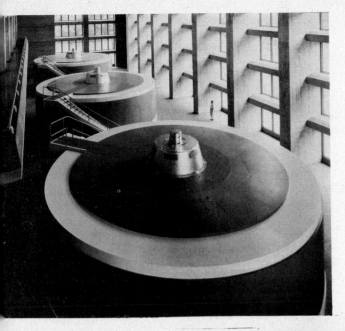

EACH ONE of these huge water driven generators at Fontana Dam, N. C., has capacity of 67,500 kw. But hydro-electric power now supplies only one-fourth of the TVA output. The remainder of it comes from coal-burning generators.

"BRAINS" of entire TVA power system is mammoth dispatching board at Chattanooga, Tenn. Operators have at their fingertips combined output of 31 dams, seven steam plants.

must use helicopters to inventory stockpiles.

And its biggest single customer is, not the farms, homes and factories of the area, but the Atomic Energy Commission, which uses more than half TVA's output.

A secondary TVA activity, but one with an impact on all U.S. farming, is its fertilizer program. It, for example, pioneered in the production of concentrated superphosphate, of which only 70,000 tons were produced in 1934 by private industry. The 1957 total was more than 1.5 million tons.

TVA policy is to develop a new fertilizer, test it throughout the country, and then, when its value is proved, turn over production to private enterprise. (The Fertilizer Development Center can switch to production of military chemicals in 24 hours.)

Flood control and improvement of navigation were among the primary legislative purposes of TVA, although in practice both are byproducts of the construction of power-producing dams.

Area residents insist that there has been no major flood damage since the system has been in full operation. (In the February, 1957, flood, it is claimed TVA installations averted $66 million damage to Chattanooga.) But critics contend that "almost as much land has been inundated permanently by the reservoirs as would have been flooded occasionally by the most extreme floods."

Ton-miles of freight carried on the improved Tennessee River Waterway have multiplied more than 60 times, from 33 million in 1933 to 2.1 billion in 1957. But much of this is coal for the TVA itself.

Economically, as well as politically, TVA probably will remain a subject of controversy.

But physically at least, and in its impact on the inhabitants of its area, TVA's accomplishments seem beyond dispute.

It has raised per capita income, in terms of purchasing power, at least one-third.

It has wiped out malaria, which once infected 25% of the population (60% in some districts).

It is restoring 2.7 million acres of forest.

The magnificent, mountain-girt lakes created by its dams have given the whole nation an outdoor recreation area unparalleled elsewhere. Visitors in 1957 totaled 33 million—plus 2783 foreign visitors who came to study and observe—and the 1958 figure is expected to top 35 million.

State, local and private recreation facilities and equipment—the TVA itself operates none—along the 10,000 miles of lake shore are valued at $72 million. Fishing and boating are the major attractions, and work of TVA biologists not only has helped improve fishing as far away as the Colorado River but given a new lease on life to two traditional local occupations—commercial freshwater fishing and musseling.

Two-thirds of the freshwater shells used by the U.S. button industry come from TVA mussels—as do most of the rare native American pearls.

FISHING is No. 1 TVA attraction, and dam outlets, where record breakers congregate, are favorite spots. TVA forestry *(r.)*, in cooperation with state and local agencies, includes resource analysis and reforestation.

BEFORE *(above)*, after, *(below)* show benefits of TVA's fertilizer program. In only two years wornout acres were producing nutritious forage.

TVA'S WATERWAYS form integral part of national system. Main section stretches 650 miles from Knoxville, Tenn., to Paducah, Ky., where it enters Ohio River. Helicopter *(below)* spreads insecticide. Since 1949 there has been no malaria traceable to TVA-bred mosquitoes.

"In the next 15 years the Soviet Land can not only catch up with but surpass the present volume of production of the most important type of goods of the U.S.A. We are confident that our Soviet people will emerge victorious in this peaceful competition."

That is the boast of Soviet Premier Khrushchev in the poster reproduced on this page.

The poster claims that, using 1913 as the starting point, Soviet production has increased twice as fast as that of the U.S. It lists, in parallel columns, 1957 Soviet output, 1956 U.S. output and anticipated Soviet output in the next 15 years, in such vital areas as steel, oil, electric power and coal.

The second poster (r.) compares alleged Soviet production growth with that not only of the U.S. but of France, Great Britain and West Germany. It claims:

"The Soviet Union already has achieved an economic position in which it can take care of all necessities.

"It now is engaged in catching up to and surpassing the more developed capitalist countries on a per capita basis."

Constantly increased per capita productivity is secret weapon by which the USSR hopes to gain world economic—and eventually political—mastery without war.

Both posters exhort the "Soviet Man" from every factory wall in the whole vast USSR.

WHY SOVIET UNION'S OUTPUT SKYROCKETS

Ceaseless propaganda urges "Beat the U.S."; piecework gears income directly to output; each worker is subjected to unending pressure

SOVIET MANAGEMENT and labor are firmly united in a single purpose — constantly increasing productivity.

Each machine and each worker is under unrelenting pressure to produce more, and more, and more.

That is the basis for Nikita Khrushchev's undoubtedly exaggerated boast to the recent 21st Congress of the Soviet Communist Party that the USSR's per capita output will surpass that of the U.S. by 1970.

It also is the basis for the grim, unquestionable fact that Soviet productivity per worker and total production, while still far behind their U.S. equivalents, are growing far faster.

Soviet Gross National Product (total of all goods and services) is, for instance, estimated to be rising at least 6% annually, compared to a 3% rate of increase in the U.S. Similarly, the USSR is reinvesting about 25% of total annual production in productive plant, as against a U.S. figure of 17%.

In the U.S., where wages far exceed those of the USSR (U.S. industrial average, $87 per *week*; Soviet, roughly $90 per *month*), the prevalent complaint is that a large segment of organized labor resists automation and other means of increasing productivity, acts to keep down output per worker and opposes all efforts to abolish useless jobs and other forms of "feather-bedding."

Soviet management, from Khrushchev down to the

240

POSTER SHOWS QUOTA SYSTEM USED IN EVERY SOVIET FACTORY

shop foreman, seems to have gained the cooperation of Soviet workers in every move to raise productivity.

One means of accomplishing this is, of course, to link pay directly to output. All Soviet industrial workers are paid by the piecework-quota system, anathema to most U.S. unions, but blessed by the USSR's All-Union Central Council of Trade Unions, actually a government department for controlling labor.

But this, which is the application of naked economic force, does not explain the apparently eager participation of the average Soviet worker in the never relaxed drive to raise individual production.

To find out the secret of the chief "secret weapon" in the Red drive for economic world conquest, YEAR's editors consulted two U.S. business leaders just back from extenisve tours of Soviet industry.

They are Lew Shalett, president of the Sheldon-Claire Co., pioneer in the employe-management communications field, and Harold Mansfield, director of public relations of the Boeing Airplane Co.

Shalett, with Soviet permission, visited many major factories, including a tractor plant employing 4000 persons and a machine tool plant employing 1000.

He states that the USSR is "utilizing the largest, most potent propaganda apparatus in the world to build worker morale."

Primary purpose, he pointed out, is to convince each worker that he or she, as an individual, is an important participant in the drive to win what Khrushchev calls the "world-historic victory of socialism in its peaceful competition with capitalism."

This theme is made concrete and competitive, Shalett says, by the unending repetition of one slogan, "beat the U.S. in production." This is blared from every plant loudspeaker, shouted silently from every poster. Shalett states:

"Posters are the basic means of communication. They are put up on the walls of all plants and public buildings. You can actually buy them in poster stores in the big cities. Many people put them up in their homes as we do pictures."

In addition to the posters, Shalett states, Soviet management uses plant public address systems, supervisory letters and a "tremendous amount of personal contact" to keep the workers keyed to the highest possible pitch of productivity.

Plant and shop managers, union officials and local representatives of Agit-Prop, the state propaganda agency, meet weekly to obtain the new government directives, and plan how to carry them out. The "line" is then passed on to the workers in the plant, in public and private meetings, in the very home itself.

To carry out this tremendous job, Shalett adds, Agit-Prop yearly trains 325,000 new field workers.

Mansfield, who described his visit to the USSR in a copyrighted series in *Boeing News*, tells how the incentive system works in one factory:

"You spot a chart on the wall. On it are listed the names of men and women in the shop. After each is a number—the man's 'social obligations' in units of work. Squares are filled in to show his work performance, with a percentage over his quota.

" 'How do you reward them?' you ask the manager.

" 'Extra pay.'

"You find there is more to the system. Another chart with the same layout shows the weekly quota, called the 'plan,' for the shop itself. Chalked in adjoining columns are the shop's actual performance and percentage over plan. The shop's record is compared with other shops. Elsewhere, the record of whole departments is charted, and that of the plant itself compared with the national plan. It is one huge, systematic production competition, man against man, shop against shop, department against department, plant against plant.

"Bonus money is provided for the individuals, shops and departments that make the best record. At the end of the year the plant itself gets a bonus to distribute if it exceeds the plan.

"The incentives in this socialist competition are negative as well as positive.

"Criticism by name in the plant paper, you learn, is only part of the grim process of collective discipline. First step is reprimanding the individual who fails to meet his quota before his friends. A later step, if necessary, is bringing him before public opinion. Removal to a lesser job or, in 'rare cases,' dismissal may follow."

Using both carrot and stick, the USSR is succeeding in increasing substantially individual productivity. Shalett said in summing up his trip:

"Unless we wake up, they are going to beat us.

"They have developed an identity of interest between management and labor. They have shown that arousing the spirit of the workers—inculcating them with a sense of pride in a job well done—produces results."

Mansfield concluded:

"You come back to America, land of the free, to find Americans taking riotous advantage of that freedom. You realize as never before that freedom requires self-discipline. Nothing less can match the discipline of a Communist regime."

EVEN THE CHILDREN are mobilized in USSR's unrelenting drive to make every ounce of materials, every moment of labor, add to industrial output. School poster, brought back by Shalett, proclaims: "Conserve material—20 cars or 160 motorcycles can be made from every ton of metal." U.S. industry makes similar efforts but drive is pallid and feeble in contrast to the all-embracing drive by the Soviets.

AUTOMATION, bugbear of many unions in U.S., Great Britain, elsewhere in West, is welcomed by Soviet Labor organizations. Poster states that "Automation makes labor easier!" Second poster *(far r.)* declares "time is the people's wealth—watch every minute."

"PEACE TO THE WORLD" is proclaimed by stalwart worker in Ukrainian factory poster brought back by Mansfield. Chief propaganda theme is that Communism can win "peaceful" world victory by economic means alone—if every worker in USSR keeps working.

East European industry is pouring consumer goods, industrial equipment and technical know-how — all desperately needed at home — into the Middle East to help the Kremlin win the economic Cold War.

RED SATELLITES DRIVE TO OUST WEST FROM MARKETS OF STRATEGIC MIDDLE EAST

Trade, aid "without strings" make friends for Soviet bloc

Throughout the Middle East, the inscription "Made in Poland"—or Hungary, Czechoslovakia or even Bulgaria—is becoming at least as familiar as "Made in U.S.A."

The Bagdad policeman on a motorcycle, the Syrian grocer telephoning in a brand new telephone booth, the passenger in a modern railway coach traveling from Cairo to Port Said, the Egyptian peasant gaping at his first farm tractor, might not even be able to find the Communist countries on a map—but he is constantly reminded that their industry is helping raise his standard of living.

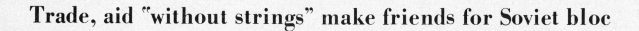

Ships for Mid East go down the ways in Polish shipyards.

Czech-trained workers man Czech-built shoe factory in Egypt.

"USSR" atop Soviet pavilion dominates night sky at Damascus trade fair. Satellites, too, display their wares at Mid Eastern exhibitions

The Soviet satellites' move into Mid Eastern markets, strategically supporting the Soviet Union's own economic offensive, has so far attracted dangerously little attention in the West.

East Europe's nationalized industry is in direct competition throughout the area with long-entrenched Western firms—and its leaders know it.

At a recent Hungarian foreign trade conference, the theme of competition with the West—and especially with the U.S.—was frankly and repeatedly stressed.

Gyula Karadi, Hungary's Deputy Minister of Foreign Trade, hailed the 1958 U.S. recession as having had an "extremely advantageous effect on our trade offensive."

And the representative of the state-owned Beloianis Telephone Company was greeted with roars of applause when he announced that it had broken Bell Telephone's "10-year monopoly of the Syrian market" with a $1.2 million order for telephone switchboards.

The satellites began to penetrate the Middle East when they sought new markets to compensate for dropping raw materials prices and diminishing Free World trade.

Today, however, Cold War economics and psychology —winning customers away from the West and boosting the prestige of the Communist world among the "uncommitted" nations—seem to have taken precedence over the satellites' own real economic interests. Consumer goods and investment capital desperately needed at home are being poured into the Middle East.

Poland, in the midst of a grave economic crisis of her own, is building a sugar factory worth $3.2 million for Iran. Bulgaria, one of the poorest and least industrialized of the satellites, has built several complete factories for Syria. And Hungary, which has one of the worst highway systems in Europe, has raised a 2700-foot bridge—the longest in Africa—at Heluan, near Cairo, for politically temperamental Egypt.

Czechoslovakia, the world's fifth largest exporter of machine tools, has trebled its trade with Egypt over the past five years and increased its trade with Syria 11 times. Bulgaria's trade with both of these United Arab

Republic members has jumped 11 times, and Poland's with Iran is up 25%, since 1955.

The satellites are offering everything from spectacular construction jobs to luxury consumer goods.

They have set up a special organization to coordinate their participation in construction of Egypt's partially Soviet-financed Aswan dam.

The Czechs are building an oil refinery which will process one million tons of oil a year and are laying 42 miles of pipeline in Syria. Entire factories they have shipped and installed in Syria and Egypt include a sugar refinery, a cement plant with an annual capacity of 150,000 tons, a shoe factory, a ceramics factory, a rolling mill and a bicycle factory. The Voice of the Arabs radio in Cairo now issues its denunciations of "imperialism" from two powerful transmitters built and equipped by Czech technicians.

Hungary is exporting machinery, motor vehicles, electric equipment, diesel engines, pumps, tractors and rails to the Middle East. Over $20 million worth of Hungarian locomotives and railway cars are in use in Egypt alone. Hungarian engineers in Egypt are building a power plant at El Tabin and three electronics factories. In five Middle Eastern countries, Hungarian matches are on sale and newly emancipated girls are wearing made-in-Hungary sweaters and lipstick.

Spartak cars from Czechoslovakia, Warsawas from Poland and Ikaros buses from Hungary are familiar sights on the streets of Beirut and Bagdad.

In exchange, the satellites are buying increasing quantities of Middle Eastern cotton, wool, phosphate, manganese ore, copper, rice and fruit.

The small nations of East Europe have a definite psychological advantage in the Mid East over the major Western powers—and even over the USSR itself. They have never played a political role in Africa or Asia, and are able to play effectively upon anti-colonial feelings.

They make much of "aid without strings" for home consumption, too.

A Czech newspaper, discussing Mid Eastern trade in a recent editorial, reminded its readers that the "other side of the export issue is equally important; we help these countries free themselves from colonial economic exploitation." And a Hungarian foreign trade official sounded the same theme in an interview: "Our exports to Africa

and Asia are significant contributions to the cause of Socialism."

But the success of the satellites' export program probably lies less in their skill in molding public opinion than in their ability to ignore it.

Their leaders face no painful debates on foreign aid; they can ignore essential domestic needs because no one asks them for an economic accounting.

Thus, they can offer the underdeveloped nations of the Middle East—and those of the rest of Asia and Africa—everything from razor blades to power stations on a barter or credit basis, with deferred payment at low interest. They can underbid Western competitors, offer quick delivery and send along squads of technicians to service equipment and train local personnel.

And their customers, naturally, come back for more. As one Syrian businessman says, "It is none of our business if they want to sell at a loss."

Hungarian production of radio sets has jumped five times since 1949—but most go to export markets

Czech-made tractors are helping mechanize Egyptian agriculture

Entire Soviet bloc is cooperating on construction of Egypt's Aswan Dam

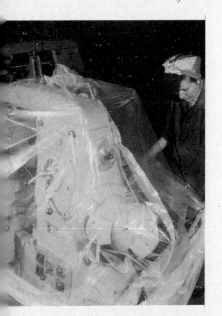

*Machine tools bound
for Iraq are plastic-
wrapped in Czech factory*

*Hungarian-made
Ikaros buses are part of Beirut's
municipal transportation system*

HUGE DAM, which will require 15,000 steel piles and 1.2 million cubic feet of concrete, inches out across the Haringvliet, main outlet for the combined waters of the Rhine and Meuse. Dam will be major link in Netherlands' 25-year, $500 million Delta Plan to eliminate all future peril from the sea.

HOW THE

$500 million Delta

EVER-PRESENT menace is graphically shown *(above)* by 1953 refugees fleeing with their cattle along crumbling dyke. First step in reclamation is closing of wave-torn gap *(r.)* by temporary dam.

AMBITIOUS SCOPE of the Delta Plan is shown by map. All waters behind four permanent dams (striped markings) will be cut off from sea, eventually become dry land. Islands which will thus be engulfed by mainland played romantic role in history. They were first strongholds of the "Sea Beggars" in Netherlands' struggle to win freedom.

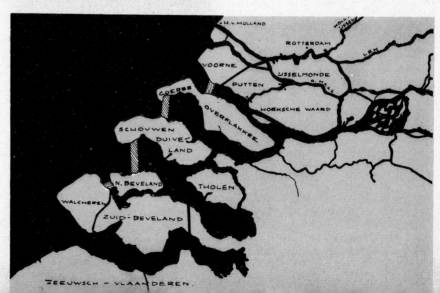

NETHERLANDS WILL TAME THE SEA

Plan will block four estuaries, shorten coast 400 miles, add acres of farmland

THE NETHERLANDS, which as recently as 1953 had 370,000 acres of its most valuable lands flooded at a cost of 1835 lives and $400 million, is determined never again to succumb to its age-old enemy, the sea.

To avert future disaster, the nation is abandoning its traditional reliance on its 1900 miles of dykes.

Instead, it plans to block off completely four important estuaries in the most vulnerable area, the Southwest Delta below Rotterdam.

The 25-year plan, which will cost at least $500 million, will join eight major islands permanently to the mainland. In the process it will add thousands of fertile acres to feed the country's swelling population.

Most of the new land will be in the province of Zeeland (Sealand), which, as its name implies, up to now has supported itself largely from the products of the ocean.

Chief sufferers will be the oyster and mussel fisheries, which for centuries have flourished in the protected tidal waters which will be transformed into farms.

Heart of the project is the construction of huge dams across the Haringvliet, largest outlet in volume of water of the rivers Rhine and Meuse, whose waters commingle in the Delta; the Grevelingen; the Eastern Scheldt and the Veeregat.

The New Waterway, chief artery of Rhine commerce and the busiest commercial waterway in Europe, will of course remain open, as will the Western Scheldt, sea link of the great Belgian port of Antwerp.

Construction of the Haringvliet dam, which alone will cost about $75 million, already is far advanced. It is scheduled for 1961 completion.

Backstopping the main permanent dams will be a huge sliding dam, the world's largest, on the main navigation link between the New Waterway and the Meuse.

Each of the two 600-ton steel slides will be 250 feet long. The dam will be used, when necessary, to cut off flood waters above Rotterdam.

The whole project will shorten the Netherlands coastline by more than 400 miles. Incidental beneficiaries will be motorists, since many bridges and ferries will be eliminated.

JOHN BULL: SCIENTIFIC FARMER

YIELD OF BRITISH DAIRY COWS IS CLOSE TO WORLD'S HIGHEST

British agriculture leads world in mechanization; production up 59%

BRITISH farming, in the doldrums since the mid-19th Century, has regained its historic position as the nation's largest single industry.

In the process, it is saving Great Britain an estimated $1.2 billion yearly in precious foreign exchange that otherwise would have to go for imported food. This development is, potentially, of great significance to U.S. business, since it frees large sums previously earmarked for such grain and meat exporters as Canada, Australia and Argentina.

Total farm production has risen 59% since 1939, and is expected to be well over $4 billion for 1958.

British agriculture today, in terms of machine-units per acre, is the most mechanized in the world. It has undergone a technical revolution whose only parallel is the 18th Century introduction by "Coke of Norfolk" and other farm pioneers of scientific crop rotation, which transformed the whole world's food production.

In 1939, for example, there were only 55,000 farm tractors in Great Britain. Today there are more than 600,000. In 1939 there were only 150 harvester-combines in the entire country, and not a single pick-up baler. Today there are more than 40,000. Before the war almost all farmers sowed by hand; today they have available 150,000 grain-and-fertilizer drills.

At the same time, to the sorrow of traditionalists, the "Shire Horse," the huge, handsome work animal which was the pride of squire and laborer alike, is nearing extinction. The total has dropped from a pre-war 500,000 to a mere 100,000.

As a result of this mechanization, which has raised farm labor productivity 62%, the increase has taken place despite a one-third drop in the number of farm workers, who total less than 700,000 compared to

WW II BOMBER FIELD, JUST HANDED BACK TO OWNER, IS RETURNED TO WHEAT PRODUCTION AS FAST AS RUNWAYS CAN BE TORN UP

STOCK FAIR STILL IS FOCUS OF FARM LIFE ALTHOUGH OWNER OPERATION IS REPLACING SQUIRE-TENANT PATTERN

more than 1 million in 1945. Today they form less than 3% of the total labor force. (The U.S. figure is 9%.)

A major part of the production rise has been caused, not by bringing new land under cultivation, but by greatly increasing yield of land already in use.

Wheat yield per acre, for instance, now averages better than 43 bushels, compared to a pre-war 34. The corresponding U.S. figures are, today, 20 bushels, pre-war, about 14. But the averages are not strictly comparable, since British wheat receives much more cultivation than U.S. And in such European countries as Denmark and the Netherlands, where the grain receives almost daily attention, the yield averages one-third more than Britain's.

Other crops have kept pace with wheat, the sugar beet yield rising 27% since the war and the potato 33%.

Almost all British farmers practice "mixed farming," with certified dairy herds a chief source of cash income. And almost everyone, even if his "holding" is under 20 acres, has the latest electrical milking and bottle washing equipment. Milk production per cow averages 27% higher than in the U.S.

Much of the resurgence of British farming is the result of government paternalism under Labor and Tories alike. Government help has gone even further than in the U.S. in price supports and guarantees, guaranteed markets and outright subsidies.

But, with prosperity, British farmers, like their U.S. counterparts, are growing restive under the restrictions and red tape accompanying government aid.

They also are nettled because they think the average city dweller regards the average countryman as a straw-chewing character living mostly on government bounty paid out of the city dweller's taxes.

Farm organizations, to publicize their contribution to the national welfare, are spending millions on publicity, even choosing U.S.-style farm "queens."

And both major parties are assiduously wooing the farm vote, which, although relatively small in itself, could hold the balance of power in a country almost equally divided politically.

FULL BEAUTY TREATMENT is given "Shire Horse" champions before stock shows. Stalwart stallions weigh up to one ton each, can pull five. But even stronger and more efficient tractor is ousting breed, which dates back to pre-Roman times. Number has dropped from half million to under 100,000. It was special pride of late King George V, Queen Elizabeth's grandfather, "Squire of Sandringham" in Norfolk county.

251

MODERN JAPANESE FISHING vessels, able to remain at sea for many weeks, are menace to survival of salmon, which breed in North American streams, but feed and grow far across Pacific. Japan may cut its catch.

TWO-WAY SQUEEZE MENACES SALMON SURVIVAL

Industry threatens boycott to cut Japanese high seas quota; dams block spawning beds

DECLINE OF THE SALMON (Annual U.S. catch, including Alaska, millions of pounds)	
Year	Total
1931	601
1939	527
1945	499
1950	329
1954	325
1955	290
1956	324
1957	257

CAN THE PACIFIC salmon, under relentless attack both on its inland spawning grounds and on the high seas where it grows to marketable maturity, come back?

The supply once seemed unlimited. But the decrease began before the turn of the century and, in the past thirty years alone, the catch has dwindled 60%.

The 1959 season, it is expected, will be the worst on record.

Only effectively enforced international agreements, plus a comprehensive program to keep the spawning waters clean and preserve the salmons' access to them, can save for the U.S. and its neighbor Canada this magnificent natural resource. (Restoring the salmon fishery is a major problem faced by Alaska's new state government. The 49th state's canneries have decreased from 120 to 40 in the past 10 years.)

The situation is becoming more and more acute with the mushrooming of world population, which both increases high seas pressure on the fish and makes it even more important that this source of protein be preserved for posterity.

The inland menace to the salmon, who return to the streams where they were hatched to breed, comes from pollution of these waters by lumbering and other industry and, of greater present menace, blocking of the streams by power and other dams.

Weyerhaeuser Timber and other giant lumber and pulp companies are spending millions of dollars to prevent pollution (one Weyerhaeuser installation removes one-and-half tons of bark, sawdust and other waste per hour from water used by a sawmill), but smaller companies cannot afford to take such measures.

This raises the question even more at issue where dams are concerned—which is more important, the salmon fishery or lumber and power?

In some cases fish ladders, fish lifts and holding pools in which the salmon are collected, and then moved around the dam by tank truck, have proved successful.

But their over-all effectiveness is dubious and, even when spawning is affected, millions of young fish are killed when swept over dams and into turbines on their way down to the sea.

Chief high seas threat to the North American salmon is Japan's wide-ranging oceanic fishing fleet. (Japan's total catch in 1957, last year for which figures are available, was 5.4 million tons, largest in the world and exactly twice that of the U.S.)

Japanese operations are particularly menacing to the North American salmon because, contrary to previous belief, huge quantities feed in waters west of the "provisional line," 175 degrees West Longitude, running down the middle of the Pacific.

Under existing agreements, Japan

has every right to take all the fish it can catch west of this line. U.S. and Canadian attempts to have it moved westward when the International North Pacific Fisheries Commission met last year in Tokyo failed.

But Japan already has backed down somewhat by announcing unofficially that it would confine its 1959 salmon catch to 170 million pounds, instead of the previously scheduled 200 million. Pressure from the Soviet Union may reduce the total still further.

Japanese pelagic fishing also is depleting the salmon which breed in Siberia's rivers, and the U.S.S.R. has for the past several years been forcing agreements on Tokyo cutting the areas open to the Japanese and the amount to be caught.

Sen. Warren G. Magnuson (D-Wash.) has introduced a bill to embargo imports of Japanese canned salmon unless Tokyo cooperates.

While the State Department opposes the bill as "basically inconsistent" with U.S. trade policies, the Interior Department favors passage on the ground that the Japanese high seas fishery is a "grave threat" to the U.S. industry, and unless it is "changed abruptly, may destroy the commercial value of the red salmon runs."

Spokesmen for the Washington and Alaskan fishermen advocate more drastic action "if talks on the diplomatic level fail to produce the necessary results." They add:

"We should refuse to handle imports, and other things. If something is not done you will see action below the level of statesmanship."

MOST U.S., Canadian fishermen capture salmon in coast waters *(below)* or in actual rivers where fish return to breed.

BIGGEST DOMESTIC THREAT to salmon survival are dams and other obstructions across rivers which they ascend to spawn. Fish ladder *(below)* helps many fish climb these obstacles, but several dams in close succession may prove too much for hardiest fish.

HAWK-FEATURED BATUTSI NOBLE (L.) IS SHARP CONTRAST TO BAHUTI SCHOOLBOY (R.)

NOBLE AND

Medieval pattern lives o

THE MIDDLE AGES, African style, still survive in the continent's heart, the 24,000 mountainous square miles of Ruanda-Urundi.

Here 600,000 cattle-breeding nobles, the famed and photogenic Batutsi, said to be the world's tallest racial group, rule almost unchallenged over a shorter, darker peasantry, the 3.5 million Bahuti.

Topping the pyramid are two hereditary kings, the Mwamis of Ruanda in the north and Urundi in the south. Their royal privileges, many anthropologists believe, can be traced back to the Pharaohs of ancient Egypt, whence the Hamitic ancestors of the Batutsi set out on their southward migration thousands of years ago.

Deep in the forest fastnesses, lit nightly by the glow of still active volcanoes, are the last sanctuaries of the tiny Batwas, the pygmies, one of the most primitive of human groups, and of the scarce, zealously protected mountain gorilla.

With an average elevation of 6000 feet, the climate is temperate. There is an almost complete absence of the diseases, such as bilharzia, which curse most tropical areas. The beautiful mountain lakes are free of the fierce crocodiles which infest most other African waters.

There is hardly any tension between natives and white settlers—there are hardly any white settlers—and the African nationalism boiling up throughout the rest of the continent has yet to penetrate the area.

Yet the pressures and problems besetting the rest of the world have begun to invade this "fly embalmed in amber," as a UN official described the isolated area.

Ruanda-Urundi is administered as a UN trust territory by Belgium. It lies on the spine of Africa — the "Great Rift" — between the Belgian Congo and the British trust territory of Tanganyika.

BEAUTY OF HIDDEN MOUNTAIN LAND IS SHOWN BY SUNSET ON LAKE KIVU. HUGE CRANE, PASSERBY ARE SILHOUETTED AGAINST HILLS

SERF

n mid-Africa mountains

The UN Trusteeship Council has become increasingly inquisitive about the progress the area, under the UN Charter, supposedly is making toward self-government.

Three successive UN missions have been increasingly critical of Belgian preparations for self-rule. They also have charged that the Belgian administrators have not made it clear to the people that they are under UN trusteeship, and not an integral part of the Belgian Congo.

The Belgian answer is to point to the roads, schools, housing and other achievements of the $75 million 10 Year Plan launched in 1950.

HARDWORKING WIFE OF BAHUTI FARMER CARRIES BABY ATOP HER HEAVY FIREWOOD

TALL, PROUD BATUTSI WOMEN STALK PAST MODERN MATERNITY HOSPITAL BUILT BY BELGIANS AS PART OF $75 MILLION 10 YEAR PLAN

HEREDITARY CULTURE of Batutsi, once wide-ranging nomad raiders, is centered about their vast herds of lyre-horned cattle. Specimens such as these (above) are treasured far above more modern and more mundane forms of wealth. Cattle number 10 million, over twice human population, itself one of densest in Africa.

NATIVE WOMEN crowd market at Kisenyi, near border with Belgian Congo. Unique coiffures are not latest styles but markings showing tribal membership.

Educational facilities, so far as they exist, are exactly the same for native as for the few white children. The integrated secondary (high) school at Usumubura, the capital, is one of the best in Africa. The Usumubura native housing development also is a model for the continent.

But the noble-serf relationship persisting between Batutsi and Bahuti remains as a barrier to genuine popular government.

The warlike Batutsi, whose privileges are slowly withering under Belgian administration, remember the very recent past when their dominance was total. Believing themselves born to rule, they would not peaceably accept the rule by the peasant majority that democratic government would mean.

Bahuti leaders fear that a Belgian withdrawal would mean, instead, an attempt to force full restoration of the rule of the Batutsi aristocrats.

The Bahutis told YEAR that, while self-government is their eventual goal, they want the Belgians to stay until education and economic change wipe out caste differences.

Poverty and explosively expanding population are more immediate problems than politics. The steepest hillsides are terraced for coffee, the only export crop, and yam and banana, the food staples. With only one town, Usumubura, the population density already is more than 160 per square mile, 15 times that of the Congo, and is expected to double before the end of the century.

Exploitation of minerals (only a little tin and wolfram are now mined) and new food and cash crops such as sugar, tea and cotton are essential to raise the living standard and make self-rule practicable.

Should the Belgians withdraw, who would furnish the needed capital and equally needed technical skill?

ECONOMIC FUTURE of overcrowded Ru-anda-Urundi is dependent on successful modernizing of agriculture. Belgians are bringing in mechanized equipment *(r.)*.

NATIVE AND WHITE children *(above)* receive modern physical training at famous secondary school in capital, Usumubura. All educational facilities are made available equally to all races. Education is major part of the Belgian program.

ATTRACTION for rare tourists are traditional Batutsi dances, which date back to days of nomad raids, incessant tribal wars. Two male Batutsi *(r.)* prepare regalia before staging centuries-old performance on the lake shore near Kisenyi.

TALKING BUSINESS

Japanese businessmen find foreign languages a vital tool; whole country studies via radio, TV

THE Japanese are fast becoming the world's most versatile linguists. They are working around the clock to master English, French, German, Spanish—and, most recently, Russian and Chinese.

Nobody is working harder than the nation's businessmen, and their reason, of course, is trade.

Tiny, overcrowded, highly industrialized Japan is doing everything it can to boost export trade—including learning to speak its customers' own languages.

Most big companies have active English-speaking societies. One young Bank of Tokyo junior executive returned last spring from a year at Stanford University to find that his first major assignment was establishment of an English club.

In the giant export-import firms of Tokyo and Osaka, proficiency in one or more foreign languages is an absolute necessity for promotion and high-paying foreign assignments.

The general manager of one company recently told its new English tutor that the three top men in his class would automatically be sent to New York this winter—and that anyone who failed would be fired. No one lost his job.

Businessmen who already have a textbook knowledge of English attend the advanced conversation courses offered by the UN Association for Japan.

UNAFJ has found that some Japanese business visitors to the U.S. have actually had nervous breakdowns and had to be sent home after a month or so of listening to soda

TOKYO language enthusiasts can study many hours a day via radio and TV, starting at 5 a.m. with "Introductory Russian, Chinese or Spanish" and finishing at 1:45 a.m. next morning with "English for Millions." French *(top)*, German *(center)* also come over the airwaves. Those who like language lessons set to music can pick up "Singing Russian" *(r.)* or "Singing French." USIA's popular "Living English" catches the nation at breakfast. Between mouthfuls of rice, pickles and fish, Japanese TV-owners can watch volunteers from Tokyo's U.S. colony demonstrate use of everyday English.

jerks' "Whadulyuhave?" and business acquaintenances' "Drop in the next time you buzz into town." So it throws out the books and concentrates on inelegant but sanity-preserving colloquialisms.

Although they emphasize English as the postwar international language of commerce, Japanese businessmen are not neglecting the other languages they need for trade with Western Europe and Latin America. And they consider the U.S.' lack of interest in Chinese and Russian either complacent or simply naive.

The business community has no monopoly on the language craze. Housewives, students, policemen and professional people are all studying, with the help of every medium of mass communication.

Television offers 17 hours of language broadcasts a week, and radio 2498 hours.

Listener polls show that 450,000 to 500,000 Japanese tune in on each of radio's 43 major language programs every week, and as many watch Nippon TV's "Living English," presented by U.S. Information Agency.

Five English language dailies are published in Tokyo, and during one month, 37 of the capital's movie theaters were showing foreign films.

Demands for language tutors crowd newspaper want ad sections.

Japan's crack school system is stepping up language training, too. A typical college entrant has 10 years of English behind him, and about half of his undergraduate and almost all his graduate courses will have heavy foreign reading lists.

U.S. COLLEGE STUDENT has Tokyo class *(above)* that includes a 9-year-old schoolgirl, a 78-year-old retired professor. On typical "Living English" show *(r.)* wife of USIA official discusses her hobby, painting.

INDUSTRY'S BILLION DOLLAR CLUB

Recession cost it $6 billion in sales, $1.2 billion in profits

U.S. industry's "Billion Dollar Club," the giant private enterprises which among them produce one-fourth of the entire Gross National Product, suffered no major damage, but was severely buffeted, in the 1957-58 recession.

Its membership, 47 in 1957, dropped to 45 in 1958. Sales and other revenue fell from $108.8 billion (25% of the $440.3 billion 1957 GNP) to $102.6 billion (24% of the $437.7 billion 1958 GNP), a decline of 6%. Profits fell more sharply, from $7.29 billion (6.7% of sales) to $6.26 billion (5.6% of sales). The drop was 14%. Employment fell from 4.99 to 4.70 million, a 6% drop.

Three well known corporations, two in steel, one in aviation, dropped, temporarily at least, below the magic billion dollar mark and from club membership. They were North American Aviation, which fell from $1255 million to $904 million, Republic Steel, $1227 million to $910 million, and Armco Steel, $1074 million to $868 million.

Only one new company joined the group. It was General Foods, whose sales rose from $986 million in 1957 to $1009 last year.

In addition, membership was firmly clinched by International Business Machines, which barely made the 1957 list with an even $1000 million. Sales jumped in 1958 to $1172 million, raising it from last to 34th place.

Food processing and sales, retailing, service, and communications bucked the recession tide by showing an upward tendency, while such heavy industries as automobiles, steel, electrical machinery and, to a lesser extent, oils, slipped back in sales and profits.

Major sales sufferers included Chrysler, Ford, General Motors, Bethlehem Steel, U.S. Steel, General Electric, Western Electric and Westinghouse.

Severe profit declines were felt by the automobile "Big Three" (Chrysler dropped from a 1957 profit of $120 million to a 1958 loss of $34 million, the only club member to report a net operating loss), Standard Oil of N.J., Standard Oil of Indiana, Gulf, Socony Mobil, Sinclair Oil, du Pont and Douglas Aircraft.

In almost embarrassing contrast was American Telephone and Telegraph, whose profits jumped $128 million to a $981 million total. Others whose profits rose substantially included Proctor and Gamble, Armour, American Can, and, as stated above, General Foods and International Business Machines.

Important sales gains were made by International Business Machines, AT&T, Sears Roebuck, Kroger, Safeway, Swift, R. J. Reynolds, Proctor & Gamble, Boeing Airplane and Douglas Aircraft.

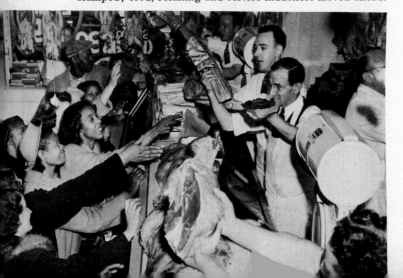

MOTIONLESS Chrysler assembly line, jammed meat market, symbolize what happened to nation's billion dollar companies in 1957-58 recession. Automobiles, other heavy industry slumped; food, retailing and service industries moved ahead.

HOW U.S. BILLION DOLLAR CORPORATIONS FARED IN THE 1957-58 RECESSION

Rank '58	Rank '57	Company	Headquarters	Sales ($ Million) 1958	Sales ($ Million) 1957	% Change	Net Profits ($ Million) 1958	Net Profits ($ Million) 1957	% Change	Employes (Thousands) 1958	Employes (Thousands) 1957	% Change
1	1	General Motors	Detroit	9522	10990	—13	634	844	—25	521	588	—12
2	2	Standard Oil (N.J.)	New York	7544	7830	— 4	563	805	—30	160	160	....
3	3	American Tel. & Tel.	New York	6771	6314	+ 7	952	830	+15	793	745	+ 6
4	5	Great A. & P. Tea	New York	5095	4769	+ 7	54	51	+ 6	145	145	....
5	4	Ford Motor	Dearborn	4130	5771	—28	96	282	—65	168	188	—10
6	7	General Electric	New York	4121	4336	— 5	243	248	— 2	250	282	—11
7	8	Sears Roebuck	Chicago	3721	3601	+ 3	166	161	+ 4	215	218	— 1
8	6	U.S. Steel	New York	3472	4414	—21	301	419	—28	223	270	—17
9	10	Socony Mobil	New York	2886	2976	— 3	157	220	—29	75	77	— 3
10	11	Gulf Oil	Pittsburgh	2769	2730	+ 1	330	355	— 7	50	51	— 2
11	13	Swift	Chicago	2648	2545	+ 4	11	14	—22	63	70	—10
12	15	Texas Co.	New York	2328	2344	— 1	312	332	— 6	52	53	— 2
13	16	Safeway Stores	Oakland, Calif.	2225	2117	+ 5	33	31	+ 2	69	67	+ 3
14	14	Western Electric	New York	2174	2481	—12	86	85	+ 1	122	141	—13
15	9	Chrysler	Detroit	2165	3565	—40	— 34	120	—128	100	130	—23
16	12	Bethlehem Steel	Bethlehem, Pa.	2006	2603	—23	138	191	—28	135	165	—18
17	18	Westinghouse Electric	Pittsburgh	1896	2009	— 6	75	73	+ 3	115	129	—11
18	17	Standard Oil (Ind.)	Chicago	1864	2010	— 7	118	152	—22	49	50	— 2
19	20	Armour	Chicago	1850	1936	— 4	5.6	3.4	+65	50	50	....
20	19	du Pont	Wilmington, Del.	1829	1965	— 7	341	369	— 9	84	89	— 6
21	23	Kroger	Cincinnati	1776	1674	+ 6	22	21	+ 5	41	38	+ 8
22	24	Boeing Airplane	Seattle	1711	1597	+ 7	29	38	—23	90	100	—10
23	21	Shell Oil	New York	1674	1773	— 6	117	135	—13	38	40	— 5
24	22	Standard Oil (Calif.)	San Francisco	1559	1651	— 6	258	288	—10	38	40	— 4
25	25	General Dynamics	New York	1511	1563	— 3	37	44	—16	92	92	....
26	26	National Dairy Products	New York	1451	1432	+ 1	46	44	+ 5	46	46	....
27	27	Goodyear Tire & Rubber	Akron	1368	1422	— 4	66	65	+ 2	100	100	....
28	29	J. C. Penney	New York	1301	1312	— 1	47	49	— 5	75	60	+25
29	28	Union Carbide	New York	1297	1395	— 8	125	134	— 7	72	77	— 9
30	37	Proctor & Gamble	Cincinnati	1295	1156	+10	73	68	+ 7	30	30	....
31	40	Douglas Aircraft	Santa Monica, Calif.	1210	1091	+11	17	31	—45	72	76	— 5
32	32	United Aircraft	E. Hartford, Conn.	1200	1233	— 3	42	51	—18	65	62	5
33	30	Sinclair Oil	New York	1190	1251	— 5	49	79	—38	24	25	— 4
34	47	Int'l Business Machines	New York	1172	1000	+17	126	89	+42	61	60	+ 2
35	35	Radio Corp. of America	New York	1171	1171	....	31	39	—20	78	78	....
36	43	R. J. Reynolds Tobacco	Winston-Salem, N.C.	1147	1053	+ 8	78	64	+23	13	12	+ 8
37	39	American Tobacco	New York	1103	1098	+ 4	59	57	+ 3	18	18	....
38	34	International Harvester	Chicago	1098	1187	— 5	43	46	— 6	63	68	— 7
39	41	Montgomery Ward	Chicago	1092	1074	+ 2	28	30	— 7	60	60	....
40	44	Continental Can	New York	1080	1046	+ 3	41	41	....	52	54	— 2
41	38	Phillips Petroleum	Bartlesville, Okla.	1067	1132	— 6	84	96	—12	25	27	—13
42	46	Firestone Tire & Rubber	Akron	1062	1157	— 8	54	62	—13	86	88	— 2
43	46	American Can Co.	New York	1037	1006	+ 3	46	42	+ 9	50	50	....
44	45	Cities Service	New York	1015	1046	— 3	45	59	—24	20	20	....
45	48	General Foods	White Plains, N.Y.	1009	986	+ 3	48	44	+10	21	21	....
		Total—45 Corporations		102,612	108,812	—5.7	6,192.6	7,291.4	—15	4,690	4,990	— 6

*Estimated ‡Weighted projection nine months basis

Scientific uses of U.S. brainpower has raised GNP many billions of dollars, transformed every phase of industry, defense, communications, distribution. Credit cards, checking accounts, food chain giants, automobile production, all are dependent on systems planning.

SYSTEMS ENGINEERING: ORGANIZED BRAIN POWER

New profession has

L EAST KNOWN—but by far most important—development in U.S. industry and defense since World War II has been systems engineering.

Expressed in terms of money, its contribution, according to widely recognized authority Israel Diamond, has been "many, many billions."

Diamond, who set up and supervises the logging system by which Broadcast Music, Inc., computes and keeps instantly available the monthly usage of its many thousands of tunes by every U.S. radio and TV station, also teaches the science at Hofstra College and the College of the City of New York. He told **YEAR**:

"In the 1940s our Gross National Product was in the $300 billions. In the 1950s it was in the $400 billions. Now, it is soaring toward the $500 billion mark.

"A very large part of this is the result of systems analysis, both because of the operational economies it effected and the new developments which would have been impossible without it."

Systems engineering has transformed every phase of production, distribution, communications and even mass entertainment. Yet the average well-informed American, even on the highest levels, would be hard put to say just what it is, and what it is not, except that it somehow involves such electronic data processing miracles as International Business Machine's 705-III system, which rents for $57,000 a month.

But, essentially, it is independent of machines. It is, to choose among definitions, the organization of any activity to produce the maximum result, present or future, with the re-

CREDIT CARD-PACKED wallet is ever-present reminder of how systems engineering is transforming U.S. living and buying habits. One card could replace all.

vital role in economy

sources available and with minimum effort in time and cost.

In the simplest case, it is merely common sense. In the most complex, such as planning for global war or the future needs of the U.S. telephone network, it involves not only present but probable future scientific developments and the intricacies of probability calculus and matrix algebra.

To the public, most apparent result of systems engineering has been the mushrooming — and coalescing — of national and now international credit cards, none of which could function without systems planning of the light-fast electronic processing of mountains of data.

Already, cards can be processed at point-of-purchase to record expenditures and changes in balance. In a few years, experts say, a single world-wide system will be feasible.

Similarly, the new science has made the checking account a mass as well as class prerogative (90% of all bills now are paid by check). Latest development is the combining of checks with credit through a rotating debit balance whose maximum depends on the size of prearranged monthly payments. Started in 1955 by the First National Bank of Boston, the plan now has been adopted by at least 50 major banks, including New York's First National City. (A similar practice has long been usual in Great Britain, but not on the same mass scale.)

Another result of systems research is mass, nationwide participation in securities trading (Merrill Lynch, Pierce, Fenner and Smith, Inc., 126 offices in 112 cities, Bache and Co., 91 in 62 cities).

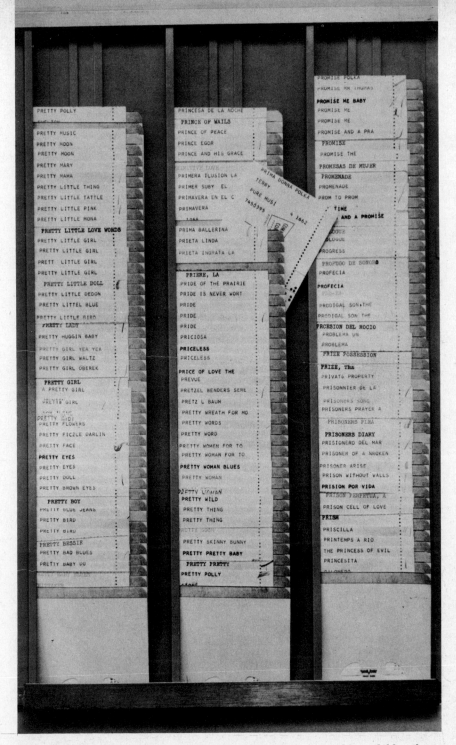

PRIMA DONNA POLKA'S complete musical history becomes instantly available when card is inserted in appropriate machine. Broadcast Music, Inc., can compute total performance of its music without insisting every station furnish daily program logs.

Still another is the recent introduction, in the northeast, of life insurance for those over 65. (Actuarial processing of statistics is one of the main systems fountainheads.)

Without systems planning successful operation of such giant food retailing chains as Grand Union and the Great Atlantic and Pacific Tea Co. would hardly be possible.

Systems experts must work out both location of stores and, just as important, most economic and efficient placing of warehouses and other distribution centers.

They must take into account, for example, present and future population trends not only in general but as they apply to each locality.

Such factors, and others, also are vital in planning the mass manufacture and distribution of clothing.

Both giant enterprise, small business profit from

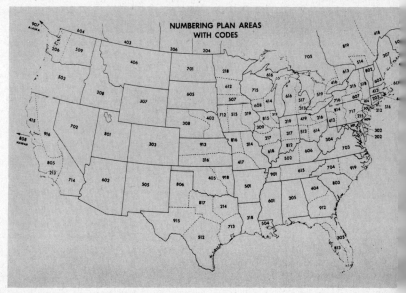

systems procedure

How many men, for instance, next year and five years from now, will wear size 43 long suits, and how will they be distributed geographically? The wrong answer can cost millions in sales, or unsaleable merchandise.

The electric fan industry, in planning production, must consider climatic changes, probable future summer weather, the spread of air-conditioning.

The automobile "Big Three," which works years ahead, must weigh indicated population growth, average purchasing power, whether or not the small car, foreign or domestic, will grow further in popular favor.

The growth rate of international airline travel has ceased accelerating. Only drastic fare reductions, according to Sir George Edwards, managing director of Vickers Armstrong, largest British plane manufacturer, can tap new passenger potential. How much should fares be cut, and when?

The Bell telephone system, with its 50 million phones and access to 11 million others in the U.S. alone, is the outstanding example of systems engineering. American Telephone and Telegraph's systems department employs 325 mathematicians, physicists, psychologists and other experts. Bell's primary systems job is planning so that the entire network will be ready to meet all future demands, whatever they are. By-products include a major role in developing the Nike anti-aircraft missiles, the Titan Intercontinental Ballistic Missile and

other vital defense contributions.

Systems analysis has effected enormous economies — and could effect more — in Armed Services procurement, stock-piling and distribution.

But systems planning can be just as important to the small private business. It has given rise to a new profession, systems consultant. One of its leaders, Lawrence B. Taylor, points out:

"Most managers are so busy doing what they are doing they have little time to consider 'why' or 'how'."

"Many procedures can be eliminated entirely by evaluation and study indicating duplication of clerical effort or lack of any important use of data produced."

Systems engineering, fundamentally, is planned use of the ultimate human asset—brainpower.

"CROSSBAR CANYON" is AT&T name for room *(above)* housing automatic Direct Distance Dialing equipment. Map shows code numbers for every area of U.S. (including Alaska, Hawaii) and Canada. Numbers are dialed before regular number. By 1965 DDD, already in operation in Washington, New York area and elsewhere, will link 95% of all the telephones in U.S.

TRACKING CONSOLES monitor early warnings in Army's systems-designed Missile Master, which controls Nike defenses of Baltimore-Washington. Ultimately, MM will coordinate every U.S. Nike installation.

CAN ELECTRIC FISHING MULTIPLY

Mushrooming world population demands vast new food sources

World's population already near 3 billion, will double by end of century. To feed them will require vast supplies from unexploited areas. Electric high seas fishing is called "the only hope."

LEADING FISH PRODUCERS	
(millions of tons; 1957 total 29.96)	
JAPAN	5.4
U.S.	2.7
USSR	2.54
NORWAY	1.7
INDIA	1.2
UNITED KINGDOM	1.0
SPAIN	0.77
WEST GERMANY	0.75
CANADA	0.70
DENMARK	0.53
FRANCE	0.51
ICELAND	0.50

CAN THE SEA, which covers more than half the earth, provide the vast new food supplies which will be needed by the world's exploding population, approximately 3 billion today, and expected to double by 2000?

Present commercial fish production, according to the UN Food and Agricultural Organization, is approximately 30 million metric tons.

While this is only about 1% of total world food production, it is of vital importance in meeting food needs.

The yield of the fisheries consists entirely of protein, diet essential which is scarcest where it is needed most, the sub-tropical and tropical regions hardest hit by population pressure.

SEA'S HARVEST?

Average diets in China, India, Indonesia, the Middle East and Africa, while approaching adequacy in carbohydrates, are woefully lacking in the proteins essential to health and energy. The shortage is growing worse.

In such over-populated areas land is too valuable to be devoted to animal husbandry, but must be used almost entirely for starch crops.

New supplies from the sea are the chief hope.

Improvement of conventional methods, according to the experts, might double present production. But this would not be enough, and already such "inshore" grounds as Europe's North Sea and Georges Bank off the New England coast are showing signs of depletion.

The Grand Banks off Newfoundland and the waters off Iceland are being unrelentingly fished by the vessels of every nation with access to the Atlantic, including modern "super trawlers" from the USSR.

HOW SCHOOL OF FISH, attracted by positive pole, swim into intake pipe and are pumped aboard ship is shown by artist's drawing of method developed by European scientists. The *John S. Cobb (l.)* is being used by U.S. Fish and Wildlife Service in electric fishing experiments off the Pacific coast.

Development of radically new fishing techniques and application of these to the vast unexploited areas of the high seas seems the only chance of increasing protein supply in step with the mushrooming of population.

Most hopeful of the new methods is "electric fishing," the application of a current to the water surrounding fish. Not only does it shock and stun them, in the same way as the discharge of the South American electric "eel," but, when properly applied, actually compels them to swim right into the net or container.

When a direct current is made to flow through water from two separated ends of a circuit, fish within its influence must swim to the positive pole just as inexorably as iron filings line up in a magnetic field.

The U.S., the USSR, West Germany and other major fishing nations are busy developing electric fishing systems. While the process was first developed for fresh water use, its economic importance lies in ocean fishing, and here West Germany has been the pioneer.

Dr. Konrad Kreutzer, former German naval officer, demonstrated in 1952 that herring and cod can be caught commercially by this method.

In the U.S., the *John S. Cobb* of the Fish and Wildlife Service has been used for experiments which combine electricity with the known attractiveness to fish of underwater lights.

Small fish were lured into the electric field by a 1000-watt light. Once in the current, they swam toward the positive pole, attached to a hose, and then pumped aboard the vessel. Top rate was 1178 fish a minute.

Large fish, and whales, cannot be handled by such a method. But tuna and other powerful fish, which, when hooked, normally struggle desperately against being hauled aboard, can be stunned into quiescence by a current sent down the line. Sharks and other dangerous fish can be killed outright.

When a whale has been harpooned, a current sufficient to kill in a few seconds can be sent down the harpoon line after the harpoon has been set. This method is said to be both quicker and more certain than the currently used explosive harpoon.

Commercial use of electric fishing is at present limited by the necessity of bringing the current within a few feet of the fish, and the fact that much more power is needed in salt than in fresh water.

But a leading Delaware fishing firm is reported already conducting large scale experiments, using Dr. Kreutzer's method.

The International Oceanographic Foundation reports that electric fishing seems to be the "one possible way" to multiply production sufficiently to meet the world's ever-mounting protein needs.

A sea harvest three to five times greater than the present 30 million tons may soon, thanks to electricity, bring food and vigorous health to hungry hundreds of millions.

SCIENCE CAN NOW CHANGE HEAT DIRECTLY INTO ELECTRICITY

TINY THERMOELECTRIC unit, powered by plutonium, spins propeller on White House desk in first public demonstration. Device was developed and assembled by Martin Company.

Thermoelectricity will transform power production, aid space flight, create new industry with multi-billion doll.

A NEW INDUSTRY with a multi-billion dollar potential, thermoelectricity, has just been born in the laboratories of Westinghouse Electric, General Electric, and other giant U.S. companies and research organizations.

An offspring of solid state physics, a true phenomenon in research, thermoelectricity is the direct conversion of heat into electricity, as Dr. Clarence Zener, Westinghouse Director of Research puts it, "simply, silently and without moving parts of any kind."

Teamed with a nuclear heat source (fission at present but, eventually, hydrogen fusion), thermoelectricity may, in the not too remote future, revolutionize electric power production everywhere in the world.

A thermoelectric-nuclear "package" could be set up in almost any size anywhere, and, without moving parts, and with little need for fuel replacement, would be damage-proof, fool-proof and almost inexhaustible.

A five-pound prototype was demonstrated Jan. 16 on President Eisenhower's White House desk.

Electric current is only one side of the coin.

The reaction, which occurs when two dissimilar materials, such as special types of ceramics or metals, are placed in intimate contact, is reversible. If a reversed electric current as applied to the end normally producing electricity, the other or "heat" end will withdraw heat from its surroundings, thus forming an almost ideal means of refrigeration.

And thermoelectricity's refrigerant uses will not be bound to earth.

In missiles and space vehicles, it can be employed to govern the temperature of guidance systems, radar and other vital electronic control apparatus, all of which are extremely sensitive to their operating environments. Within five years, experts in the field told YEAR's staff, thermoelectricity will be virtually the sole method used for missile and space cooling.

Because of thermoelectricity's almost unlimited potential, every major electric and electronics company in the U.S. and the rest of the Free World, and government and research organizations on both sides of the Iron Curtain, have established research programs.

In the U.S., in one just one phase, transformation of nuclear energy into electricity, major firms actively exploring thermoelectricity's potential include Aerojet Gen-

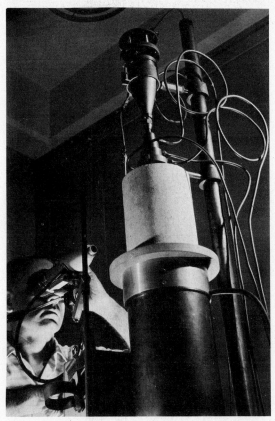

RAPID PACE of new science's development is demonstrated by General Electric's Dr. J. E. Briggs. In one hand he holds large glass converter developed in 1957, in other, tiny replacement he perfected in 1958. Westinghouse scientists *(above)* examine the ceramic material being prepared in electric furnace.

otential

eral, Atomics International Division of North American Aviation, and Northrop's Nortronics Division.

The thermoelectric reaction itself was first discovered by a German physicist, T. J. Seebeck, in 1822, and the cooling effect by J. C. Peltier, of France, in 1834. But they long remained mere laboratory curiosities.

The modern pioneers in thermoelectricity, as in other technical fields, have been Soviet scientists.

"Bible" of thermonuclear research, according to Dr. Zener, is still "Semiconductor Thermoelements and Thermoelectric Cooling," by Russia's Prof. Abram Joffe.

But the U.S., with major new discoveries in thermoelectric materials and transistor techniques, is believed to have caught up and, in some phases, to have established a substantial lead.

The impact of thermoelectricity on science and industry, according to Dr. Zener, will be both immense and unique. He stated:

"The major role the new technology of thermoelectricity is going to play in our economy is in totally new uses rather than in the mere replacement of currently used equipment."

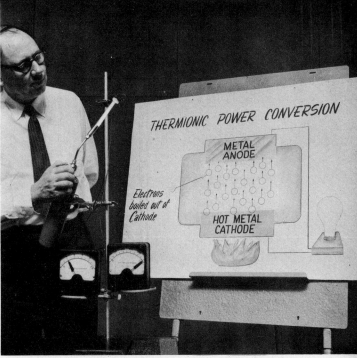

BLOWTORCH applied to thermoelectric converter produces electric current being registered on meters. Chart shows how heat produces current flow through unit, lights lamp.

269

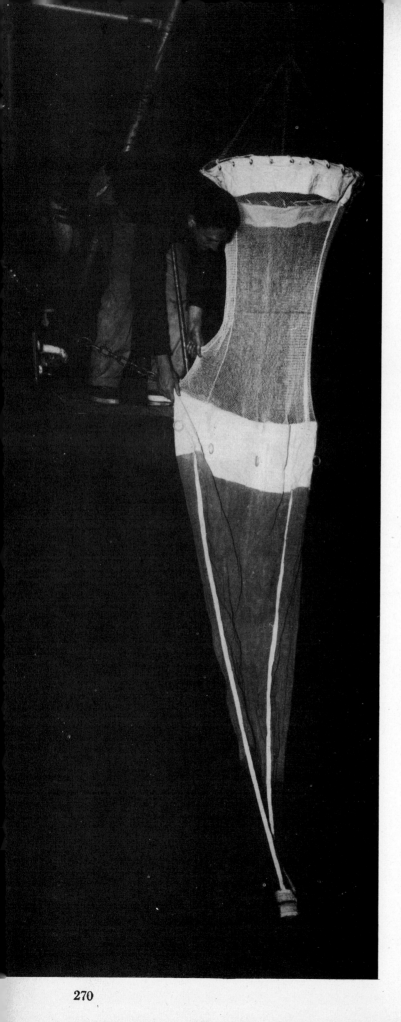

THE SEA DEEPS, NEW SOVIET PROVINCE

Net is used to collect plankton, a possible major source of food. Ocean bottom may hold large mineral wealth, like manganese (r.) photographed from bathysphere at a depth of three-and-one-half miles.

USSR now has 70 modern vessels

SOVIET SCIENTISTS, while the U.S. has been concentrating attention on outer space, have also been exploring another unknown much closer home and of much greater immediate importance—the depths of the oceans which occupy 70% of the earth's surface.

The USSR's oceanic research, called "without parallel" by Assistant Navy Secretary Garrison Norton, is being carried out by a fleet of 70 survey ships. They include:

The *Severyanka*, world's only ocean research submarine, fitted with underwater portholes, cameras and TV.

The 7500-ton icebreaker *Ob*, which has made important Antarctic discoveries.

The *Zarya*, only ship made to measure magnetic fields.

The *Mikhail Lomonosov*, East German-built, which Norton calls "probably the finest ocean research vessel afloat today." He adds that "its main emphasis appears to be on data useful to undersea warfare."

This is of ominous importance because the sea bottoms, particularly at the edge of the continental shelves, will be the refuge and operations area of missile-armed

Rare photograph shows Mikhail Lomonosov, world's best equipped, newest sea research ship. Built in East Germany, she was commissioned in 1957. USSR has some 69 other oceanographic study ships, including a special submarine.

"Core sample" of the ocean's bottom is brought up from the depths of the sea by special equipment aboard Atlantis, research vessel operated by Woods Hole Oceanographic Institute. Newest of U.S.'s 40-odd ships is over 15 years old.

plumbing areas vital to defense; $651 million U.S. crash program urged

submarines. Maps of only 2% of the total are as yet available to the U.S. (Submarines equipped with Polaris missiles are scheduled to become a mainstay of U.S. defense within the next five years.)

In addition, increased knowledge of the ocean's magnetic fields is essential to both missile guidance and undersea navigation.

In contrast to the Soviet research fleet, the U.S. now depends on 40-odd over-age converted tugs, yachts and fishing boats, none less than 15 years old.

Some are operated by the Navy, others by the Coast and Geodetic Survey, and the rest by such private organizations as the Woods Hole, Mass., Oceanographic Institute, California's Scripps Oceanographic Institute and Columbia University's Lamont Laboratory.

To remedy this "precarious" situation, a special committee of the National Academy of Sciences has just recommended a "minimum program" calling for the U.S. to spend $651 million over the next 10 years in intensive oceanographic research.

Failure to do so, the committee warns, will accentuate "serious military and political dangers" and place the U.S. "at a disadvantage in the future use of the resources of the sea."

Heart of the program is construction of 70 modern Diesel-powered "floating laboratories" which can remain at sea over long periods. Also envisaged is an aluminum submarine which can descend 6000 feet. (Limit for present steel submarines is approximately 1000 feet.)

Also planned are a host of new man-made sea monsters, including a bathysphere able to plumb the earth's deepest hole, the seven miles of the Pacific's Philippine Deep. (Existing bathyspheres have descended only half that far into the abyss.)

Ocean research could add immeasurably to the earth's food and raw materials resources, vitally important when world population is rising 25 million a year.

As the committee stated in its report, "we know less about many regions of the ocean than we know about the surface of the moon."

271

Instrumentation's volume passing $1.5
billion as space, atom and missiles swell demand

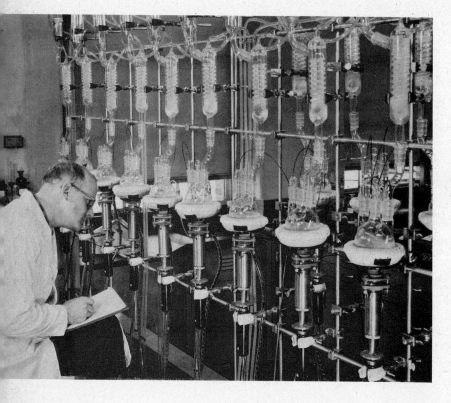

*Carpenter Steel Co. scientist
checks operation of delicate heat
transfer apparatus.*

SCIENCE'S NEED TO MEASURE CREATES HUGE INDUSTRY

SCIENCE'S "conquest" of U.S. production has created a billion-dollar industry — mass manufacture of precision measurement instruments.

The new industry, whose volume is expected to surpass $1.5 billion for 1958, received its first great impetus in World War II, and has been mushrooming ever since.

Production grew from approximately $250 million in 1947 to $1.165 billion in the year ending June 30, 1957, an increase of over 400%. Aircraft-missile instrumentation, the fastest-growing phase, jumped 1800%.

Most publicized example of the increasing demand for precision measurement instruments is ground checkout of missiles.

The countdown, so well known through TV and radio, involves hundreds, from oscilloscopes and voltmeters to graph plotters and computers, to report on the functioning of each separate "system" involved in the launching.

And still more measurement equipment is needed to insure that the missile remains in instant readiness while in pre-countdown storage.

Space/Aeronautics stated recently that the armed services have earmarked $997 million for ground support equipment for fiscal 1959, and $1.559 billion for fiscal 1960.

One-third to one-half of this, the magazine stated, would be expended for instrumentation.

And the missile field is merely one phase of accurate measurement's defense role.

Instrumentation's test segment (production of such devices as voltmeters, ohmmeters, electronic component testers, oscilloscopes and oscillographs)

*Plug-in transistors play a major role in electronic test circuitry. Units
shown were made by Packard-Bell Computer Corp. Total test instruments sales
are expected to reach some $300 million by 1961, almost $400 million by 1965.*

jumped from a volume of $55 million in 1947 to $200 million in 1957, according to a McGraw-Hill survey.

And industry, apart from defense, is making increasing use of such test instruments. Industrial sales, only about $5 million in 1947, are expected to reach $45 million by the end of the current year.

Industry employment is estimated at 180,000 to 190,000, distributed Middle Atlantic States, 63%; New England, 12%; Pacific Coast (mostly California) 11%; East North Central, 10%; and South, 4%.

This figure is expected to double in the next decade.

Development of such technologies as nuclear power, electron chemistry, cryogenics and, in prospect, space flight makes instrumentation's future especially bright—if it can keep up with their growing demands.

Progress in measurement instrumentation, according to Dr. A. V. Astin, director of the National Bureau of Standards, not only is the most accurate "gauge" of scientific advance, but an essential part of it.

He warns that, in tomorrow's world, U.S. status as a world power depends, in part, on development of new and more accurate measurement.

And he points out that, in several vital instrumentation phases, Soviet scientists today have a substantial lead over their U.S. counterparts.

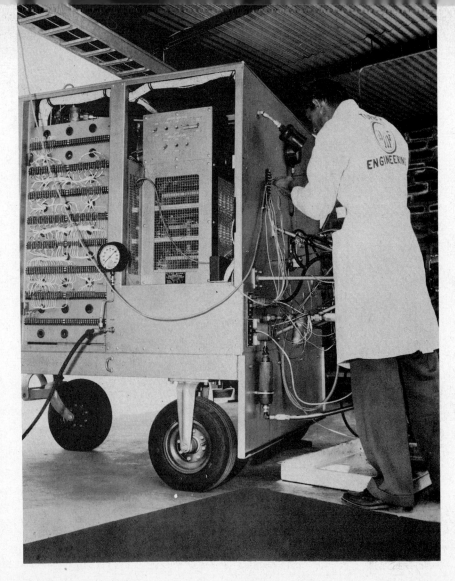

Portable electromechanical test device at Micronics Division of Elgin National Watch Co. can produce a load 3000 times that of gravity itself.

Oscilloscope is being used to check accuracy of relay. Oscilloscope sales may reach total of $45 million in 1960.

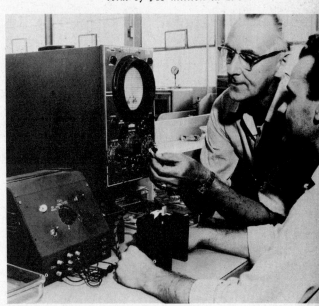

NEW INDUSTRY
SPAWNED BY SCIENCE

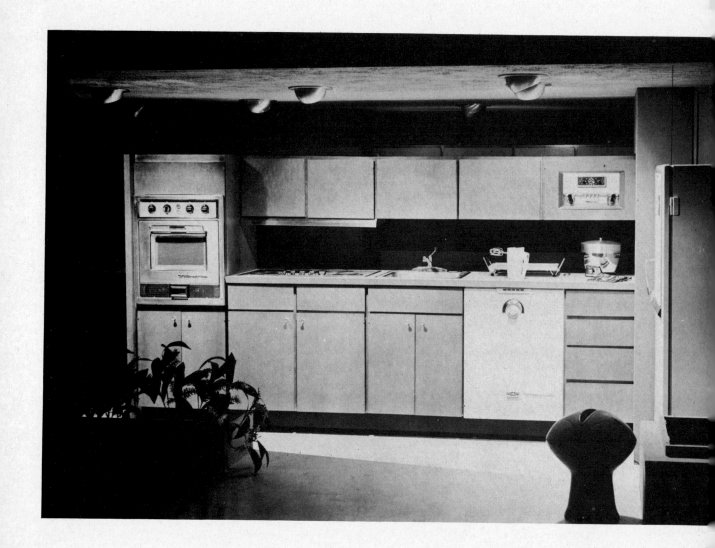

Electron chemistry's freezeless

storage revolutionizes food processing

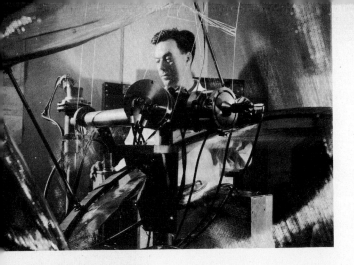

ACCELERATOR at Stanford Research Institute bombards test material with stream of electrons. Screen shields device from earth's magnetic field.

WESTINGHOUSE "kitchen of tomorrow" (l.) shows stove which cooks without heat, dishwasher that cleans without water, Electron chemistry is the answer.

NEW SCIENCE also is aiding space flight. National Space Advisory Board accelerator is being used to simulate meteoric bombardment of space ship.

Food that keeps fresh indefinitely without refrigeration, freezing or canning;

Stoves that cook in an instant without heat;

Washing, sterilization and "drying" of dishes without water or detergent;

These, for the average American, are among the most spectacular developments promised in the near future by electron chemistry, today still largely in the laboratory stage, but expected in the next few years to become a huge new industry with annual sales totaling in the hundreds of millions of dollars.

Dr. C. Guy Suits, General Electric Corp. Research Director and Vice President, predicts that electron chemistry, which uses electronic radiation to produce chemical changes, will within 10 years "make possible a host of new materials and products."

Important applications outside the food field include vulcanization of rubber without heat or sulphur heatless "cracking" of crude oil, which a top oil executive says "may prove to be the next step in petroleum processing," and replacement of the conventional heat treatment in strengthening metals and "curing" materials.

Electron chemistry currently is being used to produce hydrazine, the high energy rocket fuel used in launching the U.S. satellites, by bombarding ammonia with electrons. Stanford Research Institute scientists state that production costs already have been reduced to $10 per ton from $1000.

The Sequoia Process Corp., of Redwood City, Calif., is using electron chemistry to produce polyethelene insulation able to stand much higher temperatures than the untreated plastic.

But food, on which the average U.S. family spends 35% of its income, promises to be the chief commercial application.

Electron chemistry, using the low energy resonant transformer, "pasteurizes" food by destroying surface micro-organisms, and is of particular value in the marketing of such fresh foods as fruit, vegetables and dairy products. Its effect is to prolong "shelf life" and thus cut spoilage losses after the food has reached its market. Such foods, however, still would require refrigeration to slow internal changes.

But sterilization produced by the high energy linear accelerator would prevent even such changes, thus making possible storage for indefinitely long periods without freezing or refrigeration.

(Both linear accelerator and resonant transformer "shoot" a beam of electrons at the target material, but the former's beam is much stronger and projected at a higher speed, than that of the latter. The same energy can "cook" food by internal chemical change, and then dislodge every molecule of dirt from dish surfaces.)

The Army, faced with the problem of feeding large numbers in every part of the world under every climatic condition, is playing a leading part in electron chemistry food sterilization research. The largest linear accelerator in the U.S. has just been installed in its Ionizing Radiation Center in Stockton, Calif.

Discoloration and cost problems remain to be solved, but large-scale commercial use seems certain shortly.

PUTTING KNOWLEDGE TO WORK

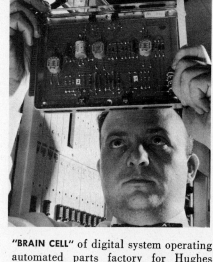

"BRAIN CELL" of digital system operating automated parts factory for Hughes Aircraft is "flip flop" circuit *(above)*. Tape "orders" controlling milling, drilling and boring operations flow through relay bank *(below)*. Computer control sharply cuts production time and costs.

Electronic processing speeds progress of science, industry

How can you know that you know? In the U.S. alone, industry, government and private institutions spend some $10 billion yearly in research of every kind, scientific and business. Many billions more are spent abroad.

In the astronomical mass of data thus accumulated—and published in literally hundreds of thousands of papers in every major language—lie the answers essential to further scientific progress, to operation of every type of large organization, even to successful advertising, public relations and selling campaigns.

Effective manipulation of such Himalayas of facts is, obviously, beyond the manual powers of the most skilled librarians and filing experts. But science, which is responsible for their ever-mushrooming accumulation, is also, fortunately, providing the way to tame them.

Their master is the new art of data retrieval, which is based on light-swift transistors and electron tubes embodied in massive computers, instead of the lagging reactions of human nerve and muscle fibres.

Data retrieval sales have jumped from $47 million in 1954 to $130 million in 1957, and are expected to double by the early 1960s.

In addition, since systems are constantly being improved and range in price up to the millions of dollars (International Business Machine's

705-III system costs just under $3 million) many companies prefer to rent them. Typical monthly fee for the 705-III is $57,000. Other rentals run from $1485 (sales price $50,000) to $22,000 (sales price $1 million).

Typical of the very large retrieval systems is that recently set up by General Electric's Gas Turbine Division in Cincinnati, Ohio.

Its magnetic tapes can store 1 million abstracts of books and articles (10 million with added storage facilities), deliver a printed abstract in less than 15 minutes and make 99 simultaneous searches.

Boeing Airplane Co. uses a "random access" accounting and control

system in its Renton, Wash., plant.

The system can store 50,000 separate items. When a card is fed to it, it checks if the item is in stock, verifies price, enters accounts receivable and other pertinent records, prepares shipping instructions and a customer acknowledgment and, if required, an invoice, all in less than one minute.

(A system of the same type was a sensation of the Brussels Fair, providing in nine languages instantaneous answers to questions on history.)

With the number of checks written annually now 10 billion, and the number of accounts 60 million compared to 27 million in 1939, data retrieval systems have become invalu-

DATA FED to, stored by IBM Ramac at Boeing Airplane is handled almost instantaneously. A complete parts accounting is provided in a matter of just a few seconds.

PRINTED ANSWER is provided by Stromberg-Carlson high speed electronic printer. Such devices usually are needed to complete computer-based systems.

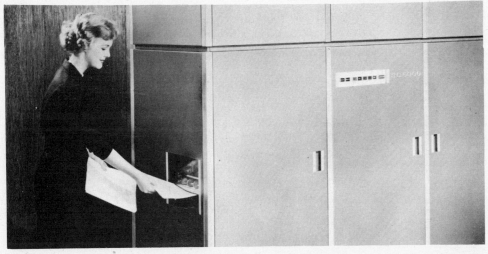

BLOCKS of libraries could not hold data stored in Northrop Corp. Univac.

able in banking. Electronic experts envision nationwide, interlocking, high speed clearing systems in the very near future.

Retrieval systems also are used to coordinate nationwide sales organizations, keeping simultaneous track of orders and inventory and funneling all data to the central plant.

Scientists expect data retrieval will end enormously costly research duplication (millions spent in one place on a problem already solved elsewhere because the knowledge is buried in a sea of paper). Lawyers hope that, some day, it will make all cases in all jurisdictions available at the turn of a dial.

SCIENCE'S

SEEING EYE

"HOT BOX DETECTIVE" mounted between tie ends on brackets records heat of journal boxes on each passing train. The device, which effects substantial savings for railroads, is made by Servo Corporation of America.

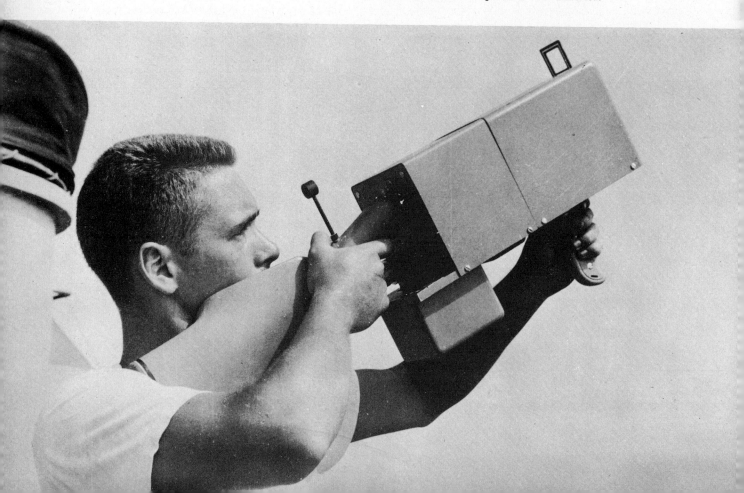

Infrared rays pierce
the dark for
research, defense, industry

HUMAN BODY'S HEAT takes place of light in these amazing infrared photographs taken at Servo Corp. laboratories during development of reconnaissance system for the Armed Forces. Brightest areas are where clothing is absent or minimum, as in faces and girl's legs (c.). Infrared camera can penetrate even areas where light is blocked or absent.

INFRARED RADIOMETER aboard U.S.S. Stickwell was first to detect reentry into atmosphere of Jupiter missile fired May 18 in "Operation Gaslight." Destroyer was stationed in South Atlantic 1500 miles southeast of launching site, Cape Carnaveral, Fla. Distance, height, direction and speed of an object can be quickly calculated after device picks up 'glow'.

INFRARED RADIATIONS—invisible heat waves below the threshold of sensation—are enabling the Armed Forces and industry literally to "see in the dark."

Most publicized present infrared application is guiding missiles to their targets by "homing in" on a jet engine exhaust or other heat source .

But this accounts for only a part of the estimated $100 million being spent by the Armed Forces this year on infrared research, and many millions more by industry.

Major military use in the future, many scientists believe, will be to supplement or even replace radar in missile detection. First demonstration came May 18, 1958 at 1:06 a.m., an Army Jupiter was successfully launched from its pad at Cape Canaveral, Fla.

On a ship 1500 miles distant in the South Atlantic, a group of Barnes Engineering Corporation scientists aimed their infrared radiometers, developed as part of "Operation Gaslight," north into the starry night.

Fifteen minutes later, substantially ahead of any optical device, the radiometers detected the re-entry into the atmosphere of the three parts into which the Jupiter had separated, nose cone, instrument "package" and rocket body. In daylight, when the sun would mask atmospheric friction glow, infrared detection would be even more valuable.

First big military application was the World War II "snooperscope," used for night sniping. It was a rifle equipped with a heat source which focussed infrared radiations on a target and an optical device which converted them, when reflected back, into visible light. The soldier using it actually could aim in the dark.

But application today, both military and industrial, has discarded such "active" devices for the "passive" forms which detect external heat sources.

Infrared "homing" devices are used not only for missiles but for submarine-seeking torpedoes.

Infrared aerial reconnaissance cameras, which in effect convert heat into light, can penetrate camouflage or blackout. Every area where energy is being used, and is thus a scene of activity, betrays itself in outline on the exposed plate. Use of semiconductors permits detection, even at substantial distances, of objects only a few degrees warmer than their surroundings.

One of the most widespread single industrial applications of infrared is the Servo Corporation of America's Servosafe Hot Box Detector. Scanners alongside railroad tracks check each bearing for overheating as trains roar by, and send their findings to a permanent recorder.

Many major railroads use the device, which prevents costly delays by quickly spotting hot boxes.

The same technique is being used in power plants to detect corroded connections, overloaded or defective switches and furnace wall flaws.

Another important industrial use is in accurate measurement without contact with the object measured. Infrared gauges, accurate to within 0.003 inches, are finding ever wider uses in steel and other metallurgical plants, and in the glass, rubber and oil industries.

Most spectacular demonstration in the near future will be when the U.S. launches its moon probe rockets.

Infrared cameras will be aboard to record the lunar landscape, including the unknown "far side of the moon."

PROBING INFINITY

Radio telescope may help discover basic structure of universe

U.S. SCIENTISTS expect very shortly to project an actual physical object, an instrument-laden rocket, 240,000 miles into space to reach the moon.

And they also plan, by 1960, to probe unimaginably further, more than 5 billion light years, a distance in miles of 30 followed by 21 zeroes.

The new science which will make this possible is radio astronomy, which is based on the fact that many bodies in space—in theory, all—emit the entire electromagnetic wave spectrum, radio as well as light.

The tool they will use to penetrate the depths of the universe, and thus perhaps learn the secrets of its birth and basic structure, will be the world's most advanced radio telescope which will be erected at the National Radio Astronomy Observatory, Green Bank, West Virginia.

Completion of the telescope, which will cost $5 million, is scheduled for the spring of 1960.

Its parabolic "bowl," actually a vast directional radio antenna, will be 140 feet across, tower 205 feet above the ground at its highest point.

Its supporting "yoke" will contain 1202 tons of steel and ballast, and its polar axis shaft—which must at all times be exactly parallel to the earth's north-south axis—weighs 780 tons.

The entire weight of these and auxiliary units, a total of more than 2500 tons, will float on an oil film only .005 of an inch thick.

No point in the bowl, which will be composed of aluminum plates each 25 feet by 12 feet and have an area of about three-eighths of an acre, can vary more than a quarter of an inch from a perfect paraboloid.

Radio astronomy was born, and a new window opened onto the universe, in the early 1930s, when Karl Jasky, a Bell Telephone Laboratories engineer, discovered that certain radio waves causing circuit interference came from apparently fixed points in space.

World War II, with its tremendous advances in reception equipment, gave impetus to the new science. Means for analyzing the cosmic data thus received were established in 1944 by a Netherlands astronomer, H. C. van de Hulst.

He calculated that hydrogen atoms, the most prevalent in the universe, emitted radio signals at a frequency of 1420 megacycles.

In 1952 two Harvard physicists, Harold Ewen and Edward Purcell, succeeded in picking up this hydrogen radiation. Shifts from it enable radio astronomers to measure distance and speed of radiation sources, just as shifts in the light frequency of a known element aid optical instrument astronomers.

The new science will greatly extend the range of astronomy, since radio waves can pierce both the interstellar "dust clouds" and obstructions in the earth's atmosphere which block light.

The Green Bay radio telescope may help discover whether the universe is bounded or infinite, curved or flat, and its recession speed.

It will be operated by Associated Universities, Inc., which operates the Brookhaven National Laboratory, under contract with the National Science Foundation. Manufacture and installation will be carried out by the E. W. Bliss Co., of Canton, Ohio.

RADIO TELESCOPE AT GREEN BANK, W.VA. WILL BE ONE OF LARGEST PRECISION INSTRUMENTS EVER BUILT ANYWHERE

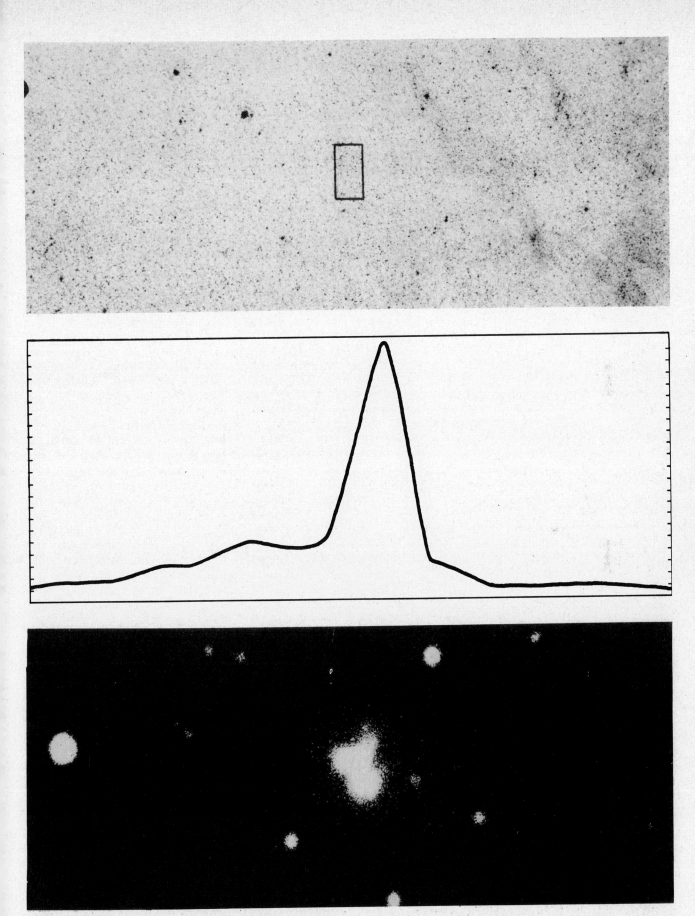

RADIO ASTRONOMY'S most spectacular achievement was discovery of two colliding universes. Top picture shows Cygnus A sky area *(in box)* as it appeared in pre-radio film observations, a mass of ordinary stars. Center graph *(peak)* reveals area's radio strength. Bottom shows galactic collision after optical astronomers pinpointed instruments on Cygnus A.

FAMOUS
MAKES

J OHN D. Rockefeller, Jr., and his
five sons are writing a new chapter in their family success story.

Nelson Rockefeller's landslide election victory, in which he won the New York State governorship by half a million votes while GOP candidates all over the country were going down to defeat, was more than a personal triumph.

It was proof positive that the Rockefellers have transformed their name from a symbol of ruthless power into one of wealth dedicated to the public good.

Fifty years ago, John D., Sr., was a national bogeyman. Rockefeller meant Standard Oil, Standard Oil

OLD JOHN D. (above) gave $19.31 to charity in his first year as a 50c-a-day bookkeeper. He founded the University of Chicago (1890), Rockefeller Institute for Medical Research (1901), General Education Board (1903), Rockefeller Foundation (1910). John D., Jr., (r.) restored Colonial Williamsburg, built the Cloisters, $15 million medieval art museum, established national parks from coast to coast, donated the land (worth $7.5 million) for the UN's New York headquarters. Nelson (far r.), his brothers and sisters all have their own favorite money giving projects in U.S. and abroad, have added the Rockefeller Brothers Fund. He is probably worth well over $100 million, gives away $20,000 of his estimated weekly income of $60,000. As N.Y. governor, he will get $50,000 yearly salary.

FAMILY FRIENDS

among top assets

LEFT TO RIGHT: JOHN D. JR., DAVID, NELSON, WINTHROP, LAURANCE, JOHN D. III. RARELY PHOTOGRAPHED TOGETHER, THEY GATHERED FOR JOHN D. SR.'S FUNERAL IN 1937.

meant monopoly, and monopolies were evil. The old man himself was seen as a harsh, stingy tyrant who had nothing but contempt for the ordinary citizen.

Nobody gave him much credit for his contributions to charity, which had already passed the $1-million-a-year mark in 1892.

Popular fear of the Rockefeller empire did not begin to recede until 1911, when the Standard Oil trust was "busted" by the Supreme Court.

Then, in 1913, came the incident that John D., Jr., himself has called "one of the most important things that ever happened to our family."

A strike broke out in the Colorado Fuel and Iron Company, of which John D., Jr., was board chairman.

The strike was long and bloody, and when the Colorado militia fired into the workers' tents, fury against the Rockefellers mounted to such a pitch that Congressmen were demanding John D., Jr.'s execution.

Old John D. refused to intervene. "We do our own dictating," he shouted at a board meeting when the directors timidly suggested that public opinion had been outraged.

But "Junior," under urging, decided to go to Colorado and see for himself. He spent two weeks there, wearing denim and listening to the workers' stories—and came back determined to break down the barriers that he felt his family's millions had created between it and the rest of the world.

Over the past 45 years, the Rockefellers have won friends and influenced people with imaginative philanthropy (at least $2.5 billion worth), conscientious public service, and the help of a succession of skilled public relations men, beginning with the now-legendary Ivy Lee.

It was under Ivy Lee's tutelage that John D., Sr., then in his 80's, began endearing himself to the public by passing out dimes to children.

John D., Jr., gave the family's public relations stock an even bigger boost when he began construction of Rockefeller Center in New York City during the darkest days of the depression, giving badly needed jobs to thousands of workers.

And his sons have refuted H. L. Mencken's charge that rich men's children are trained only for "polo and polygamy."

They are not only giving away money as enthusiastically as their father; they have also held literally dozens of directorships and trusteeships in business and non-profit organizations and government jobs at home and abroad.

When "Junior" had lunch with President Taft in 1911, his name was so far from being a political asset that he had to enter the White House by a side door. His second son has been welcomed in the front door under three administrations—and some day, may even live there.

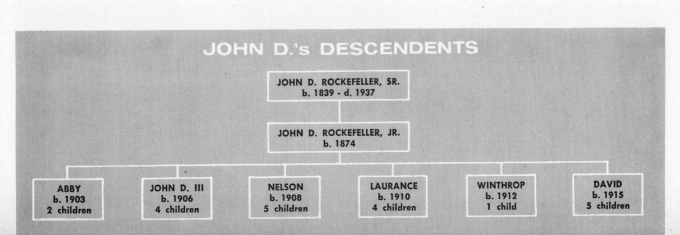

JOHN D.'s DESCENDENTS

JOHN D. ROCKEFELLER, SR.
b. 1839 - d. 1937

JOHN D. ROCKEFELLER, JR.
b. 1874

| ABBY b. 1903 2 children | JOHN D. III b. 1906 4 children | NELSON b. 1908 5 children | LAURANCE b. 1910 4 children | WINTHROP b. 1912 1 child | DAVID b. 1915 5 children |

KOREAN CHILDREN go to school in burnt out YMCA. New one will cost $750,000; Koreans will raise half themselves.

YMCA SPELLS HOPE TO WORLD'S YOUTH

In underdeveloped, "uncommitted" areas,

organization mans key

outposts in front lines of freedom

He seems incredible, but he represents two-thirds of mankind...he is

WILL THE YOUTH of the world, particularly of the two-thirds of mankind both "uncommitted" and hungry, choose freedom or Communism?

Many millions of them are bitter, sullen, suspicious; they can be won to the side of democracy, not by resounding slogans, but only by patient understanding, concrete example, hard, selfless work.

One of the Free World's most important assets in this struggle are the 10,000 branches of the Young Men's Christian Association, which in 76 nations are training freedom's future leaders in the classroom, on the playing field and, most important of all, in the trade school.

The YMCA was started in 1844 in London by George Williams, a religious young draper's assistant, who organized Bible reading classes to improve the spiritual life of the young men of the period.

The movement spread to this continent in 1851 (first branches were in Montreal and Boston.) Today the 2000 YMCAs in the U.S. and Canada participate in a joint program called World Service, which, working through the central YMCA agency in Switzerland, helps establish and support branches all over the world (since its inception in 1889 it has established 42 centers.) In 1959 World Service will send $1.7 million to 36 of them.

In addition, World Service has pledged $5 million to the $19.9 million "Buildings for Brotherhood" drive. The campaign, which provides for construction and expansion of 180 centers in 39 countries, will restore such war damaged buildings as the one in Seoul. Saturated

THE WORLD'S AVERAGE MAN

2/3 of the world's population go to bed hungry

45% of the people in the world

cannot read or write

One out of every 40 is a refugee

900 million are living under communism

700 million in 16 nations

have won independence since 1945

with oil and burnt by the Communists in 1950, the roofless, roomless shell in Korea is school for 1500 youngsters.

Basic principle of World Service is to help people to help themselves. Distribution of funds is considered as "seed money" planted in foreign branches to help them eventually grow into self-supporting, self-directing entities.

As its major contribution, World Service sends secretaries abroad to set up new branches and train local leaders to take over as soon as possible. Last year 38% of its budget went towards salary and maintenance of 56 secretaries at an approximate cost of $12,000 a man.

In underdeveloped areas the YMCA's work often extends far beyond the immediate needs of youth to actual

LARGEST YMCA in Europe is in Salonika, Greece, where boys *(l.)* study math. Although war damage left it partially unusable, it houses three schools, due for repairs.

ENTRANCE REQUIREMENT for stray boys in India is a shower. One rural center in Indukurpet, outcast village, is a "Boys' Town," houses 120 young "untouchables."

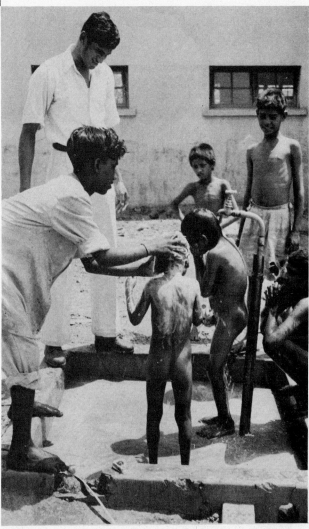

COLLEGE STUDENTS *(above)* organized under YMCA program bring technical know-how into Philippine backwoods. Boys *(below)* learn to play basketball at Hong Kong YMCA.

improvement of the economy of the section. World Service funds for such projects as rural reconstruction have gone into the development of scientific agricultural techniques at rural centers in India, which proved so successful they were adopted as standard UN practice.

YMCAs strategically situated in global hot spots help absorb the shock of international upheaval; to them World Service sends emergency funds—$58,000 last year. Uprooted refugees in Hong Kong flock to the YMCA for language courses, job-training and recreation. The YMCA school in Jordan provides the sole opportunity for education for refugee Arab youngsters. In Seoul the YMCA's "Boys' Town" shelters war orphaned boys.

Essential part of all Y programs is to build strong bodies, teach sportsmanship and combat juvenile delinquency through athletics. Both basketball and volleyball were invented by secretaries of YMCAs in Massachusetts; the former by James Naismith in 1891 and the latter by William Morgan in 1895.

Through its classes, clinics, camps and vocational training programs the YMCA has opened the way for countless young people. International figures whose boyhood experiences at YMCAs shaped their thinking include Carlos Romulo, Philippine ambassador to the U.S.; Syngman Rhee, president of Korea; and Charles Malik of Lebanon, president of UN assembly.

WALIANGULU tribesman, caught at side of carcass, seems unperturbed at prospect of jail term for poaching. It is hoped tribe, who live off elephants, can be converted from poachers into legal hunters.

DOOM OF THE GREAT BEASTS

AFRICA'S elephant, largest of the world's land mammals, seems doomed to extinction—except for a comparatively few survivors in zoos and closely guarded game preserves.

So do such other unique beasts as the African rhinosceros and the Cape buffalo.

No more than 200,000 elephants survive of the millions that once roamed unchallenged over the continent (they had no enemy but man) and average life has been cut from the fabled century to 50 years.

Most spectacular enemies of the great mammals are the native poachers, who cannot understand the necessity of conservation, and whose poisoned arrows, spear-studded deadfalls and antique shotguns take a toll of scores of thousands yearly. (In 1957, in a single area of Kenya, poachers slew 1000 elephants.)

NATIVE game ranger sergeant looks over some of valuable elephant tusks seized in recent mass anti-poacher drive in Kenya.

But actually a much greater threat is the mushrooming increase of the native population — and the consequent inexorable encroachment on remaining wild areas to provide new land for food crops and pasture and waterholes for cattle.

In Kenya and Uganda, for instance, buffalo have been slaughtered wholesale to eradicate the tsetse fly and open the way for native herds. In Amboseli, within sight of the snows of Kilimanjaro, and in the Ngorongoro Crater area, Masai cattle have been herded in by the tens of thousands, driving the elephants, rhinos and smaller game — and even the regal lions themselves — away from the waterholes into the desert.

The war for land and water, scarcest of African commodities, is raging between the wild fauna and man and his domestic animals everywhere from the Sudan to South Africa.

An added complication is that in many tribes prestige is based entirely on cattle ownership. Their enormously excessive herds, almost entirely unproductive, not only crowd out wild game but occupy thousands of square miles needed for crops for the expanding native millions.

POACHERS had begun butchering elephant when surprised by game rangers.

SPONTANEOUS DANCE OF JOY is staged by exultant Waliangulu as smiling comrades prepare to remove tusks from slaughtered elephant. Poison from arrowhead often takes days to complete the kill.

WARDEN JAN ALLEN sniffs *(above)* at captured arrow to detect poison brewed from leaves, dead animals. Other poachers use clever traps, short-range shotguns. Light plane *(r.)* acts as spotters for rangers. It is permanently stationed at Voi, anti-poacher headquarters in Kenya.

CRISIS OF HUNT is loosing of arrow at huge victim which gazes unsuspecting in bush a few feet away. Chance for shot was preceded by days of patient stalking to enable the poachers to draw near enough for kill. Waliangulu are trained from infancy to trail and shoot wild animals.

Elephant ivory and rhino "horn" (actually tightly packed hair) have been treasured throughout Asia for thousands of years, the latter as the most powerful of aphrodisiacs.

The poachers sell their loot to Arab traders, who smuggle it out at night by dhow. (Cargoes, despite the vigilance of warships and police, sometimes still include "black ivory," young female slaves.)

Whole tribes are poaching "specialists." The pygmy-like Waliangulu live off the elephant, tracking it for days until it drops from a poisoned thrust, selling the ivory and gorging on the meat in 10-day-long meals.

The Kenya and Tanganyika governments, in particular, wage ceaseless war on the poachers, even using airplanes to spot them at work. But so vast is the area, and so high the profits, that experts are convinced poaching will end only when the animals themselves are extinct.

GARGANTUAN TOOTH EXTRACTION is practised by poacher "specialists" trained in quick tusk removal. Carcass is then carefully cut up for elaborate banquet where the feasters will eat selves unconscious.

RHINOCEROS, TOO, faces extinction despite vigilant protection. It is being pushed into the desert lands by native cattle herds, is favorite poacher target.

Boy on left listens attentively as teacher lures cobras from basket. He will shortly make his own first attempt with gourd flute he holds.

BOLDEST

Mulladabad moppets sta

Mulladabad, India: *Pop. 2000.*
Principal export: *snake charmers.*

TEDDY BEARS and other usual toys make small children cry with fright in Mulladabad, India.

But cobras, pythons and other dangerous snakes cause the local toddlers to laugh with delight and rush forward to fondle them.

In isolated Mulladabad, India's snake-charming "capital," the reptiles are the children's only playthings, and training in handling them begins at the age of three.

From then on, the tots are encouraged to handle snakes, to let them coil around their tiny bodies, even to share with them their milk.

Little girls, who, when they grow up, will care for the snakes their husbands and brothers display in public, are taught to feed them the goat milk,

European child watches gravely as Mulladabad playmate proudly displays her favorite toy.

Snake charmers of Mulladabad are famous throughout India. Chief snakes they train, handle are python (l.), king cobra (c.).

There is no pet like a huge rock python—if you are three years old and happen to grow up in Mulladabad.

PROFESSION

essons in snake charming when only three

termites, leeches and live frogs which make up the diet of the small varieties, and the squirrels, ducks, kids and lambs swallowed whole by the huge pythons.

Boys are trained to play the eerie, plaintive flute music by which the charmer lures his venomous charges from the wicker baskets in which they are carried.

When the boys reach 10 or 12, they are taken on snake hunts in the jungle. Bare-armed and bare-legged, they are taught to capture the snakes with their hands.

Their only protection from the angry reptiles is quickness of eye and lightning agility.

Cobras, one of the world's most poisonous snakes, are caught when they are most dangerous—during the breeding season.

When the boys approach manhood, they learn the most important Mulla-

dabad secret — how to remove the poison glands. This knowledge is handed down from father to son, and must never be divulged to outsiders. Mulladabadis also have their own secret antidotes to poison, and ignore modern anti-venom serums.

Adult Mulladabadis form the bulk of snake charmers throughout India, and wander not only to Pakistan and Ceylon but as far away as Burma and Malaya. But Mulladabad is home, and they invariably return.

The charmers form a special sub-caste, and are ruled by a hereditary "king," 72-year-old Amar Nath.

He settles disputes, approves marriages and grants divorces, and woe betide the snake charmer who defies his authority.

The proud Mulladabadis prefer to ignore the Indian courts and police—after all, most of *their* personnel is afraid of snakes.

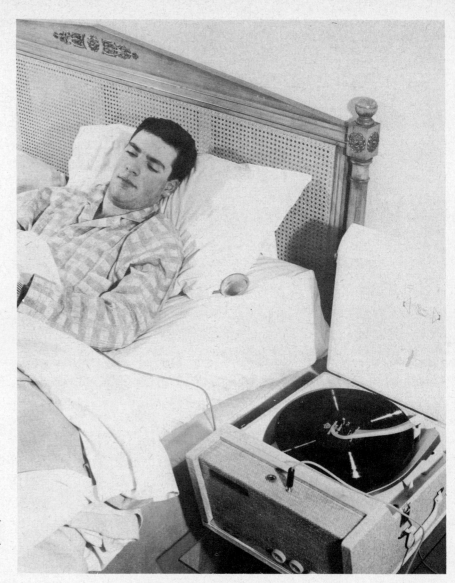

NEW WAY TO STRETCH THE DAY: STUDY IN YOUR SLEEP

Recorded courses can have sleeping students learn Russian, pass a real estate brokerage exam or give up smoking

"Sleep teaching" record industry is shooting for $50 million sales volume by 1965, hopes acceptance by business users will spur growth.

DORMIPHONE RECORD PLAYERS (*r.* and *l.*) are equipped with clock-timers which automatically turn records on and off while students sleep. Early studies indicated that subconscious mind was most receptive in "twilight" or semi-conscious state, more receptive during light sleep than heavy. According to recent research, however, learning goes on even in deepest sleep, periodic repetition is most effective help.

ACTRESS JOAN CRAWFORD (*below*, with Modernophone founder Max Sherover, who died in May, 1959) has used sleep learning to memorize scripts. So have Gloria Swanson, Paul Winchell, Rudy Vallee and others. TV star Art Linkletter learned enough Mandarin Chinese in a 10-day trial to chat with a visitor from Nationalist China in video demonstration.

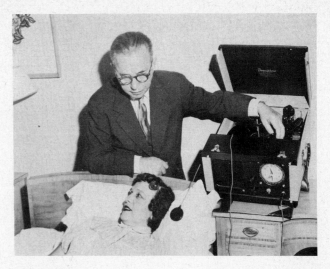

THE EXECUTIVE who complains that there are never enough hours in the day can now absorb statistics, learn a new language for a foreign assignment or give himself a psychological shot in the arm *while he sleeps*.

Under-pillow speakers and bedside record players have been on the market since the early 1940s, helping students learn their lessons and actors memorize scripts—but businessmen have only recently discovered that "sleep learning" can be a painless and profitable kind of overtime.

Salesmen are finding that recorded "self-help" courses played during the night help bolster their confidence during the next day's rounds.

Major corporations like United Fruit, Ford International, Chrysler Overseas Corp. and Gulf Petroleum are encouraging men headed for overseas posts to study languages in their sleep.

And leading aircraft manufacturers are reported to have set their key engineers to "sleep-learning" the Russian they need for technical reading.

Modernophone, Inc., a New York firm founded by the late Max Sherover and now headed by his son, Charles, appears to be the pioneer of sleep education. Sherover developed Linguaphone, the first of the recorded language courses for the wide-awake, 35 years ago. He became interested in the technique of sending recorded messages to the subconscious mind when he found that his grade school-age daughter could memorize the poems that he read to her while she dozed.

Today, Modernophone sells 6-7000 machines and accompanying courses a year in Mexico, Sweden, Norway, France and Italy. The firm keeps its U.S. sales figure to itself, but says it is well above the foreign total.

A Modernophone Dormiphone Record Player costs $149.50, or $157.50 with stereophonic sound. (Stereo does not hasten the sleep-learning process; Modernophone offers it because many customers use their equipment for ordinary daytime record-listening, too.) A Memory Trainer tape recorder, for users who want to record their own study material, costs $159.50.

Prices of records range from $7.50 for a single disc containing a talk by the Rev. Norman Vincent Peale to $57.50 for a complete Linguaphone language course to $165.00 for the longest personality development course.

Modernophone does not claim that a student can completely master an academic subject in his sleep with no daytime study at all. The records do, however, virtually eliminate time consuming and tedious drill, and greatly hasten the learning process.

Smaller companies from coast to coast are also selling sleep education materials and equipment. Most seem to be riding the do-it-yourself psychiatry boom and concentrating on self-help. The Breckenridge Institute and Master Productions, in California, and Unifonics Corp., New York, are probably Modernophone's closest competitors.

"Wage earner" shoppers pay extra for security of known brands.

WHY SELLING MUST BE CLASS

Media preferences, purchasing patterns vary sharp

JUDY O'GRADY and the Colonel's Lady are not sisters under the skin. And the entire advertising industry is currently utilizing all the tools of social research to determine how their backgrounds affect shopping habits.

Before an advertiser can sell with maximum effect at different social levels, he must first of all understand the differences between social classes—who buys what and why, how much buying power each has and how it is apportioned, who makes the buying decisions at different levels and how media preferences vary.

A man's income alone is not sufficient indication of his social class. Today, hourly paid workers like painters, plasterers and bricklayers average $35 more a week than most white collar bookkeepers, bank tellers and office managers. A more accurate measure of social class was developed by Dr. August B. Hollingshead of Yale University, who worked out an Index of Social Position based on occupation, education, residence neighborhood.

In an exhaustive study of social stratification of the population of New Haven, Conn., Hollingshead developed these five distinct classes:

Class I—$10,000-$50,000; major executives and professional men; college education; some inherited wealth.

Class II—$6,000-$10,000; executives of national organizations, business owners and lower-paid professionals; college education.

Media preferences of sample New Haven families, ranked by Hollingshead "Index of Social Position"

	Class I	II	III	IV	V
Radio news and commentary	35.1	23.4	13.9	9.1	7.8
Serious music	27.3	27.5	13.4	9.0	7.2
TV crime drama	2.6	11.0	20.9	27.6	24.9
TV sports	28.6	46.9	58.9	65.3	59.2
Literary, Education and Information magazines	39.0	28.9	9.6	4.1	1.2
Women's escape fiction	0.0	0.0	1.2	3.4	6.9
New York Times	50.6	40.3	24.2	8.7	4.0
New York News	1.3	6.6	9.6	16.5	15.1

Status-conscious shoppers pay extra for prestige symbols.

CONSCIOUS

by social class

Class III—$3,000-$10,000; white collar workers, small business proprietors; high school graduates.

Class IV—$3,000-$5,000; hourly paid workers, skilled and service workers; 8-12 years of schooling.

Class V—$2,000-$4,300; factory hands and unskilled labor, grammar school education.

What confuses the class picture is what Hollingshead calls the "upward mobile" segment of each category which aspires toward a higher class. These are the social climbers who shop across class lines and buy the prestige brands symbolic of the group they are aiming at. Upper and lower classes are least status conscious. Old-line Class I members, bending over backwards to demonstrate "under consumption," are more likely to choose a foreign car, a Chrysler Imperial or a Lincoln than a Cadillac, the No. I prestige symbol to Classes II and III. Most intense social aspirations are found among the "newly arrived" members of Class I and the majority of Classes II and III, striving to keep up a good front. These are the consumers most susceptible to products advertised

with liveried chauffeurs and country clubs in background.

Social ambitions, according to Thomas Kemm, of W. R. Simmons & Associates, Research Inc., explain why two products of almost identical quality and price appeal to different markets. Camel cigarettes, for example, have always been the "workingman's smoke." Before filters came on the market, Pall Mall was the prestige cigarette. Justerin & Brooks Scotch and Jack Daniels bourbon have within the past year become the status whiskies, far outselling equally expensive brands which lack "prestige."

Advertisers also need to know how purchasing decisions vary on different social levels. Greatest autonomy, here too, exists at both extremes of the social ladder. At the bottom household expenditures are completely the wife's responsibility and, at the top, economic freedom eliminates the need to debate purchases. In Classes II and III purchases are joint decisions with responsibility shared between husband and wife.

Macfadden Publications has drawn a sociological profile of its readership—women hourly paid workers and

295

CLASS BUYING

their families—to acquaint the upper echelons of business, far removed from the social orbit of this group, with its market potentialities.

The "Wage Earner" group has in the past 10 years increased twice as fast as the total population. Weekly wages have increased 57% to an average of $78.33.

What is most significant about this group, according to Macfadden, is that it has 62% of the nation's discretionary spending power (money available to the family after the basic fixed living costs). Free from such Class II and III financial burdens as college tuition, country clubs, extensive insurance and homes in the "right" neighborhood, wage earners often have more "loose" money they are free to spend as they please.

Wage earners live in two-family houses in older sections and in new suburban developments. Uninterested in a "good" address, they want to live in a "friendly neighborhood—not too ritzy—close to the job." The wife, in handling household finances, often uses a "gimmick economy"—small cash savings in teapots and envelopes. She tends to be more dependent on her family's approval and therefore indulges it more. There is an overabundance of food on her dinner table and more toys and treats for her children. Primarily an impulse shopper, she is attracted by cute novelties and often dissipates money on knick-knacks. She pays her bills in cash and is paying $32 a month for instalment purchases. She manages to save $10-$20 a month.

Camels are No. 1 cigarette in working class market. But ads use "he-man" appeal to attract other classes too.

THE INCOME IS THE SAME ...

Wage Earner Family of 4

	OCCUPATION	INCOME	TAXES
Husband	Tool & Die Maker	$ 5,262.40	$ 737.00
Wife	Housewife	–	–
Son (23)	Truck Driver	4,305.60	684.00
Daughter (18)	Receptionist	3,016.00	427.00
	Total	$12,584.00	$1,848.00

TAXES	LIVING EXPENSES	OTHER
$1,848.00 (\$139 less)	$4,880.00 ($1,839 less)	$5,856.00 ($1,978 more)

Living expenses are broken down into family household expenses, and fixed expenses outside of home accruing to son and daughter.

Savings are invested in home, furniture, clothing and the family car. As the family's true purchasing agent, she is working towards the "Great American Dream" — a "pretty" home equipped with every electric device and gadget for modern living. A 12-city survey of appliance stores showed that 56% of all appliances were sold to wage earner families. She wants her kitchen "fixed up nice" because it is the center of family social life.

The housewife in Classes II and III is more confident in her relations with her family and the outside world. She feels obligated to contribute to the success of her husband's career. And she guides her children with goals rather than gifts—a child's future success in the world is sufficient reward for being a good mother.

A "good" neighborhood in these classes is a fashionably correct one. Savings are invested in homes, insurance policies and savings accounts. The housewife is not as wrapped up in her home and devotes a good deal of time to community affairs.

She, too, wants modern kitchen equipment but for very different reasons than the wage earner wife. To her, labor saving devices are a means of cutting down time spent in the kitchen and getting out of it as quickly as possible.

Members of different classes, while often buying the same things, do so for different reasons and therefore must be reached through different advertising appeals. It appears that some homework in sociology is a must for advertisers who wish to penetrate specific markets.

THEY SPEND IT DIFFERENTLY

White Collar Family of 4

	OCCUPATION	INCOME	TAXES
Husband	Bank Vice Pres.	$12,584.00	$1,987.00
Wife	Housewife	–	–
Son (23)	Law School	–	–
Daughter (18)	College	–	–
	Total	$12,584.00	$1,987.00

TAXES	LIVING EXPENSES	OTHER
$1,987.00	$6,719.00	$3,878.00

Living expenses include son's and daughter's tuition and campus living costs, landscaping, and other necessities to "keep up with the Jones".

Department of Marketing and Research, Macfadden Publications Inc.

Knowledgeable people buy Imperial

—and they buy it by the case

Whiskey by Hiram Walker

Imperial Whiskey ad appeals to status-sensitive consumer. Ad stating "Knowledgeable people" buy it confers prestige.

endorsements: NAMES THAT MAKE NEWS MAKE SALES

Celebrities are selling everything from toothpaste to trucks. Agencies find that ads starring "big" names catch attention and gain acceptance for a product. After a vigorous clean-up campaign, testimonials are flourishing—7640 products have been endorsed by 14,000 celebrities in the past 15 years. An endorsement, to be successful, must be honest, believable.

HARPER'S MAGAZINE ADVERTISER.

SARAH BERNHARDT

The great French actress and woman, is so pleased with the delicate bouquet and flavor of

"Gold Seal"
America's Best CHAMPAGNE

that she wrote to a friend:

" I find the Urbana Wine Co.'s Gold Seal Champagne excellent—in fact, equal to many French Champagnes. It surprises me that such a fine wine can be produced in America."

Sarah Bernhardt

New York, April 7, 1901.

GOLD SEAL is served in every first-class café and club, and sold everywhere at half the price of French wine

MME. BERNHARDT.

URBANA WINE CO., Urbana, N. Y., Sole Makers

SARAH BERNHARDT patronizingly testified in a 1901 ad for a domestic champagne—which was trying to cut into sales of imported brands—that, to her surprise, it equalled many French varieties. For this she received the modest fee of $500.

ELSA MAXWELL provides her guests with Hudson paper napkins, J. Edgar Hoover wears a Cyma watch and Donald Douglas drives a Lincoln. Such illustrious examples, the advertising industry assumes, influence Mr. and Mrs. John Q. Public to buy and use these articles also.

Testimonial advertising—endorsement of a product by a satisfied user—is as old as advertising itself. Earliest modern day example was the Pear's soap ads in 1889, which had both the Rev. Henry Ward Beecher and actress Lily Langtry testifying from their diverse experience about the excellence of Pear's.

In the early 1900s testimonials were in full flower. But they fell into disrepute because of blatant abuses and excesses. Deceased persons were lending their names to patent medicines. "Royal" personages unknown to the Almanach de Gotha were invented at the drop of a press agent's

Mr. Douglas with his Lincoln Premiere Landau—and the new Douglas DC-8 jetliner

"Design is the vital thing— and Lincoln proves it beautifully,"

says planebuilder Donald Douglas, chairman of the board, Douglas Aircraft Company.

World pioneer and already legendary leader in aircraft production. Dynamic designer and engineer. Rugged individualist. Sportsman. This is the man who directs Douglas Aircraft. The kind of man for whom we planned and built the magnificent 1959 Lincoln.

A man who responds to Lincoln's classic, dramatically simple lines. And who can fully appreciate the luxurious spaciousness provided in this distinctive design. A spaciousness that lets you step in and out with ease. That gives you more head room, more leg room and foot room than any other car in America.

And Lincoln furnishes its spacious interiors with unparalleled elegance. You sit in seats the height of a fine armchair. You are surrounded with specially loomed fabrics, handcrafted leathers and superb coachwork.

Donald Douglas, a man accustomed to the finest, is quick to recognize value and distinction and refinement. We invite you to do as he did—compare Lincoln with any of the other fine cars. We feel sure that you, too, will find this is the year to change to Lincoln.

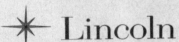 **Lincoln**

Classic beauty...unexcelled craftsmanship

LINCOLN DIVISION · FORD MOTOR COMPANY

Donald Douglas seated in his office with models of two of his most famous planes, the DC-3 which made aviation history—and the DC-8 jetliner, another Douglas masterpiece of design and construction soon to be introduced.

DONALD DOUGLAS, CHAIRMAN OF THE BOARD, DOUGLAS AIRCRAFT CO., POSES WITH A LINCOLN AND A DOUGLAS JET, TOO

hat. And in one fruitful day actress Constance Talmadge endorsed 400 different products.

In the past 15 years, however, the Federal Trade Commission has helped the industry scrub behind the ears and attain the dignity of long pants. Since 1945 more than 14,000 celebrities have endorsed 7640 products at a total media cost of $1.2 billion.

About 60% of all testimonial campaigns are handled by Jules Alberti, president of Endorsements Inc., a unique organization which grosses about $1 million annually solely from bringing advertisers (through their agencies) and endorsers together.

After being called in by an agency, Alberti goes through his celebrity file (marital, moral and professional status are all noted) and comes up with a "name" most suited to the product. Fees to celebrities range from nothing (a plug for a forthcoming picture or book is sometimes sufficient) to a fat $25,000 for a big name star.

Celebrity testimonials lend authority to advertisers' claims, if personality has logical connection with product

Alberti's fees, which range up to $30,000 for a several-stars TV campaign, are based on the celebrity's fees plus the amount of time and expense involved in signing him up.

The remaining 40% is handled by publicity agents on a free lance basis and by advertising agencies themselves. J. Walter Thompson Co. is the only one with a separate celebrity department. Lux toilet soap and Pond's cold cream, endorsed respectively by Hollywood stars and society women, are two "old timers" at Thompson's. More recently, the agency has been handling the United States Line campaign. Prominent industrialists, photographed testifying to the pleasures of the crossing, do so simply because they *are* pleased—no fee is involved.

To be successful, according to Alberti, self-appointed watchman of the industry, an endorsement must be honest, believable and, above all, properly cast, with a logical connection between product and personality. It was asking too much of subway riders, he says, to believe Lady Iris Mountbatten when she appeared on subway cards claiming she loved Warren's chewing gum. Alberti convinced the Airwick Co. that a testimonial from a movie star's housekeeper would be much more credible than one from the star herself, who knew little of household chores.

Does Mickey Mantle really smoke Viceroy cigarets?

Prime requisite for an honest testimonial is that the endorser be a valid user of the product. The FTC established that a 30-day "user" is a legitimate one. Usually a month's or more supply of the product is sent to the celebrity; if, after use, he reports he likes it, the requirement is satisfied. Some advertisers, however, are even more exacting. American Tobacco sent out questionnaires to potential celebrities for a Lucky Strike campaign, asking among other things, their brand of cigarets. Only those who answered "Luckies" were considered. Rounding up seven southern farmers who were long-time users of a particular laxative involved a manhunt originating with drug distributors and ending in local druggists' charge files.

A celebrity is required to sign a release of the endorsement (preferably with as few time and media restrictions as possible). The contract also bars him from endorsing a similar or competing product for a year.

A study which compared attention-getting value of 100 testimonials with that of 100 non-testimonial ads in five leading magazines over one year revealed that endorsements attracted much greater attention. Celebrity ads with highest scores had identification in *small* type, little or no comment.

Movie, TV and stage stars are most in demand. Sports figures, society leaders and fashion and interior designers appeal to special markets. Use of titled persons, once in great vogue, is becoming negligible, although the Duke of Argyll has kept

PERSONAL PRESTIGE of James Farley, former Postmaster General and present chairman of the board, Coca-Cola Export Corp., lends authority to Carte Blanche's claims. Ad omits testimonial comment. If used, is best left in endorser's own words.

For men of responsibility
like James A. Farley

CARTE BLANCHE

The Hilton All-Purpose Credit Card—
Your Finest Credit Credential

TOUGHEST ASSIGNMENT for Alberti was getting Gen. MacArthur's "name" for Cyma watch. He reached MacArthur at Waldorf, when General checked in after Korean dismissal. This is only time MacArthur, who received $1000 watch, lent his name. Ad was designed as honor award; involved no testimonial.

STANDING ORDER from McGregor requires Alberti to obtain Open Golf champion every year. Current title holder Tommy Bolt wears McGregor jacket.

DOUBLE BARRELED "sell" in Hertz ad plugs Esther Williams' International Swimming Pool Corp. at the same time she endorses Hertz auto rental service.

busy autographing a brand of Argyll socks and the Duke of Bedford (in Great Britain) endorses anything and everything to pay off $16 million death duties on his father's estate.

Statesmen are the toughest names to deliver. "Bringing them back alive" is Alberti's specialty. For the Cyma Watch Co. he rounded up Philippine Ambassador Carlos Romulo, Gen. Douglas MacArthur and Mrs. Eleanor Roosevelt. And for the Zenith hearing aid ads he obtained Mrs. Roosevelt, the late Charles Edison and noted author Rupert Hughes.

Such distinguished names lend prestige to the entire industry, which has come a long way since the Lydia Pinkham ad at the turn of the century. The testimony from a much-married beauty read:

"I have taken three bottles of Lydia Pinkham Compound and feel like a new man."

THE PACKAGING PICTURE
INDUSTRY VOLUME: $15 billion in 1958 for all materials, manufacturing, services.
AMONG TOP DESIGNERS: Egmont Arens (N.Y.); Donald Desky (N.Y.); Karl Fink (N.Y.); Frank Gianninoto (N.Y.); Walter Landor (San Francisco); Lippin-

DESIGNING

YESTERDAY'S corner grocer *(below)* helped his customers make choices, recommended brands. In today's giant supermarkets *(above)*, customer is on her own. Packages must be bright and attractive enough to sell themselves, and making sure they do is job of top designers like Egmont Arens *(r.,* with 73 of the 748 experimental packs he developed when Philip Morris switched to red, white and gold in 1955).

cott & Margulies (N.Y.); Raymond Loewy (N.Y., Chicago); Jim Nash (N.Y.).

AMONG TOP RESEARCHERS: Center for Research in Marketing (N.Y.); Color Research Institute (Chicago); Institute for Motivational Research (N.Y.); James M. Vicary (N.Y.); A. J. Wood (Phila., N.Y.).

POST TOASTIES packages span 50 years: early 1900s *(l.)*, 1936 *(c.)*, new design with "appetite appeal" for 1959 *(r.)*.

STAR SALESMEN

Dollars spent on keeping packages up-to-date pay big dividends in today's market

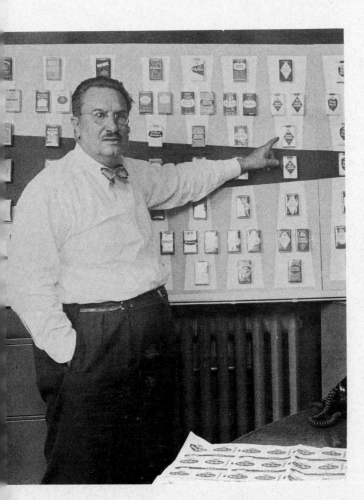

THE RIGHT package can do just about as much to build sales as the quality of the product inside—and manufacturers of consumer items from cereal to cigarets are becoming more and more concerned with making sure that they get full value from their packaging dollars.

Seventy-five years ago, when grocers stocked crackers in barrels, flour in sacks and butter in tubs, take-home boxes were a novelty.

Their design, as often as not, was the fruit of the company president's own imagination. It ran to curlicues and fancy lettering, photographs of bewhiskered founders, roses and violets for the ladies, and (forerunners of today's cutout-covered cereal boxes) comic pictures for the children, who were often sent to the corner store.

The do-it-yourself era of package design, which lasted until the 1920s, produced plenty of top management men who were also advertising geniuses, like American Tobacco's George Washington Hill, and trademarks so good that they are still household favorites.

But with the rise of mass production and distribution and big-time advertising, manufacturers began taking their packaging problems to professional industrial designers (Donald Desky in 1928 and Raymond Loewy in 1929 were among the first to set up shop).

In the 1930s, the designers gleefully began stripping Victorian furbelows from their clients' packages in favor of big, clean type, simple, striking layouts and bright colors. They encountered plenty of resistance from some manufacturers, who failed to see how grandpa's design could possibly be improved upon, but they usually won.

Packaging turned into a really big business after World War II, when supermarkets, which had been around since the mid-1930s, became a national institution.

Today, the independent designer's "intuitive rightness" is still highly respected—and well paid. (A design firm's retainer, which in most cases covers many services besides packaging, may run as high as $5000 a month.)

But everybody is getting into the act—even a small package change calls for consultation with the client's top sales management (and sometimes his own "captive" design force), packaging materials supplier, advertising agency and market researchers.

303

MINIATURE SUPERMARKET at Jim Nash Associates' New York office lets clients (like Rath Packing's Wesley W. Johnson, *l.*, with Nash vice president Gerald Frisch) see their new packages under point-of-sale conditions.

PANEL OF HOUSEWIVES meets to discuss old and new Lipton Soup packages with staff psychologist at Peekskill, N.Y., office of Center for Research in Marketing.

The trend toward teamwork in package development is leading to the establishment of packaging committees in many big organizations.

Nabisco, which pioneered the team approach, gives committee seats to top men from all departments concerned with packaging—advertising, laboratory, production, purchasing, sales and special products. It gets this group together with representatives of its design firm, Raymond Loewy Associates, and its own art department to confer on all packaging problems.

One indication of management's increased interest in packaging is the appearance of more than 4000 presidents, owners, partners and directors at the American Management Association's 1958 packaging show. (The AMA greeted more top level guests this year, April 13-17 at Chicago's International Amphitheater.)

A second trend is toward increasing emphasis on market research.

The researchers have analysed the behavior of the housewife in a supermarket as enthusiastically as anthropologists studying a group of South Sea Islanders.

Her "blink rate" has been clocked by James M. Vicary (eye-blinking is a sure-fire index of nervous tension, and the shopper's rate ordinarily drops so low as to indicate that she is practically in a trance). Other observers have found that it takes her only 1/50 of a second to pass a counter, and that two out of three of the packages she takes home are "impulse purchases."

A package has to be pretty eye-catching and appealing to get picked off the shelves under these conditions—

especially since it is competing not only with other national brands, but also, probably, with the store's private brand, which gets the best display. And its job has only begun when it reaches the checkout counter.

It must look handsome, and be easy and practical to use, in the color-coordinated kitchen or bathroom at home—or even on the informal dinner table.

In other words, it has to keep on selling itself until it gets thrown out with the trash.

It must be effective and easy to identify in magazine, newspaper and television advertising.

And no matter how good it is, in the vast majority of cases, it has to keep getting better all the time.

DOES PACKAGE CHANGE BOOST SALES? When Egmont Arens scrapped Colonial Sugar's plain brown pack (*r.*), designed bright new version, sales quadrupled in two-and-a-half years.

BORDEN TRADEMARK, Elsie the Cow, recognized by 81% of all adult Americans, got a yellow daisy frame from Frank Giannioto in 1952 when he redesigned entire milk carton series.

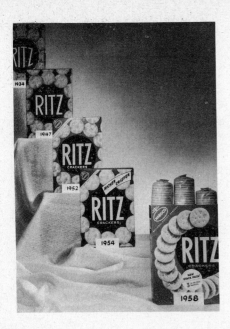

NABISCO'S RITZ has changed its package five times in 15 years. Latest Loewy version features new "stack pack" wrap.

BRILLO SOAP PADS, on the market since 1913, with only one minor package change, got new Arens design in 1958.

FASHIONS IN BABIES as well as in packages have changed since 1900, when first Ivory Baby *(above)* appeared in advertisements. Jim Nash's handling of Baker's Cocoa can *(below)* shows how popular trademark can get modern poster-style treatment, still keep identity. Nash also redesigned Swansdown Cake Flour's 1930-model box *(bottom)* to give swan trademark star billing, then to add appetizing cake slice. New redesign, with bigger piece of cake, smiling swan, will soon appear.

SOCIETY BANDS SWING TO FAST TEMPO OF $15 MILLION ANNUALLY

Veteran leaders, booked years ahead, are permanent fixtures of social

Society has its own style of dance music—old favorites played in fast fox trot tempo—as opposed to the dragging "business man's bounce." Catering to the 400's taste has become a multi-million dollar business; a top maestro often sends out 12 bands a night.

Duke of Windsor, shown dancing at Waldorf, also enjoys a turn on the drums. Favorite song is "It Had To Be You."

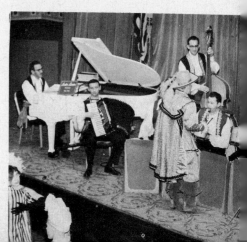

Debutante cotillions have largely replaced lavish individual debuts, but society bands continue to play on at both.

scene everywhere in U.S.

KEEPING SOCIETY hopping at a fast fox trot tempo is big business. Society dance bands' over-all gross in 1958 was more than $15 million, and 1959 promises to be even more tuneful—and profitable.

Big time band leaders like Lester Lanin and Meyer Davis in New York, Ruby Newman in Boston and Ernie Hecksher in San Francisco are contractors as much as they are musicians, supplying bands of any size at any time for charity balls, cotillions, college proms and private parties.

At the peak of the social season, both Lanin and Davis often have as many as 26 bands playing in 11 different cities in one evening. Working

Lanin and band often turn up in masquerade costumes at informal affairs. At college proms he gives out zany crew hats to dancers.

with permanent staffs around which they build bands, each can draw on a large stockpile of musicians when engagements get heavy. The American Federation of Musicians estimates that society dance bands provide employment for 12,500 men— 5% of its membership. Lanin's payroll alone totals 800.

Cost of paying the piper varies from $50 for a single accordion player to $15,000 for a large orchestra. Costs are higher when the leader himself puts in an appearance—exacting hostesses who insist on Lanin's or Davis' personal services will often book a date 10 years in advance.

The average band today is about 15 men, but they are sometimes as large as 75. Complicated wage scales set up by the A.F.M. are dependent upon where musicians are playing— home or hotel—, and playing time per hour—normal is 40 minutes, continuous 55. A 10-man band playing for a four-hour Saturday night dance at a country club in the New York area gets from $700-$1200.

Meyer Davis, who is the "grandfather" of society band leaders and is known as the "millionaire maestro," started out in Washington, D. C., over 40 years ago. In addition to six orchestras on the luxury liners *United States* and *America,* there are Meyer Davis bands at such posh resorts as Palm Beach, Swampscott and White Sulphur Springs. Meyer Davis music is also a White House habit; Presidents Harding, Hoover, Coolidge, Roosevelt and Eisenhower all danced to his tunes at inaugural balls.

Lester Lanin, who cut his teeth on the drums in his father's society orchestra at Philadelphia Main Line

Cabots and Lowells dance to Ruby Newman's music in Boston. Newman played at both James and John Roosevelt's weddings.

parties, is perhaps the biggest name in the dance band trade today. In addition to setting the tempo of many of the most important balls in the country, he enlarged his audience as of three years ago with an on-the-spot recording of the Monte Carlo Ball in New York—scene of the announcement of Grace Kelly's engagement. Since then his albums have become the No. 1 best seller in the dance band field.

Although, obviously, maestros cannot personally wield the baton at every engagement, sub-leaders and all members of the band are so thoroughly schooled in the organization's particular style, phrasing and arrangements that the music is uniform. As Lanin puts it, "my orchestras are like canned soup—the same wherever you buy it."

Society music is distinguished by its brisk tempo and well marked beat as opposed to the "businessman's bounce," which has a moderate tempo with a dragging beat. The only change in tempo is made for the college crowd, which prefers its music somewhat slower and dreamier than their elders do. The repertory is basically show tunes and old favorites rather than a reflection of current hit parade selections. Occasionally a waltz may be played, and some Latin American tunes may turn up later in the evening, but rock-and-roll is frowned upon at any hour.

Leaders, who know their social register from Astor to Vanderbilt, can judge the mood of a crowd and keep a party from falling flat on its face. They are thoroughly familiar with the preferences of the people they play for. Lanin knows, for example, that Henry Ford cannot resist leading the band to "When the Saints Come Marching In." Harvey Firestone likes to beat out a tune on the maracas and John Hay Whitney enjoys "teasing" the clarinet. Col. Sergei Obolensky enjoys the reputation of being a superb waltzer. Henry Ford usually runs away with the jitterbuging honors.

Harold Vanderbilt's favorite tune is "In Little Old New York." Francis du Pont invariably requests "Who." Ali Khan calls for "I Concentrate On You." But Barbara Hutton does not enjoy "I Found A Million Dollar Baby in the Five and 10 Cent Store."

SCIENCE, ENGINEERING LEAD HIGH SCHOOL JOB PREFERENCE LIST

But teenagers consider "egghead" worst term of reproach

THE AVERAGE high school boy (56.5%) plans to go to college, would like to work in science or engineering (38.7%) and picks General Electric (18.3%) as the company for which he would most like to work.

His coed classmate also expects a college career (44.8%), but is more likely (27.1% to 14.6%) to look for a job immediately after graduation from high school.

Her first job preference is teaching (19.7%), followed by secretarial (10.8%), retail business (8.7%) and science or engineering (8.4%). She also (16.6%) would like to work for General Electric.

None of the boys, and only a tiny fraction (1.6%) of the girls, now plan marriage.

This profile of the average teenager is the result of a survey just completed by *Scholastic Magazines*, and is based on replies from 5000 students (75% in 11th and 12th grades) in 43 states.

Boys, the survey reveals, prefer (66%) to work with things and girls (72.5%) with people.

Very few (6.7%) in either group want to work with ideas, and both boys (31.1%) and girls (32.6%) consider "egg-head" the worst term of reproach.

Both boys (44.2%) and girls (57.1%) consider savings banks the best place for savings, followed by government bonds (boys, 33.3%, girls, 31%) and life insurance (boys, 10%, girls, 7%). But both (boys, 9.2%, girls, 3.3%) consider stocks as a possible investment.

The high school population of the U.S. is presently estimated at 16 million, and is the nation's fast growing group. As a market, the teenagers themselves now spend $6 billion a year, influence even greater family purchases.

COMPANY PREFERENCE (%)

Company	Boys	Girls	Total
General Electric	18.3	16.6	17.4
General Motors	11.2	7.1	9.1
du Pont	6.3	7.4	6.8
Westinghouse	3.6	3.7	3.7
Bell Telephone	3	3.9	3.4
IBM	2.2	1.6	1.9
Ford	2.2	1.3	1.7
Kaiser	2.2	0.5	1.3
U.S. Steel	1.8	1.9	1.8
Chrysler	0.7	0.3	0.5
Miscellaneous	15.8	16.3	16
No answer	32.7	39.4	36.4

CAREER PREFERENCE (%)

Field	Boys	Girls	Total
Science or Engineering	38.7	8.4	23.5
Manufacturing	8.2	2	5.1
Teaching	7.3	19.7	13.5
Retail	7	8.7	7.8
Mechanics or Crafts	5.7	....	2.8
Religious or Social Work	3.5	7.6	5.6
Farming	3	....	1.5
Armed Services	2.2	0.3	1.2
Law	2.2	0.1	1.1
Architecture	1.2	....	0.6
Secretarial	....	10.8	5.4
Nursing	0.1	7	3.6
Office Work	....	4.5	2.3
Airline Stewardess	....	2.9	1.5
Beautician	....	2.9	1.5
Marriage	....	1.1	0.5
Miscellaneous	9.7	4.3	7
No answer	8.1	10.5	9.4

NAME PROUDEST OF (%)

Name	Boys	Girls	Total
Democrat	24.5	27.8	26.2
Capitalist	17.3	9.6	13.4
Republican	14.3	19.1	16.7
Conservative	12.8	14.7	13.8
Liberal	11.1	11.5	11.3
Fundamentalist	5.3	4.7	5
Radical	3.1	1.5	2.3
Politician	2.3	1.6	1.9
Socialist	0.8	2.5	1.7
No answer	7.2	6.5	6.8

NAME RESENTED MOST (%)

Name	Boys	Girls	Total
Egghead	31.1	34.1	32.6
Proletarian	10.5	7.9	9.2
Spendthrift	10.4	11.6	11
Reactionary	9.7	9.5	9.6
Huckster	8.6	10.6	9.6
Capitalist	8.1	8.7	8.4
Politician	5.3	3.3	4.3
Strikebreaker	3.1	3.1	3.1
Wall Streeter	2.4	2.4	2.4
Millionaire	2.2	0.7	1.4
No answer	8.6	8.1	8.4

PREFER TO WORK WITH (%)

Field	Boys	Girls	Total
Things	66	13	39.5
People	23.2	72.5	47.9
Ideas	6.7	6.7	6.7
No answer	4	7.8	5.9

ATOMS FOR TREES

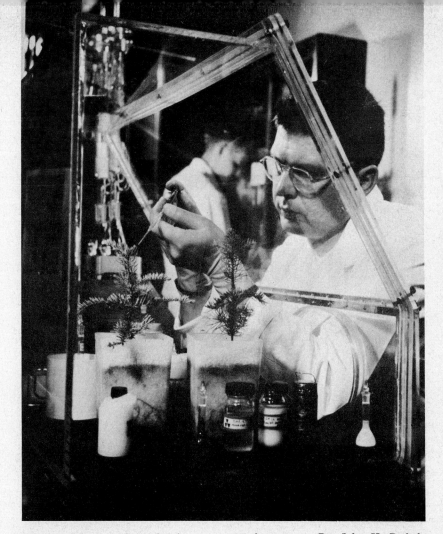

ATOMIC power is helping trees grow in the state of Washington.

At the Centralia, Wash., Forestry Research Center of Weyerhaeuser Timber Co., radioactive isotopes have become a valuable experimental tool.

Research foresters are introducing identifiable isotopes into trees and following their paths to determine their behavior.

Use of these tracers is giving a clearer understanding of the growing process — how green plants use the carbon dioxide in air, water, soil nutrients and the sun's energy to form the compounds essential to life —and is throwing new light on seed germination and genetics.

MAN IN CHARGE at Centralia forestry research center is Dr. John H. Rediske (*above*, handling tiny seedlings with gloved hands, his face shielded by glass). Weyerhaeuser Timber's use of radioactive isotopes to grow higher quality forest products at a faster rate is example of wide range of atoms-for-peace research.

The isotopes are also helping determine how chemicals may be used to stimulate tree growth, kill weeds without damaging the trees, and prevent damage by insects, disease or animal pests.

Animals, especially deer and wapiti, are one of the worst menaces to growing seedlings. Radioactive materials are being used to develop a repellent which will keep these animals away from the young trees.

If current experiments with selenium, a non-metallic, sulphur-like element, prove as successful as they now seem to be, young seedlings will stand a much improved chance of growing into full-sized trees for lumber and pulp.

Reports from Centralia indicate that radioisotopes will contribute even more to the forestry research of the future, helping to protect and develop one of the world's most precious natural resources.

ATOMIC EXPERIMENTS at center are surrounded by every possible safeguard. (Dr. Rediske enters restricted area.)

PHOTOGRAPHS of beta-particle radiation are being used to find weapon against parasitic dwarf mistletoe, pine enemy.

"FUN"

PARK REVOLUTION

New amusement centers stress fantasy and education; big companies chief investors

"FAMILY STYLE" amusement parks, without a roller coaster or a penny arcade in sight, are attracting major U.S. corporations as million-dollar investors.

The new, king-size parks, inspired by Walt Disney Productions, Inc.'s highly successful Disneyland, offer their visitors imaginative exhibits based on history, folklore, fairy tales and science fiction—and many of these are sponsored by public relations-conscious companies.

At Disneyland itself, Richfield Oil, Trans World Airlines, Kaiser Aluminum, Monsanto Chemical and American Motors are among the corporate concessionaires that have boosted the park's investment total from $17 million to $23 million in three years.

Disneyland's chief California rival, the newly-opened, 28-acre, $10 million Pacific Ocean Park at Santa Monica, is owned jointly by Columbia Broadcasting System and the Los Angeles Turf Club, operator of the world famous Santa Anita race track. Coca-Cola sponsors its "Neptune's Kingdom," which features a "visit to the bottom of the sea," and Westinghouse Electric is planning to open an "Enchanted Forest" there later this year. In the "Forest" will be found a "home of tomorrow," complete with automated appliances, and a 100-foot replica of the atom

submarine, Nautilus, which (with a Westinghouse reactor) recently sailed under the North Pole.

Texas boasts a $10 million, 100-acre park in Dallas, "Texas Under Six Flags," which counts Rockefeller Center, Inc., and real estate giants Webb & Knapp among its investors. Its star attraction is a mock Civil War battlefield where visitors can ride between the front lines of the Northern and Southern armies.

The prime mover behind the coast-to-coast spread of the big parks is Marco Engineering Co., Inc., of Los Angeles, headed by C. V. Wood, a former Disneyland vice-president. Marco already holds contracts worth $45 million for construction of "family style" playlands in Denver, Houston, San Antonio, Florida and even Venezuela and Mexico.

A $6 million park in Caracas, Venezuela, will have as its theme the story of Columbus and the discovery of America; one in Mexico City will tell the "Story of the Conquistadores."

All these—and a number of others—will be open for business in 1959 or 1960. Traditionalists can only hope that they will not ban such indigestible fare as cotton candy and crackerjack.

HISTORY AND LEGEND come delightfully to life in new amusement parks. Disneyland offers a full-scale replica of an old-time full-rigged ship *(opposite page)*, a model turn-of-the-century small town *(l.)*, and, for future space pioneers, a fanciful "Tomorrowland" *(c.)*. Another California playland is Santa's Village (r.), located in San Bernardino Mountains.

Old-time canteens now luxury chain
serving G I families throughout free world

PX FACE-LIFTING

UNCLE SAM runs the world's largest discount chain — the Army and Air Force Exchange Service.

Its 12,429 outlets, scattered across the entire Free World, have annual net sales of $830 million. They sell servicemen and their families everything from diapers ($2 million worth in 1957) to mink coats.

The old time PX whose stock in trade was cigarets and razor blades has had a dramatic face lifting. Today 80% of all servicemen are married; consequently family merchandise now makes up 30% of PX inventories. Exchange stores now carry a stock as luxurious as that of any big department store.

Bargain basement prices (20% lower than retail stores) are based on the historic tradition of "service to the serviceman at the most reasonable cost." Volume purchasing, plus waiving of state and municipal taxes in this country and immunity from U.S. taxes overseas helps hold costs down. Cigarets are 10¢ in a German PX.

To appease local retailers who cry unfair competition, A&AFES has set up a rigid Authorized List limiting items that *domestic* exchanges are permitted to stock. In addition, PXs

FAMILY FUNCTION of PX is shown as kids visit Santa while mothers shop for clothes. A&AFES is big business today; PX at Fort Knox grosses about $10 million annually.

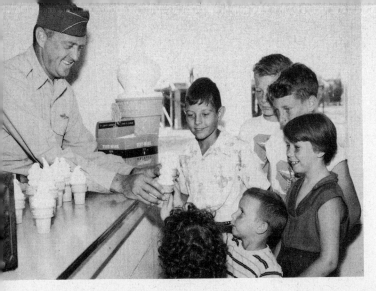

TREATS for kids are far cry from early days when sutlers peddled snuff to troops. PXs were run by individual military units until '41, when they were coordinated under morale branch of War Dept.

FORT SAM HOUSTON's huge PX is typical of modern exchanges. 16¢ of average G.I. dollar spent in PXs goes for tobacco (cigarette sales were $100 million a year), 15¢—clothing, 9¢—beverages, 4¢—magazines and stationery, 4¢—jewelry.

give a healthy lift to local economies by purchasing in the area—in 1957 Fort Sam Houston bought $2 million worth of goods from San Antonio merchants. PXs, whose employees are 99% civilians, also create huge local payrolls—in the U.S., 1957 total was $20 million. Service units such as barber shops, shoe and watch repairs, laundry and cleaning, and garages often are leased to local businessmen. Some 3000 concessionaires at domestic PXs did a combined volume of $85 million last year.

In overseas areas local merchants' cries that they are being robbed are even louder. In the post war period PXs, oases of abundance in deprived areas, were glaring foci of irritation as well as rich sources for the black market. However, as local economies improved, tensions have lessened.

PX purchasing agents overseas buy a good deal of local merchandise. Bases in Greenland report a run on totem poles and sealskin kayaks (Eskimo canoes). PXs in Japan are doing a land office business in "happy coats," fingertip length smoking jackets worn at parties. In Saudi Arabia GIs are buying up camel saddles to use as TV chairs.

The overseas PX is more than just a glorified bargain counter. It actually spells home for lonesome service families. Here a GI wife can buy the latest stateside version of the chemise while her teenager can find the newest rock and roll record. When the recent hoopla over hula hoops spread overseas, GI children sent out an S.O.S. for hoops from the States. Shipping was a problem because of the space required but PX officials

met the demand just as they had that for Christmas trees from GIs in Eritrea "Dreaming of a White Christmas."

Exchange snack bars take the place of the corner drug store for GIs at foreign stations. Last year the European Exchange System (the largest retail chain in Europe), which serves troops in France, Italy and Germany, sold 55 million hamburgers, 26 million hot dogs, 30 million doughnuts and 3.5 million gallons of ice cream.

Set up as an autonomous corporation, A&AFES is completely supported by its GI customers, who spend approximately 20% of their monthly pay at exchange stores. In turn, PXs are geared to produce a 6%-7% net profit. They hand over the major portion of this—$50 million in 1958—to welfare service funds for recreational and athletic activities.

ELECTRIC
CARS
ARE COMING BACK

First of new, small electrics goes on market this year; manufacturers look forward to sales of 60,000 to 150,000 units a year for 1000-lb., $1000 car

BETTING ON

STINSON AIRCRAFT TOOL & ENGINEERING (San Diego, Cal.): first on the market with electric passenger car, the Charles Town-About; deliveries: July 1959; price $2800
CLEVELAND ELECTRIC VEHICLE (Cleveland, Ohio); first electric truck, the C-V; deliveries this year.
NU-WAY INDUSTRIES (Lansing, Mich.): taking orders for delivery of $1500-$1800 Nu-Klea car.
ELECTRICAR (Freeport, N. Y.): new golf car, the Envoy, costs $1100, is sturdy enough for off-the-links use.
BOLSEY RESEARCH & DEVELOPMENT (New York): has Bolsey Shopper-Commuter on the drawing boards; looking for financing to mass produce, sell at $750.

DISPLAY MODELS of Cleveland Electric Vehicle's new C-V trucks are already in operation. Company is only one of early electric manufacturers to have stayed in business throughout the lean years.

THE electric car, which gave the gasoline-powered "horseless carriage" a run for its money down the dusty roads of the early 1900s, is due for a spectacular comeback.

At least three brand new electric-powered passenger cars and one electric truck reached the market by the end of this year, and a half-dozen more are gleaming in the eyes of would-be manufacturers. (All are listed in the chart above.)

The goal most manufacturers are working toward—and none have as yet reached—is an electric car that will weigh not more than 1000 pounds and sell for about $1000.

Such a car should, its boosters believe, grab off a very substantial share of the small-car market. They are looking forward to sales of 500,000 units in the next five years, and to a long-term demand by the

OLD AND NEW ELECTRICS, the 1959 model Nu-Klea Starlite *(r.)* and a 1915 Milform, appeared together in Lansing, Mich., centennial parade. First battery-powered car was built by William Morrison of Detroit in 1892, and industry's heyday came before turn of the century; gas-powered cars took sales lead in 1901. Electrics from 36 different manufacturers (Studebaker, Waverly, Raush & Long were famous names) sold briskly until WW I. Cars were built until 1923 and trucks till 1933.

ELECTRICS:

ELECTRIC EQUIPMENT & ENGINEERING (Denver, Colo.): working on kit for do-it-yourself conversion from gas to battery power; 1959 delivery.

YARDNEY ELECTRIC (New York): has experimental electric on road, plans commercial model with 240-mile range.

NIC-L-SILVER BATTERY (Santa Ana, Cal.): has electric model in the works; no details.

ELECTRIC STORAGE BATTERY (Philadelphia): supplying batteries for Charles Town-About and C-V; working with other firms on research and development of electrics.

AMERICAN MOTORS (with SONOTONE) and DE SOTO: long-range development of electric "dream cars."

VETERAN ELECTRIC TRUCKS carry heavy loads on short hauls for Curtis Publishing Co., Philadelphia. Average age of the 27 trucks in Curtis fleet is 40 years; oldest was built in 1912, and nine are pre-World War I. Electric trucks and other industrial vehicles were in fairly common use even during years of electric passenger cars' virtual disappearance; today, they number well into the tens of thousands.

public for 60,000 to 150,000 or more a year.

Electrics still labor, to some extent, under the disadvantage that drove them off the road 40 years ago—their batteries run down and have to be recharged over night. But batteries available today can keep a car running for up to 100 miles—a great improvement over the 25-30 mile capacity of the old-fashioned kind. And, in a two-or-more-car suburban family, a runabout with a 100-mile range can earn its garage space making short hops to supermarket, station and school.

The electrics coming on the market today are not very fast, either—60 mph is the top speed of most. However, this is not a serious disadvantage for short hop driving, and might be considered a positive advantage by elderly drivers or by fathers who

want their teen-age sons to have a car with a built-in speed limit.

Battery-powered cars also have unique advantages.

They are safe—no danger of flash fires from gasoline or carbon monoxide poisoning—and simple to operate —no gear shift or clutch, no stalling, easy braking.

They are compact—in most cases about three feet shorter than conventional cars.

And they are extremely economical. The average electric will probably cost only about half as much to operate as the average gasoline-powered car. In the first place, electricity is a much cheaper source of automotive power than gasoline. Cost of gas has risen 80% since 1940, while lead batteries have gone up only 20%, and price of residential electric power has actually gone down. And also,

electric cars have fewer moving parts, offering lower maintenance cost and longer life.

The comeback of the electric has undoubtedly been sparked by the popularity of small electric golf cars —used by the nation's most famous golfer, President Eisenhower, and by thousands of others. (There are probably about 60,000 golf cars—and several thousand more miniature electric passenger vehicles, for invalids—in use in the U.S. today.)

If and when the 1000-pound, $1000 model appears on the market, the electric car will almost certainly be back on the road to stay.

And the day may come when "dream" electrics driven by fuel cells or by self-recharging super-batteries will make the gasoline-powered car look as old-fashioned as the electric itself did a few years ago.

INDEX

317

PICTURE CREDITS

The following list credits the source of each picture used in YEAR's 1959 Edition. Credits are listed picture by picture for each page—left to right, top to bottom. Each picture starting a new line across a page is preceded by a dash (—); each picture following on the same line is preceded by a comma (,).

Abbreviations used are:

WW—Wide World
UPI—United Press International

2 – UPI. 5 – YEAR, INC. 8 – UPI. 9—WW. 10—UPI—UPI. 11—UPI, WW. 12—UPI—WW, WW. 13—WW. 14—WW, WW, WW—WW—UPI, UPI. 15—WW, WW, WW—WW, UPI—WW, UPI. 16—WW—UPI. 17—WW, UPI—WW. 18—UPI—WW, WW. 19—WW. 20—WW. 21—UPI, UPI, WW, WW—UPI. 22—WW. 23—U.S. AF, WW. 24—WW—WW. 25—WW, WW—WW, UPI. 26—UPI—No. American Aviation, UPI. 27—WW—Kaman Aircraft Corp. 28—Bethl'm Stl. 29—WW. 30—Dickey & Waidley, WW—WW. 31—WW—WW, Tata Steel Works. 32—UPI—WW. 33—UPI, WW—WW—Philip Lesley Co. 34—WW – UPI – AP. 35 – WW, UPI – WW, WW. 36—YEAR, WW—UPI. 37—WW—UPI, WW. 38—UPI—UPI. 39—UPI, UPI—WW. 40—WW. 41—UPI. 42—UPI. 43—UPI. 44—UPI. 45—WW. 46—UPI. 47—WW. 48—UPI—UPI. 49—UPI—WW, WW.
50—UPI, UPI—WW. 51—WW—WW. 52—UN—UN. 53—UPI, UN, UPI—UN, UN. 54—WW—YEAR. 55—WW—UPI, WW. 56—WW. 57—WW—UPI. 58—WW, WW—WW, UPI. 59—USSR Mag. from Sovfoto—UPI—WW. 60—UPI, WW—UPI, WW. 62—WW. 63—UPI, UPI—WW, WW—WW. 64—WW. 65—WW, WW—WW, UPI. 66—UPI. 67—WW, UPI—WW, WW. 68—UPI—WW. 69—WW. 70—UPI. 71—UPI, WW—UPI, UPI. 72—WW. 73—WW, UPI—WW. 74—WW—UPI. 75—WW. 76—WW. 77—UPI—WW, WW. 78—WW—WW, UPI. 79—WW, WW—WW, UPI—WW. 80-81—WW. 82—AP—UPI, WW. 83—WW. 84—UPI—WW—WW. 85—UPI, WW. 86—WW. 87—Israel Info. Office, WW—WW—Israel Info. Office. 88—YEAR, Chas. Miller. 89—WW. 90—WW—UPI—WW, WW. 91—WW. 92—A Matheson, A. Matheson—WW, WW.
93—UN, WW—WW, UPI. 94—WW—UPI. 95—Info. Service of India. 96—UPI. 97—UPI—WW. 98—WW—Laurence P. Atkinson—WW. 99—WW—WW. UPI, UPI. 100—UPI, WW. 101—Graphic Arts Photo, China Photo. 102—WW, China Photo—UPI. 103—WW—WW—UPI, WW. 104—UPI—UPI—WW, UPI. 105—Consulate Gen. of Japan. 106—WW. 107—UPI, UPI—WW, UPI. 108—UPI, UPI—WW. 109—WW, Australian News Bur. – same – C. P. Smith. 110—UPI—WW, UPI. 111—Brazilian Govt. Trade Bur.—UPI. 112—UPI—UPI, UPI—Hamilton Wright. 113—UPI. 114—UPI, WW—UPI, WW. 115—UPI, WW—WW, WW. 116—WW. 117—WW, UPI—WW—Mexicana Airlines. 118—WW, WW—Nat'l. Film Board of Canada. 119-121—WW. 122—WW—UPI, WW. 123—UPI, UPI—WW—UPI, UPI. 124 Std. Oil of N.J. 125—UPI. 126—WW, UPI. 127—UPI—WW, UPI.
128—United Press Internat'l.—WW, WW. 129—UPI, WW—Hughes Aircraft. 130-131—WW. 132—UPI, UPI—UPI, WW. 133—WW. 134—UNESCO—UPI. 135—UPI—WW—WW. 136—UPI—WW. 137—WW—Doubleday, Bobbs-Merrill, Farrar, Straus & Cudahy. 138—Geo. Cserna—Sussman & Sugar, WW—WW—Scribner's. 139—French Govt. Tourist Office, WW. 140—Hurok Artists—WW. 141—UPI, UPI—Lincoln Center Performing Arts. 142—WW, Len. Bernstein—NYC Ballet. 143—UPI, UPI-WW.

144—UPI, WW – Friedman – Abeles. 145—WW – Friedman – Abeles. 146 – UPI. 147 – WW – Frank Goodman—Friedman—Abeles. 148—Couture Group of N.Y. Dress Institute, UPI, UPI. 149—UPI. 150—Peter Fink, Maxwell—Gray, UPI—Rose Marie Reid, WW. 151—UPI, Capezio-Couture Group of N.Y. Dress Institute, WW. 152—WW. 153—WW—Conant.
154—N.Y. World-Tel. & Sun. 155—Univ. of Chicago, WW—WW. 156—WW. 157—WW, UPI—Religious News. 158—Pan Am.—Preston. 159—Puerto Rico News, Japan Tourist Assoc.—WW, Trans-World Airlines. 160—WW—WW—Horizons. 161—Herald Tribune—UPI, WW. 162—Goldman—United Artists. 163—Goldman, United Artists—Goldman. 164-165—Goldman. 166—UPI. 167—WW. 168—UPI, UPI—UPI, WW. 169—WW. 170-172—WW. 173—WW, UPI—WW, WW. 174—WW. 175—WW, UPI—WW, WW. 176—GM. 177—Nash-Studebaker, Chrysler—Cadillac. 178—Renault. 179—UPI, WW—Mercedez-Benz, WW. 180—Tip Top Bread—Ford. 181—El Al Airlines, Calvert Distillers—Cole of Calif. 182—UPI—WW. 183—WW, NBC—WW. 184—UPI—WW, CBS. 185—NBC, UPI—WW. 186—P. E. Guerrero. 187—P. E. Guerrero, UPI—UPI.
188—Robt. Lautman, WW—UPI, Brazilian Govt. Trade Bur. 189—WW, UPI—WW—Amer. Academy of Arts & Sciences, WW. 190—UPI—WW. 191—WW. 192—WW, WW—UPI. 193—UPI—WW, WW. 194—WW—UPI. 195—UPI, WW—UPI, UPI—UPI. 196 – UPI, WW – WW, UPI. 197-198 – UPI. 199-201—WW. 202—WW, UPI. 203—UPI. 204—UPI—WW—WW. 205—WW. 206—UPI. 212—Std. Oil of N.J.—Drake Well Mem. Museum. 213—Shell Oil. 214—Std. Oil of N.J.—same. 215—Tex. Mid-Cont. Oil & Gas Assoc.—Texas Co. 216—British Petroleum. 217—Union Oil—Standard Oil—British Pet. 218—Pittsburgh Ch. of Com. 219—Same. 220—Community Redev. Agency (LA), St. Louis Globe-Democrat. 221—Dept. Report & Info. Comm. Detroit, Louis Alexander, same. 222-224—USAF from Louis Alexander.
225—Lockheed—USAF from Louis Alexander. 227—USAF from Louis Alexander. 228—NEWS FRONT. 229—WW. 230—Sikorsky Aircraft. 231-233 —U.S. Army. 234—WW, WW—UPI, WW, WW, WW, WW. 235—WW. 236-239—TVA. 240—Sheldon Claire Co.—Harold Mansfield. 241—Sheldon Claire Co. 242—Harold Mansfield – Sheldon Claire Co. – Harold Mansfield. 243—same. 244—Eastfoto. 245—USSR Mag. from Sovfoto. 246—UPI, Paul Lendvai. 247—Eastfoto, Paul Lendvai, Eastfoto. 248-249—British Info. Serv. 250-251—Paul Lendvai. 252—WW. 253—Homer Hathaway. 254-257 – Alastair Matheson. 258-259 – Hamilton Meserve. 260-261 – Columbia Univ. 262-263—Broadcast Music. 264—AT&T. 265—U.S. Army. 266-267—Stevens Hammer. 268—CBS. 269—MBS, CBS—NBC—ABC. 270—British Info. Serv.—Philip Drew. 271—British Info. Serv.
272-273 – Irwin Stambler. 274 – Stanford Research Inst.—West. Electric—Varian Assoc. 275—same. 276—Hughes Aircraft. 277—Boeing Airplane —GD Stromberg Carlson Div.—Northrop Corp. 278-279—Ed Diamond. 280-281—E. W. Bliss Co. 282—WW. 283—WW. 284-285—YMCA. 286—Kenya Info. 287—same. 288—same. 289—Kenya Info—Alastair Matheson. 290-291—Lawrence P. Atkinson. 292-293—June Aulick. 294-295—WW. 296—R. J. Reynolds Tobacco. 297—Hiram Walker. 298-300—Endorsements, Inc. 302—Grand Union—WW. 303—Egmont Arens—Gen. Foods—same—same. 304—Jim Nash—Center for Research in Marketing—Egmont Arens—Frank Gianninoto. 305—Nat'l. Biscuit—Proctor & Gamble— Brillo—Jim Nash—same. 306—WW, N.Y. Pub. Lib.—Lester Lanin. 307—Ruby Newman. 308—Scholastic Magazines.
309 – Weyerhaeuser Timber. 310-311 – Irwin Stambler. 312-313—Army & Air Force Exchange. 314—Carlisle Carver, Cleveland Electric Vehicle. 315—Carlisle Carver, Curtis Publishing.